Jesus' View of His Father
A Perspective for the Thinking Christian

William M. Livingston

D1059741

Jesus' View of His Father:
A Perspective for the Thinking Christian
© Copyright 2016
Brotherhood of Christ Church

Printed by Sure Print & Design, Canada
First edition
ISBN 0-692-70277-6
ISBN 13 978-0-692-70277-2

In the beginning was the Word, and the Word was with God, and the Word was God. The same was in the beginning with God. All things were made by him; and without him was not anything made that was made. In him was life; and the life was the light of men.

John 1:1-4

Preface

As we enter into a period of history where in many places throughout the world a Christian genocide is underway, it becomes expedient that people address their need for spiritual empowerment. In John 14:12, Jesus said, "*Verily, verily, I say unto you, He that believeth on me, the works that I do shall he do also; and greater works than these shall he do; because I go unto my Father.*" The people of the early church often fulfilled this expectation of Jesus. However, Christianity soon lost the ability to give sight to the blind, heal the withered hands, and raise the dead.

It is the author's position that those spiritual powers can be restored if people will examine Jesus' view of His Father and His personal definition of salvation. How did Jesus actually view His Father? What does that view have to say to us today? How did Jesus define salvation in His own words? And what effect did modifying that definition in the Gentile Mission have on the empowerment of the saints?

This book is a transcription of a series of eleven sermons that were taught in our church from November 2014 through March 2015. They address the answers to those questions. Editing has been done for concept clarification where needed but otherwise the style of the speaker to a live audience has been preserved. This entire study is scripturally based using the King James Bible. This penetrating study has deep ramifications for people today. Elder Livingston examines the origins of Judaism and Western Christianity to look for the source of this disempower-ment. He has been a keen Bible student for more than 50 years and studied the foundations of the early Church for more than 30 years. He lives in our modern day Essene Community where he is the senior teacher of righteousness.

In Session 1 the Christian lifestyle is discussed in order to lay the foundation for actually doing something practical with expressing Jesus' view of His Father. Session 2 lays out Jesus' view of His Father and Christ's definition of salvation. In Session 3 the scope of the study is outlined with the focus on the discourse of Stephen in Acts chapters 6 and 7 being the launching point to explain, within the context of the Bible, the meaning of Christ's views and definitions. Here Stephen expresses to the Sanhedrin four basic issues that the early church brought to the public debate. These issues were substantial and he gave his life in order to proclaim them. It is the understanding of these four basic issues that can lead Christians to spiritual empowerment. These issues are expressed in terms of four blasphemy charges against Stephen. They are blasphemy against Moses, the temple, the Law, and God. Each of these topics is addressed in separate Sessions 4-8. This study takes the Bible student into some uncharted territory in the Western Christian tradition. Sessions 9, 10, and 11 are a current expression of the Essene view of the Creatorship of Jesus, a topic entirely undeveloped in Western Christianity. In these final sessions we have authorized the author to make public the Essene theology and world view. Elder Livingston opens up the Biblical evidence of the Creatorship of Jesus, the ancient Hebrew definition of righteousness, and the pre-Flood concept of the separation of powers – again all this from the Bible record of Jesus' view of His Father.

It is altogether reasonable that such an inquiry be made in the context of the pre-Gentile Mission period of the early church where the clearest expressions of spiritual empowerment were demonstrated by Jesus and many others of the church. Those who actually walked with Jesus and were subject to His ministry of salvation and His view of His Father healed the lame, gave sight to the blind, and raised the dead. In the last sessions Elder Livingston explains how an empowered person can do these very things and he shares real life examples of such occurrences that happened during his own life and ministry. Historically, the Essene sect has been private in its teachings and scriptural knowledge. We have been a functioning Essene community for nearly 30 years and have followed this pattern of privacy until now, so the text you hold in your hands is a work that provides a unique perspective and opportunity to today's faithful. It is essential and timely that this light and truth is made available in these troubled times. Our prayer is that you will carefully and prayerfully consider the ideas presented here. Thank you.

The Council of the Community
Brotherhood of Christ Church

Session 1
Preparing Ourselves to Live Jesus' View of His Father
November 23, 2014

I would like to welcome all of you this morning; those of you in our church community and also those who hear this series. This series is called <u>Jesus' View of His Father: A Perspective for the Thinking Christian</u>.

I want to talk today about the kind of things people need to know to create an effective Christian life. This will be the first session of a ten or eleven part series. Before I talk about Jesus' view of His Father I want to talk to you about your view of Christ. How you view Him is central to how you live; and there are lots of different views of Christ. How people conceive of Him is guided by tradition, guided by denominational doctrines, and by life circumstances. For everyone, how we view the Lord is basically going to influence how we live, even for those who don't believe in Him. Even that lack of belief has influence on how a person lives.

Of the people who do believe in Him there are many different kinds of expressions of belief. Different Christians focus on different aspects of Christ's life - some by necessity, some by training, and some by choice. The vast majority of Christians who are fully engaged in the society at large haven't got time to view Him in a way that will allow them to completely live their lives based on Him. In this country, and also in many parts of the world as well, that means that both parents are working away from home, and the education system, the media, and the day care centers are raising their children. And if they are fortunate, they have time to go to church on Sundays; especially on holidays like Christmas or Easter.

And that becomes the way they live – based on their view of and their interaction with Christ. Most of them view Him essentially in terms of His death, so if they believe in Him and they confess Him with their mouths, then they have an assurance that they will go to heaven and be saved because His blood applies to them. For a lot of people that's all they can feel inclined to do. They are consumed by paying bills; they are busy pursuing wealth,

7

busy accumulating and consuming what society has to offer. So to a great extent society is supplying their children with its values and world view that is largely void of any view of Christ and what He stands for. And society is in a **continual state of moral flux**.

These Christians, by the example of society, pursue the satisfaction of possessions. They are so busy paying for all they accumulate and for their debts and working for money that their children are taught their way of life by society, and they are enculturated by society in their education. God deeply loves these Christians for all the efforts they make to love Him.

But there are other people who not only see value in Christ's death but also in His life. So their Christ view is a little more effective. Their view of Christ is bigger because they have more time. It takes time to live in Christ. They are not so fully engaged in society and their possessions don't mean as much to them. They take time to pray and they sometimes attend prayer meeting and classes during the week and on Sunday night. They try to follow Christ's life example and try to be good every way they can and they like to read about Christ's ministry. They like to teach their children stories from the Bible and the Lord dearly loves them because of everything they do to try to be good and be the kind of people they feel they need to be. So the view of Christ gets a little bigger when you include His life.

And for still others what He taught and preached is yet more important. Not just that He died. Not just that He lived. But there are important stories about Him, telling what He said and did and what He showed by example.

I am going to read from John 14:23-24: *"If a man love me, he will keep my words: and my Father will love him, and we will come unto him, and make our abode with him. He that loveth me not keepeth not my sayings: and the word which ye hear is not mine, but the Father's which sent me."*

This is a Christ view that is broader yet. These people want to keep His sayings and that which He taught. They are still involved in society but they are less involved. Their possessions can be almost out of mind and they trust the Lord to add what they

8

need when they seek first the Kingdom. They are in society but they are more involved with Christ and His teachings; so that they work in soup kitchens, they are ministers, they send care packages, they sing in the choir, they volunteer to go to Africa to fight Ebola. They do things more involved with what Christ taught. And so the Lord loves all those efforts. He loves those people who try to, in these ways, serve others.

Christians in today's world are forced socially and legally to acquiesce to their exposure to horrific expressions of morality. Any expression of prayer is now routinely belittled in the media. The Lord expects His people to stand for the highest levels of holiness and virtue and these social forces are compromising Christians' relationship with God.

And Christians who are still engaged in society often can't fully keep the First and Second Commandments. When you are engaged in society how do you love your neighbors as yourself when you don't even know their names? Maybe you are afraid of them.

Let me read to you Mark 12:29-31: *"And Jesus answered him; The first of all the commandments is Hear O Israel; the Lord our God is one Lord: And thou shalt love the Lord thy God with all thy heart* (which is your feelings and emotions), *and with all thy soul* (which is with all that you are), *and with all thy mind* (which is always underlying all your thoughts,) *and with all thy strength* (which means in all you do): *This is the first commandment. And the second is like, namely this, thou shalt love thy neighbor as thyself. There is none other commandment greater than these."*

And in another place He says, *"and all the law and the prophets hang on these two commandments."* So when you are in the world; some of us have lived there, we would hear loud noises coming from the neighbors and raucous music; we wouldn't dare go talk to him when he was abusing his kids – he would be angry. Here, in community, we love our neighbor as ourselves.

How do you deal with persons that you live with when society feels like it is an insult to reprove someone, or even care about their lives? Is what they do none of your business? Should

9

you say anything? If you do will they get even with you? How do you love God with all your heart (that is all your feelings) while living in the world when you are forced to feel things that aren't like Him? When you view the way people are dressed, or are exposed to their morals, or when you hear their music, when you are around and see the things that are going on, your feelings are caught up in those things, especially if you watch TV. For example I remember once crying watching an episode of Gunsmoke back in 1957 and thinking "this is stupid. I should be crying over something that is real instead of fake things coming out of a TV." The visual media can be absolutely overwhelming.

So you loving Him with all your feelings or with all your heart is hard in the midst of society – if not impossible. Society forces a lot of feelings upon you. And those feelings have to run their course in your daily life. And you can be certain that they have an effect on your relationship with God. You can't just have a huge feeling about something and then turn it off or completely isolate yourself from it. I remember once sitting in our van in the parking lot at Wal-Mart and watching a dad come out with two little girls. They were just little things and he had them by the hands. And he stood them on the edge of their open van door and he held up dresses to them that he'd just bought. And they were sexy, like you would see in a night club or something; for two little girls. I'm thinking "where are their lives going to go, Lord?" and I remember praying for those girls. I remember thinking what the Lord had to feel to know that those little treasures of His were going to grow up having a hard life with their womanhood being compromised. I was feeling with Christ, but those moments are rare in the world setting. You can do that only so much or you become emotionally spent. That experience stayed with me for days.

So you can't love God with all your mind in the world because the world infringes on your mind. I remember working as an inspector in welding and fabrication for Caterpillar tractor and I had to make my rounds every hour. And I would find ways to go as fast as I could and do as good a job as I could so that I could accumulate about ten minutes every hour and go out in the night on a loading dock and just think about the Lord and view the stars. I worked the night shift and I did this so I could have 10 minutes out of every hour for Him because it required all my mind to do my job fully. I had to inspect big equipment and make sure they were correct in every detail because they were getting shipped all over the world and they had to be right. And I had a good department but I could not love the Lord my God with all my mind. Fifty minutes of my mind belonged to the world every working hour. Never mind that I was helping build equipment for war.

And so the world regularly requires all of who you are, to be other than what God created you to be - you can't love Him with all your soul. So what does a person do? How do you find a Christ view where you can live Christ? Don't be shocked; you can live Him. He can be the entire way you live, the way you think, the way you eat, the way you love, the way you dress, the way you talk, the way you pray. He can be the absolute, all consuming center of your life. And you can follow the Lamb withersoever He goes taking no thought for your life as John writes in Revelation. Not many people are willing to put that much effort into their spiritual lives, but for those who long to do so there are places to start. First of all you can't walk in everyday society. You are going to have to find a way to withdraw.

I want to read a scripture from Isaiah 8:11, *"For the Lord spake thus unto me with a strong hand, and instructed me that I should not walk in the way of this people."* Here Isaiah is told by God to withdraw from walking in the way of the people. Now this is a prophet. This is somebody who is living in the days when prophets had a big influence in Israel and he is not supposed to live like they do. He is supposed to bring himself out of the way they live. How can you do that?

The writings of John are very important in terms of finding a Christ view to build a community on or a self-supporting church group; or being able to live your life for Him totally and completely so that you can keep the First and Second commandments. And so the Lord has provided John's writings for us. I am going to read some things about John and tell you some things about him. The Lord has provided truth for His people, through the writings of John in a special way, so that we would have access to the kind of Christ view that will allow us to live our lives totally for Him, in our case, here in community.

I want to read first another scripture in Isaiah 48:20. This is a rather unique scripture, Isaiah writes, *"Go ye forth out of Babylon."* What is unique about this verse is that it was written about 125 years before Israel went into the Babylonian captivity. Isaiah was long gone when Israel went into Babylon. In Isaiah 52:11-12 it says this again, speaking concerning Babylon, *"Depart ye, depart ye, go ye out from thence, touch no unclean thing; go ye out of the midst of her; be ye clean, that bear the vessels of the LORD. For ye shall not go out with haste, nor go by flight: for the LORD will go before you; and the God of Israel will be your rearward."* This was said before the time of Jeremiah, who lived over a century later, when they went into captivity into Babylon.

So why would Isaiah say to the Israelites to come out of Babylon, when they hadn't even gone there yet? Remember when the Lord had told him earlier to not walk in the way of the people? *"Go ye forth out from Babylon,"* Isaiah said, when they were not even in Babylon yet. He said this very clearly in the two places I have cited. Well, the reason is that Babylon is not just a city or a nation. And when you look into it, and you study it, you will find out that Babylon is an economic system, a religious system, a political system, and a legal system. It is an entire social system that began in the ancient city of Babylon and never quit clear into our day. And the Jews had already entered into this social system before they ever went into captivity. They already had money, and banking with interest, and they could buy insurance, and they could mortgage their house and property. They had marriage licenses and birth certificates. They had legal signatures. All those things and much more began in Babylon. And the Jews were already doing all that in Isaiah's day. You can read in the Bible that in the days of Isaiah they also had certain weights for their money. They had the Levitical law that largely came from Babylonian law that formed the framework of their religion.

So 125 years before they went into Babylon Isaiah was preaching to them to come out of it. I personally think that because they were already in Babylon spiritually it was just natural for them to be carried there physically. And then 500 years after the ancient city of Babylon fell John is still asking people to come out of her. Let me read it, it is Revelation 18:4-5: *"And I heard another voice from heaven, saying, Come out of her, my people."* He isn't asking the wicked to come out; it's the Lord's people who should come out, the ones who love Him, who are involved in society but who can't love Him enough for Him to protect them there. They can't raise their children the way He wants. *"Come out of her my people, that ye be not partakers of her sins, and that ye receive not of her plagues. For her sins have reached unto heaven, and God hath remembered her iniquities."* It seems to me that it is becoming more and more incumbent upon Christians to make every effort to create their own unique Christ-like living environment.

So John is saying this 500 years after Babylon the city was laying in ruins. Today, the Lord is still saying to you to come out of Babylon; because it is not just a city and it is not just a symbolic word. Most Bible dictionaries say it is a symbolic word that refers to a society that is against Christians. It is not symbolic – it is literal. Babylon started the banking system and insurance. They had surveyed property lines and land titles. All the things society has today Babylon started in ancient times and it has never stopped. So we have to come out of her. According to my Bible Isaiah wrote around 713 B.C. and 588 B.C. is when Israel was taken into the Babylonian captivity. So John is clearly writing in harmony with the early prophets.

By the way, none of the other gospel writers except John deal with the Old Testament prophets in terms of their theology. Matthew quotes 44 times that Christ's action in regard to some occurrence has *"thus fulfilled the prophets."* And so he was most involved in that kind of expression. There are only eight such times in the Gospel of John. So the style in Matthew was more along the lines of fulfillment of prophecy, not theology. But John dealt with the theology of the prophets.

So Babylon has continued without interruption. And Christ, John, Isaiah – and others – put the importance of coming out of Babylon squarely in the terms of the last days. When you read Isaiah 13:1-14 he puts the idea of coming out of Babylon in context with the sun being darkened and the moon not giving its light and the stars falling from heaven. And Christ does the same thing in Matthew 24:29 and John in Rev. 6:12. So the idea that the Lord's people should come out of Babylon squarely applies to our day, because all three of them used that call to come out in relation to the

13

last days when those unique conditions would be present. There is no time in history when the sun will be darkened, and the moon not give her light, and the stars fall from heaven than the day in which we live. Also a great earthquake is involved in all those things. There is no other time when those conditions are all present together according to John, Christ, and Isaiah. We simply live in a day when we cannot afford to walk in the way of the people.

Why do so many Christians still interact with the world in ways that curtail or severely limit their relationship with the Lord? So far I have addressed Christians' view of Christ. The revelation of Jesus Christ has yet to be fully comprehended by almost all the world's Christians. The key to opening the Christ revelation lies in Christ's view of Himself and His Father as expressed in your Bible, especially in the New Testament and specifically in the writings of John. For some reason Christ's expressed view of Himself and His articulated perspective of His Father has largely escaped Christianity. And I am convinced that the full potential of the Christian life in any environment cannot be realized without a careful and diligent understanding and acceptance of His position in these two matters.

When you can begin to grasp the meaning of how Christ viewed His Father you will be empowered from on high. That empowerment is what this series is all about. Jesus' Father is basically a Christian enigma and I would like to explain to you how important it is to change that. The reason I am beginning with calling attention to your relationship with the world is because I know from experience that discovering Jesus' Father will require a holy lifestyle; one that is engulfed in His Spirit routinely every day.

So what am I saying from a very practical sense? I will say it plainly. If you are on the outer fringes of salvation by believing that you have professed with your mouth that Jesus exists and therefore you are saved, move in toward the center by starting to learn about Jesus' life. Begin to use Him as a role model in your behavior. If you are a person who is already doing this move more to the center of salvation by studying the life of Jesus and begin to order your lives to live more like He would live if He was in the flesh today. If you are among those who are already doing this then begin to alter your lifestyle so you can become involved in an active

14

Spirit-led church. Abandon those influences that rob you of your time for the Lord. If you are already doing this begin to change how you feel about your possessions and your career. Order your life to do and keep the sayings and words of Jesus in all your daily walk.

Remember Jesus said, *"If a man love me, he will keep my words and my father will love him and we will come unto him and make our abode with him."* If you are among those who are already doing this then turn your attention to the lives of your children. There are huge waves of filthiness waiting to wash over your children destroying who God created them to be. Consider that there is no change in your lives that is too drastic to save them from those influences. Move your family if need be. Change how they are educated. Abandon careers and lifestyles if that is what it takes for you to raise your little ones up unto the Lord. This is not something you can do overnight. The Lord has to guide you step by step, but you will never break away from the captivity you are subjected to unless you begin to consciously, inside your soul, express remorse for those influences in the lives of your families that are not centered on living Jesus.

Remember Isaiah said, *"For ye shall not go out with haste nor by flight, for the Lord will go before you and the God of Israel will be your rearward."* So send your cries to the Lord for deliverance. He will answer. Study, study, study and pray, pray, pray – not out of fear but in faithful confidence in Him. If you can't find a church where the Spirit leads and all that is there is the dry, mealy droning from some denominational headquarters, get together with like-minded people and worship among yourselves. There are very few Christian communities that have the environment that allows for keeping the First Commandment. But in all your walk the Lord can lead you to places of invigorating enlightenment and safety. My heart goes out to you and yet I know, nothing doubting, that the Lord can and will lead you forth to times and places of refreshing. All this is what it means to *"come out of Babylon my people."* I commend you into the safety and loving hands of the living God.

So now we will move right into Jesus' view of His Father. First, I want to talk to you a little bit more about John, because his

15

writings are the primary source of the foundations of the Christian revelation. Not that you should ignore everything else, but his writing are very unique. And there are certain aspects of his writings that I think the Lord provided for a people who want to live in Christ and give their lives completely to the Lord. John was very mild and a sweetheart of a man; a very kind person. He didn't record any of the harsh conversations that are attributed to Christ in the other Gospels. He didn't have Jesus say "Woe unto" anybody in the Book of John. Christ didn't curse the fig tree in John. The words "hypocrites" and "vipers" are not in the writings of John. John never writes that Christ uttered the words "scribes" or "Pharisees."

There are none of the confrontations that are written in the other Gospels. And in Luke, Christ was invited to dinner at the home of a Pharisee. And the fact that they would want to eat with him was a major expression of respect, because they were careful who they ate with. They wouldn't eat with the Samaritans; and they wouldn't take anything out of their hands either. They invited Jesus to eat with them. And Jesus was also content to eat with them, which is a very personal act of respect in His culture. And you can read in Luke were Christ went in there to eat and Luke writes that He cursed them seven times and calls them fools. Luke 11:44, *"Woe unto you, scribes and Pharisees, hypocrites!"* and He said this over and over seven times while all the guests who were present were carefully observing Jesus' behavior. To seven someone with curses has special cultural and religious meaning in Israel. By the way, Matthew in Chapter 23 records the very same dialogue, but not at a meal, but before a crowd in the temple. Perhaps Matthew was more cognizant of the Hebrew culture.

John would never record anything like that. He recorded a lot of things that no one else recorded. John is the only one to record the healing of the nobleman's son. You remember Jesus said *"go thy way thy son liveth."* Now the nobleman was an enemy to the Jews. He was one of the Romans who was suppressing their country, and he said, My son is dying can you come? And he went and he found out his son was healed at the very same time Christ said that. He is the only one to record that Christ baptized. John liked to record the Lord blessing His enemies and loving those who were not accepted by their society.

16

John gives other stories where Christ actually blessed His enemies. John is the only one to record the story of healing the man with the withered legs on the Jew's Sabbath where He expressed His Sonship. John is the only one who records the story of healing the man who was blind from birth where He went later and found the man in the temple. And Jesus said *"do you believe in the Son of God"* and the man said *"who is He that I may believe in Him?"* Jesus said, *"It is He that talketh with thee."*

John is the only one to record the event of turning water into wine. That story is a personal glimpse of Jesus with His mother. Believe it or not, John is the only one to record the raising of Lazarus from the dead. As central as that incident was to the circumstances surrounding His triumphal entry into Jerusalem, John is the only one to record that event.

He is the only writer to record the story of Nicodemus to bring us the knowledge that we must be born again. Only one other author in your Bible, in the Old or New Testament uses the phrase "born again" – John speaks of it seven times, and Peter does once in I Peter 1:23. Peter's letter was written long after John's Gospel, but Peter was certainly well aware of the visit by Nicodemus. Any born again Christian is dependent upon John for that information and of course Peter mentioned it also. He is the only one to give us Christ's prayer of infinite blessing on the way to the Garden of Gethsemane. He is the only writer to do all those things. John is the only person who allowed Christ to proclaim who He was Himself. This is a fact of major importance. There is no other author that allows Christ to say "I Am" – only John. *"I am the Living Bread which came down from heaven."* I am going to go through those, but before I do that I forgot one point on John's exclusive list.

John is the only one to record the story of the woman at the well. And this story is so wonderful that I am going to depart for a moment here and talk to you about this incident, because there is no finer example of a tenderhearted and loving John and his ability to show you Who the Christ is. So Jesus came to the well on the way through Samaria and He met a woman at this well. He asked her to give Him a drink. Jews do not take things from Samaritans; they ignore Samaritans and won't even talk to them. Did you ever know why? I have read that the Samaritans had come down from the children of Jewish women who were sexually abused during the Babylonian captivity and they were seen to carry the stigma of shame for Israel.

So now I'll keep going with my story. And Jesus asked her for a drink. He is just there, alone with her. His disciples are gone to get food in town. And she says, why are you asking me for something to drink when you are a Jew and you don't have anything to do with Samaritans? And He said, If you knew who I was you would know that I can give you the Living Water. And she said, How can you draw water when you have nothing to draw it with and the well is deep? Finally Jesus said to her, I can give you Living Water so you will never thirst again and live forever.

Now I am going to read this story to you. This account is so amazing. It is John 4:1-42: *"There cometh a woman of Samaria to draw water: Jesus saith unto her, Give me to drink. (For his disciples were gone away unto the city to buy meat.) Then saith the woman of Samaria unto him, How is it that thou, being a Jew, askest drink of me, which am a woman of Samaria? for the Jews have no dealings with the Samaritans.*

Jesus answered and said unto her, If thou knewest the gift of God, and who it is that saith to thee, Give me to drink; thou wouldest have asked of him, and he would have given thee living water. The woman saith unto him, Sir, thou hast nothing to draw with, and the well is deep: from whence then hast thou that living water? Art thou greater than our father Jacob, which gave us the well, and drank thereof himself, and his children, and his cattle?

Jesus answered and said unto her, Whosoever drinketh of this water shall thirst again: But whosoever drinketh of the water that I shall give him shall never thirst; but the water that I shall give him shall be in him a well of water springing up into everlasting life.

The woman saith unto him, Sir, give me this water, that I thirst not, neither come hither to draw. And He did. He immediately reproved her and thereby called her to repentance, which is the very first part of the Living Water. *Jesus saith unto her, Go, call thy husband, and come hither.*

The woman answered and said, I have no husband. Jesus said unto her, Thou hast well said, I have no husband: For thou hast had five husbands; and he whom thou now hast is not thy husband: in that saidst thou truly. The inclusion of number five in this statement that the women had been now with six men who were not her husband is very likely written here to promote the stereotype of promiscuity amongst Samaritans.

The woman saith unto him, Sir, I perceive that thou art a prophet. Our fathers worshipped in this mountain; and ye say, that in Jerusalem is the place where men ought to worship. Jesus saith unto her, Woman, believe me, the hour cometh, when ye shall neither in this mountain, nor yet at Jerusalem, worship the Father.

Ye worship ye know not what: we know what we worship: for salvation is of the Jews. But the hour cometh, and now is, when the true worshippers shall worship the Father in spirit and in truth: for the Father seeketh such to worship him. God is a Spirit: and they that worship him must worship him in spirit and in truth.

The woman saith unto him, I know that Messias cometh, which is called Christ: when he is come, he will tell us all things. Jesus saith unto her, I that speak unto thee am he."

Ok, so this woman is sorry for her sins and He forgives her. And she is born again. She leaves her water pot and she hurries back to town. And she is not ashamed of what He said to her. She told the people in town, this man told me everything that I have ever done. This woman said I am alive. I am clean. I am free. I am forgiven – come and see Him. Here was a woman who they all knew, who walked among them in shame – daily. Hanging her head in shame and being reticent and hardly speaking to anyone and now she is forward and confident. She had indeed new life welling up within her. The Living Water is reproval, repentance and forgiveness; a flowing process.

19

And so the Samaritans came to see Him. And as Christ saw them coming He thought, "Well I'm here at this well I might as well give my disciples some Living Water, too." So He reproved them and called them unto repentance. *"Say not ye, There are yet four months, and then cometh harvest? behold, I say unto you, Lift up your eyes, and look on the fields; for they are white already to harvest. And he that reapeth receiveth wages, and gathereth fruit unto life eternal: that both he that soweth and he that reapeth may rejoice together. I sent you to reap that whereon ye bestowed no labour: other men laboured, and ye are entered into their labours. And many of the Samaritans of that city believed on him for the saying of the woman, which testified, He told me all that ever I did.*

So when the Samaritans were come unto him, they besought him that he would tarry with them: and he abode there two days. And many more believed because of his own word; And said unto the woman, Now we believe, not because of thy saying: for we have heard him ourselves, and know that this is indeed the Christ, the Saviour of the world."

And He said to them the most outstanding call to evangelism recorded in your Bible. He saw them coming and He said, *"the field is white and ready to harvest."* The very people who they thought He shouldn't even be talking to, He wants them to *"thrust in [their] sickles and harvest"* for the day is short. And to love those people who you thought you shouldn't even talk to or eat with. And they repented before the Lord and spent two days with them. They ate with them, stayed in their homes and ministered to them. These things someone in the temple religion would never do. In those moments a part of the disciples' hearts were also born again. And they converted many of the Samaritans for it says *"many in that place believed on Him."* So He gave His disciples Living Water, which again is reproval, repentance and forgiveness.

Now there is more to that story in John 4:7-23 than meets the eye, because the Samaritans were rejected by the Jews, they couldn't come to the temple to hear Him teach, on pain of death. They couldn't be there when He healed and multiplied the loaves and fishes. They missed the Sermon on the Mount. They couldn't be at His entry into Jerusalem. They were not there to behold Him

20

after He was resurrected. They could not see the empty tomb. **And neither can you**. All of you have a kindred faith with the Samaritans, because you can't be there either. You can only read about it. They couldn't even read about it.

So you see John has in his writings feelings about the Lord that no other person has recorded. He is a strong voice calling you to have faith. Can you have the faith of a Samaritan?

Only John records that Christ is called God – he writes this twice. Christ is called the Only Begotten Son of God in John ten times. The only other time in the Bible is found in Hebrews 11:17. Christ is said to be equal with God four times in John and he is the only Gospel writer to record this. John states four times that Christ never sinned. Only John indicates that Christ is eternal. He says that Christ is able to resurrect the dead and that all judgement is given to Jesus. Also in John, he and Peter are shown to have a special relationship between them. This is expressed four times: 1) John brings Peter to the court of the High Priest, 2) they run to the tomb together, 3) John is the first to recognize Christ on the shore after the resurrection and Peter jumps in the water, and 4) Peter asks the Lord whether John will tarry.

Now I want to go back and go into the "I Am's." He said I Am the Living Bread come down from heaven. I Am the Resurrection. I Am the Light of the world. I Am the true vine. I Am The Way, the truth, and the life. I Am the door of the sheep fold. I Am the One who can give the Living Water. He also said, I Am the Good Shepherd and my sheep hear my voice. I Am known of mine, He said. And He says that from the voice of a stranger they will flee. I Am Messiah. And finally before Abraham was I Am – which is to say I Am Eternal.

Now, before I go any further, I want to give you some important background information so you can better understand the real intent of Jesus when He used the words "I Am" to describe Himself. Jesus, in the context of the culture of His day was very old fashioned. He would be viewed as extremely conservative by His fellow Hellenized countrymen. All throughout His ministry He exemplified the old Hebrew culture. So did John the Baptist. Remember He came to restore all things. Jesus was, in effect, part

21

of a subculture in the midst of a larger culture. So here we find the real meaning behind the great "I Am" statements.

Let me explain. In the world there are very many cultures – probably thousands. All cultures have what is called a "culture base." By that I mean an underlying component of previewed value that defines the culture. Amazingly, all the world's cultures fall within just four culture bases. These can be expressed as cultural orientations. There are **object** oriented cultures; **action** oriented cultures; **precept** oriented cultures and **relationship** oriented cultures. The old Hebrew culture Jesus expressed in His ministry was a relationship oriented culture. Let me give you the briefest idea of how cultures springing from these four culture bases could be understood. In an object oriented culture, a mother teaching her child to speak would roll a ball across the floor and say, "Can you say **ball**?" A mother with an action oriented culture would say, "Can you say **roll**?" A mother from a precept oriented culture would say, "Can you say **round**?" And a mother in a relationship oriented culture would say, "Can you say **share**?" The Hebrew meaning for the word "ball," as used in Isaiah 22:18, is *pure*, #1754 coming from the root word #1752 *to remain* or *to dwell*. Or that is to say *to live the circle of life* – which is a relationship. This is a vastly different definition of a ball than the other cultural orientations.

So keeping this in mind one can come to better understand what was on Jesus' mind when He defined Himself by saying, "I Am." Every I Am is an appeal for us to join in a very important life relationship with Him. In almost every case modern Christians cannot respond to do so. The purest form of the Christian culture anywhere in the world must be a subculture.

So let me go on and explain what I mean. First as I do this I can think of no better way to help you understand than to give you examples of relationships we have here in Community. I am a bit cautious to do this because I do not want to come across as promoting our community in this series. I am promoting a close relationship with Jesus and His Father instead. But be that as it may, I will try to explain some of the meaning behind Jesus' appeal to you when He said, "I Am."

Now I want to give you an idea of how a lifestyle that is in many ways apart from the society at large, can join you to many of the feelings expressed in the life of Jesus and those in the early church. Please don't be discouraged by our example but be reminded that we have been at this a long time now. You too can find ways to join with A Way that can bless you to feel the richness of life the Lord desires for you and your family. So this is my example of what I mean: In our community we know what it means when He said "I am the good shepherd." We raise sheep: we watch them be born, we shear them, we make clothing from their wool, and we know they will flee from the voice of someone who they are not acquainted with – a stranger. The sheep are a good example to us. So we know how to not listen to any other spirit except His Spirit. We know we can call the sheep and they will follow us to a new pasture. We know that. We live it. That relationship with Jesus is part of our way of life. It is a constant example to us to listen to His Voice and not one of a strange spirit.

We have carefully developed the ability to identify His voice in our hearts from those voices that are not of Him. And we know how important it is that each person learns to know how to hear the Lord for themselves. There isn't one sheep that hears the shepherd for the others. It is that way in our community. We have learned and can teach the difference between a voice inside our heart and mind that is the Lord's and a voice inside our heart that isn't. We know that because we experience what He said in real daily life – like that example when He said "I Am the good shepherd." This statement defines the entire scope of our relationship with Him in how He leads us.

And so we follow the Lamb withersoever He goes, taking no thought for our lives. We also know what it means for Him to be **the living bread come down from heaven**. This "I Am" defines our view of life as we interact with the life that He came down from heaven to give us, as it says in John 6:33. We do not experience the alienation that one does by living in the world. In the world you go and buy bread. You don't know who made it. You don't know where it came from. It could come from China. Who knows where it came from, who knows what is in it? Who knows what feelings are there being put there by those who baked it? Who knows what the person felt who grew the grain? Was he going out on his wife?

23

Was he angry or selfish when he planted the wheat? Did he put those feelings into the ground when he put those seeds in the ground? Was he cursing his neighbor?

We know what it means for Jesus to be the Living Bread. We pray over our ground when our horses plow it. We pray over our men and our horses and over our care of the equipment. We can watch the wind blow over a wheat field and it waves in beautiful ripples. We know what it means for a field to be white and ready to harvest. And the horses cut and bind the wheat. The Lord leads us to know when to harvest. We pray over the safety of the threshing crews and the horses grind the wheat into flour in our mill. And the person grinding it allows the Spirit of God to lead him so he produces good flour.

And in all of this process, all are laboring for the Lord and for the love of His people. Our men are not doing it to earn any money. Nobody as earned any money yet with our wheat or bread. And in the entire process of the life of the wheat they are doing it because the Lord wants to feed His people and give them life – because He is the Living Bread. And they pray over their roles as caregivers. So we know that Christ as the Living Bread is an integral part of our lives. We can feel it and we are not strangers to the life He put into our bread. It isn't a commodity that one pulls off the shelf of a stranger. The gentle loving hands of our mothers and women make the bread and bake it over a fire that is especially dedicated to the Lord when it is kindled.

We also know that **He is the true vine**, because we have a large vineyard. This "I Am" defines our pathway that we are to cling to as we travel through our lives with Him. Some of the men here have pruned, fertilized, and watered wild grape vines. No matter what they do they bring forth wild grapes. I think my real vines are going to bring forth wild grapes the way the cows have been chewing them off. So we know what it means for Jesus to be the true vine. Only Jesus can bring to our lives real, deep and profound relationships in happiness; or that is to say abundant life and loving kindness.

We know what it means for Jesus to bring **the Living Water**. This "I Am" defines our constant relationship with Him

24

and our day by day awareness that we are loved by Him and forgiven when we are humble and repent to love better, cleaner lives each day. We prayed over every place where the well diggers drilled wells on this property before they drilled them. It turned out that the Spirit could tell us where each village well would be. Now we couldn't know on our own because we do not know how to dowse for water. But the well driller was really good at that. He would come and we would have a little spot where we identified and where we had prayed over. And he would say, "That's funny. The best water is right in this spot you have marked." That happened in all our villages. So then we watch him drill the well. We have prayed and sung over the ground he is drilling, just like Abraham did; he was a well digger. We see the water come gushing in like a new birth of a living soul. One of our men had to go down and retrieve a dropped chain and the well man had to pull him out before the water came up around him to overtake him it came in so fast. And then we go to the well and we draw the water with a bucket on a well spar.

It is cold and sweet and good. It doesn't come out of some unknown place, from a pipe with poison chemicals in it that cause illness and disease. It doesn't come at a price so if you don't pay your bill they come and shut your water supply off. It is the Living Water because **it doesn't come in an environment where a person is insulted to be reproved**. Job 5:17 says, "*Happy is the man whom God reproveth in any manner.*" It comes just like it did to the woman from Samaria. She said, Sir, give me this water; and the cycle of living the gift of life flows.

With people who live the First Commandment the cycle of reproval, repentance, and forgiveness must be viewed as sacred; so that reproval is sought after, repentance is routine, and forgiveness flows to give life like a pure flowing fountain. So when the woman asked for the Living Water Jesus reproved her to start this cycle in her life. And He did it so kindly and so wonderfully that it changed her whole life and that of many of her people. If she would have been offended at a Jewish stranger reproving her it would have affected them all to miss their salvation and an intimate moment with the very Son of God. That kind of comfortability with reproval is one of the primary things the world will eliminate from your life. Now more about the Apostle John.

25

John is the only one to call Christ the Lamb of God. He is the only one to describe the Holy Spirit as the Comforter. He is the only one to allow Christ to define salvation Himself. Christ's definition of salvation is in your Bible. In the red letter edition everything Jesus spoke is in red ink so it is easy to identify just what He said. Christ defines salvation very differently than that which is presented by some authors in the New Testament.

John is the first one to record that Christ is the Creator, in John 1:1-14. He is the first one to expound on it. It is also in Hebrews 1:2, Ephesians 3:9, and Colossians 1:16-17 and I Corinthians 8:6. I want to read you the one in Colossians. It is also in Revelation and in I Timothy, by some scholars' accounts. Here is the one in Colossians 1:16-17 and this came because of John and that which he recorded. *"For by him were all things created, that are in heaven, and that are in earth, visible and invisible, whether they be thrones, or dominions, or principalities, or powers: all things were created by him, and for him: And he is before all things, and by him all things consist."*

The account written in John of Christ being the Creator predates the Colossians scripture by some 38 years according to the dates in my Schofield Bible. You are, I'm sure, all familiar with what John says but I am going to read it anyway just because it is so wonderful to hear. *"In the beginning was the Word, and the Word was with God, and the Word was God. The same was in the beginning with God. All things were made by him; and without him was not anything made that was made. In him was life; and the life was the light of men." (John 1:1-4)* And again in verse 10: *"He was in the world, and the world was made by him, and the world knew him not."*

So John could record this because somewhere along the line Christ openly taught that He was the Creator. And those people who wrote of it, like the authors of Hebrews, Colossians, Ephesians and Corinthians wouldn't have written that He was the Creator if He hadn't taught it. But there is no record of Him teaching it.

So, in the future, in one of these sessions one of the topics I plan to speak on is: Why didn't God create the world Himself?

Why did He have His Son do it? There is a very profound reason why Christ is the Creator. Almost universally Christians ignore the Creatorship of Christ and that which He instructs regarding salvation. First and foremost, above everything else, **above your salvation – Christ is the Creator.** If He didn't create you and your world what would salvation be? How could He forgive anyone if there was no world with its peoples? How can He redeem someone who doesn't first exist? First He created you.

So what does it mean for Christ to be your Creator? Why was He the one to create the world? Why didn't God just do it Himself? I have a little saying that may be startling but "I don't think God was Man enough to create the world Himself." I think He needed a man to do it. Somebody who experienced our lives with us, who knew we needed the cycle of the living water and the bread of life, someone who knew that we like sheep have all gone astray and needed to be guided by a gentle shepherd. Someone who knew we would need to be resurrected. Ok, should I go further? I will in another session.

So I am going to do a sermon on Christ as the Creator, because it is very essential to the Christian life. For you to have a relationship with the Christ that is in and through all things, by whom all things were created, you must come to comprehend the Creatorship of your Redeemer. This is so you can experience Him where He is and what He is doing there. He is in the wind and in all things. You can experience Him and interact with Him in the creation around you.

So the Lord has said *"come out of her my people"* for a reason, because Christ views that the majority of the Christians in this world have an inadequate view of Him and His Father for His Father to be able to take care of them in these violent times. Right now, as I speak, millions of Christians all over the world are being driven from their homes with nothing. Terrorists go into nations and come to a Christian's home and they would spray paint on it "this home belongs to our God." That family has twenty-four hours to leave that house. They can only take what they can carry. They then go through check points and everything they are carrying is taken away from them. They leave with nothing or they'll be killed.

27

What is happening to Christians around the world is so terrible that I cannot describe it here in the presence of so many tenderhearted people. Right now, it is happening to millions of Christians. Egypt used to be 15% Christian. Now they are one percent of the population.

All these things are happening to Christians because they are so fully engaged in Babylon. *"Come out of her that you receive not of her plagues."* They are involved in Babylon and partaking of her sins. So the Lord says to come out of her because He wants you to live with Him, to feel Him, know Him, experience Him, to ask Him questions, to hear His voice, to get real answers by the Spirit, and thus be able to find safety and security; to follow those answers, to follow what His Spirit gives you to know and feel; the voice inside your heart that you can come to recognize that is Him and not a stranger; it is that which will guide you to rich happiness and to be endowed with power on His behalf. We all need to live this way in these trying times. We need to raise our children this way. The Lord wants this because He loves all of you so much.

The time is now. The moment is upon the world's Christians to grow strong with Christ's view of Himself and His Father. As I end this session let me say a few words about the Gospels. Of course two of the four were written by Apostles who actually were with Jesus during His ministry: Matthew and John. Mark in all probability did not live during the lifetime of Jesus. His gospel is very impersonal about Jesus and offers no support for Jesus' view of His Father. Luke says in Luke 1:2 that he was not himself an eyewitness. His writings however have places that are very supportive of Jesus' view of His Father.

As we launch out into this series we will be going into what will be for many uncharted territory. Jesus' view of His Father that is expressed in the Gospels and in John has been obscured by tradition and evolving beliefs in the period following the Ascension of Jesus. You will find that I will be very respectful of the message of Jesus. Also, His view of His Father is heavily supported in the Book of Acts and the other Gospels, which will add greatly to our studies.

As I conclude let me say that I will be citing occasionally information from several Bible Dictionaries. I use the very old Smith's Bible Dictionary printed in the late 1800's. In its day it was considered very liberal, but of course, is not now. I use the New International Bible Dictionary which is liberal and the conservative Nelson's Bible Dictionary also. The Jehovah's Witness Study Aid sometimes is very helpful because they are good Bible students, even though many times their view is narrow. I will also be using the Strong's Exhaustive Concordance of the Bible throughout this series when referring to the meaning of biblical words. I am not learned in the Hebrew language but I do know how to use the Strong's Concordance. And there may be an occasion when I use Jeff Benner's book on the Ancient Hebrew Language and Alphabet for the paleo-Hebrew meaning of words. And of course, I exclusively use the King James Version of the Bible. Later on in the series I may reference some of the writing of the early church as found in the Dead Sea Scrolls, however, when I do that it will be to only add support for something found in the Bible. Thank you.

Session 2
Discovering the True Nature of Jesus' Father
December 14, 2014

Good morning. Welcome to this second session of our Christ View series. There are times when I feel pretty old. A few days ago I was clearing brush in our eastern most village and I scuffed up my finger. It was chaffing inside my glove and getting dirt in it. So when I got home I washed the finger real good and put salve on it and a band aid. About an hour later I noticed my finger still hurting. I looked down and saw that I did all that to the wrong finger. So there are sometimes when the effects of age are obvious.

Well, last time we talked about the Christ view that the Lord's people need in order to keep the First and Second Commandments and to not walk in the way of the people. And you will notice we talked about how John, in his writings, let Christ say many unique things such as all the "I Am's." There were a couple of times where He didn't actually use the words "I Am" such as I Am Messiah, but He said "*I Am He*" when He was asked about being Messiah. Also, He said in Matthew 12:8 "*The Son of man is Lord even of the Sabbath.*" There were a couple more that I didn't mention. So the writings of Apostle John are very unique.

In this session I want to talk about the view Christ has of His Father that comes from Jesus Himself defining salvation, among other things. And John in his writings presents a different message than some of the other New Testament authors. I've told you a lot of things about what is in John and what isn't. Other scriptures do not have Jesus' words recorded the same way as in all the times that I have cited. I can tell you a little bit more concerning John's writings that are unique. In the writings in the Gospel of John Christ refers to His Father by using the word "Father" 119 times. In Matthew it is there only 16 times, Mark only 4 times, and in Luke 14 times. So there is a huge difference in the message and the feeling and writing style in the Gospel of John, with complete emphasis on the Father of Jesus. He also refers to His Father as "*the One Who sent me*" 44 times. That phraseology is only in Matthew twice, Luke twice, and Mark only once. Christ is found actually referring to His Father in the Gospel of John 163 times in total.

So what is the significance of His referring to His Father in such markedly different ways than in the other Gospels, especially compared to the Book of Mark when such references occur only 5 or 6 times in the whole book? Why is Christ portrayed in John as speaking or referring to His Father so much? That is something we are going to look at in this session.

So Christ talks about "the One who sent me." In other words He is not speaking for Himself. He is always representing somebody else. He is representing His Father. The perspective John gives us of Jesus' entire purpose and ministry is to show that, in the mind of Jesus, His whole mission is to reveal His Father to mankind. He does so with all that He says and teaches and in all that He does out of love and compassion. By John's account Jesus has no other earthly task. Everything from start to finish in Jesus' heart and mind is to reveal His Father. Writers other than John often give the impression that Jesus is representing Himself to be the destination in our pathway to salvation.

Now also in the Book of John the word "believe" occurs 98 times and all the other gospels combined there are only 29 such references. So it occurs three times as often as all the other gospel writings combined. Matthew, Mark, and Luke use the word "faith" a total of 29 times. In John the word "faith" does not occur. So what is behind His appeals and statements regarding belief? He is anxious for us to believe that Jesus is **demonstrating the character of His Father**. When Jesus speaks of believing in His Father this is precisely the specific thing about Him that He wants you to believe. By the way, the word "life" is the same way, it occurs in John more often than all the other Gospels combined and that word is very attached to His effort to reveal His Father. And so looking further in John, Jesus is twice called God and ten times called the Only Begotten Son. There is only four other times in the whole New Testament that He is called the Only Begotten Son. So John is actually identifying something about Christ that is unique to his writings. It is not just a difference in writing style. It is a difference in the message and for Christianity a very significant difference.

32

So Christ went through a lot of trouble to see that He would make a clear point that He only represented His Father. You will find this out when you study; that He only and always represented His father. Everything about Christ points to his father. His name Jesus means "God has saved." So His name is in reference to His Father. In John He is called "the word of God" in the first verse of John. So he is the word of somebody else.

Ok, all through Christ's life from beginning to end He made a point to only represent his Father. The first time recorded in your Bible is in Luke 2:49 when he was 12 years old. He was in the temple and he said to his parents "*wist ye not that I must be about my Father's business?*" And also, as I have indicated, His entire ministry as recorded in John was focused on His Father. And at the end of His earthly ministry in the Garden of Gethsemane when he was summing up His life, He said "*I have finished the work which thou gavest me to do. I have manifested thy name unto the men which thou gavest me out of the world.*" So he said He has done His Father's work. So from beginning to end, that is what he was doing very purposefully.

The name for **Jesus** in Greek is the Hebrew word **Joshua** and it comes from Strong's #3091 *Jehovah has saved.* So in both languages His name is not referring to Him being the destination, but it is referring to His Father. He is not where you are going, He is **the Way**. Again, He is who you are going with. And He made a great effort to make sure that people would know that He is the One that you are going with. He is not where you are going. This is a very important point, because later on in the New Testament that began to change. He didn't view Himself as the end; He viewed Himself as the One who takes you somewhere.

So I want to read a little bit of that. He has a task when He is taking you to His Father. And he had a particularly difficult task because the people he ministered to, both Jews and Gentiles didn't know His Father. It is much the same way with Christians today. How do you take somebody somewhere when they don't know where they are going? So He had to clearly illustrate to them that they didn't know his father. So I am going to read a few references citing Jesus' addressing this. There are lots of them. But I am just going to read seven or cite seven if I don't read them all. And I am also going to do this so you can get a feel for John and how much Christ dealt with the fact that the people didn't know his father. Now I am going to give you these references. So you will be getting a lot of information today to better enable you in your studies.

I am going to go to John 12:44-45. "*Jesus cried and said, He that believeth on me, believeth not on me but on him that sent me. And he that seeth me seeth him that sent me.*" The Lord here is certainly not promoting a belief in Himself. This has important implications for understanding His definition of salvation. So he is clearly saying that He represents somebody else.

And again in John 10: 37-38, "*If I do not the works of my Father, believe me not. But if I do, though ye believe not me, believe the works: that ye may know, and believe, that the Father is in me, and I in him.*" You will find the word "works" here is one of a few important incidents of a translation that obscures Jesus' intent. The word "works" in the Greek, the word they used to translate to the word "works" has two definitions. One definition is "*to labor in an occupation,*" like a brick layer. The other is "*to do kind deeds.*" So it actually should have been written, "*if I do not the kind deeds of my father believe me not.*" That is actually the best translation because he is not laboring like a brick layer; He is doing kind deeds to demonstrate His Father's character. So the word "works" is a little misleading. That may be helpful to remember.

Another one is in 5:31. He is telling people he is not the destination. He said "*If I bear witness of myself, my witness is not true.*" So He is actually saying, I am representing somebody else. I am not *where* you are going. I'm just the one who can take you there; I am **The Way**.

Another one is in John 12:49-50. There are so many I am just reading a few to give you an idea of how extensive this is. "*For I have not spoken of myself; but the Father which sent me, he gave me a commandment, what I should say, and what I should speak. And I know that his commandment is life everlasting: whatsoever I speak therefore, even as the Father said unto me, so I speak.*" So he is saying, I am not even representing myself in what I am saying. In all the things I teach and say I am representing my Father in what I say and that which I speak. So he is making it clear that His Father is telling Him **what** to say. He even couches it in terms of a commandment. And then in 5:30, " *I can of mine own self do nothing: as I hear, I judge: and my judgment is just; because I seek not mine own will, but the will of the Father which hath sent me.* "

So again He is saying He is pointing to where you are going. And in the same chapter in verse 36 it says, "*I have greater witness than that of John (the Baptist): for the kind deeds which the Father hath given me to finish, the same kind deeds that I do, bear witness of me, that the Father hath sent me.*" So He is saying everything I do is bearing witness of somebody else. It is not me but my Father. So He is doing these acts of kindness to demonstrate what the character of His Father is like in view of the people not knowing Him.

And then in John 6:44 is the last one that I will read. Amazing how many times he said it. "*No man can come to me, except the Father which hath sent me draw him.*" So He is saying even people who come to Him it is not His doing but the doing of His Father. So He is making a clear point that He is not **where** you are going. He is just **the one to take you there**. He is again representing somebody else.

That changed drastically in some of the later portions of the New Testament. He became the focus. He became the destination. And the lack of knowing His Father carried over into Christianity. But in John, Christ is saying it differently. This is something that needs to be listened to because this is certainly His desire.

Now He is also constantly referencing "*He who sent me.*" as you can see. Remember there are 44 times this is said, I am going to read you seven. I will just cite them without having to read some of them. In 7:29, He says, "*I am from Him and He has sent me.*" 8:26 "*He that sent me is true.*" You are going to notice as you read John that John is one of only three places in the Bible, counting the Old Testament, where "the true God" phrase is used; "the One True God." I will get into that in a little bit. So when you see this word "true" come up you should pay particular attention. John 8:29, "*He*

35

that sent me is with me." 8:42, *"Neither came I of myself, but he sent me."* 9:4 says, *"I do the kind deeds of him that sent me."* And again, *"The servant is not greater than his Lord, the one that sent him."* And 17:23 says, *"That the world may know that* **thou** *has sent me, and* **hast loved them,** *as thou hast loved me."* He is constantly referring to the one who sent Him. There were some Pharisees that came to Him and asked Him, "From whence came ye" they said. And he answered and said, You know where I came from. And they said what we shall answer because we are sent. What shall we tell those who sent us? So it was clear that they understood what it was like to represent somebody else. He is not representing Himself.

So now, all of this is laying the foundation for His definition of salvation; because if He was the destination in the salvation process then salvation would have one definition but when His Father is the destination and Christ's task is to take you to Him, then there is another definition of salvation. So Christ described His Father often in terms of being "the One True God," like I said before. In John 17:3, Christ talks about the One True God. And in another place in II Chronicles 15:3, it says this *"Now for a long season Israel hath been without the true God, and without a teaching priest."* That term "long season," just happens to reference a period of 500 years that they had been without the true God. I have found only twelve places in the Bible that use the phrase "God is true."

So Jesus proclaimed over and over to the Jews that they did not know His Father, the One True God. It has now been a longer period than the one in II Chronicles. And there begins to emerge a very interesting pattern when you begin to progress through the instances of it in the Gospel of John; that is of him telling people that they do not know His Father. A very interesting pattern. He starts out by telling one person. In John 4:22 He told the women at the well, *"Ye worship ye know not what."* Then as this pattern begins to progress, Jesus starts to tell bigger groups of people. He continues and He tells his Apostles and then larger groups up to the leaders of the Jewish temple religion and finally Jesus tells His Father that the people do not know Him. So this pattern is really interesting as you read through John.

So I am going to read in John 5:37, "*And the Father himself, which hath sent me, hath borne witness of me. Ye have neither heard his voice at any time, nor seen his shape.*" This has far reaching implications to the Jewish view of the Sinai experience by Moses. "*And ye have not his word abiding in you: for whom he hath sent, him ye believe not.*" There really is a significant verse right there, "*Ye have neither heard his voice at any time.*"

How did they get the Old Testament? What voice were they hearing? He said you have never heard His voice at any time. You will find it was one who is called The Angel of the Presence.

Now back to the pattern in John. Then He spoke to a larger group of people that were there in a synagogue in Galilee. Now He is going to talk to a larger group yet of people in 7:28-29 in the temple. He is going to tell them the same thing. "*Then cried Jesus in the temple as he taught, saying, Ye both know me, and ye know whence I am: and I am not come of myself, but he that sent me is true, whom ye know not. But I know him: for I am from him, and he hath sent me.*" So there He is telling a large group of people in the temple. He is telling them that they do not know God. It started out with one person, then a small group and now a large group.

Then in 8:54-55, He is telling the very pious religious leadership. He is telling the religious leaders of the Jews. "*Jesus answered, If I honour myself, my honour is nothing: it is my Father that honoureth me; of whom ye say, that he is your God: Yet ye have not known him; but I know him: and if I should say, I know him not, I shall be a liar like unto you: but I know him, and keep his saying.*" So He is telling the religious leaders of His nation, who live in a high priest palace and walk around with an entourage. Their high priest went through Jerusalem on foot and when he went he had a man behind him carrying the scroll of the Levitical Law, it was his main scribe who was also considered a lawyer. When he went into the temple he had people who would walk with him who carried a pillow for him to sit on. He owned all the booths of the concessions in the temple and took a percentage of all the transactions by the money changers. So he was a man of high position and here he is being told that he does not know God; he says this to the very man who thinks that his mission in life and his occupation and his status is to teach people who God is. That is a big deal.

Then in 15:21 He is telling His Apostles, "*But all these things will they do unto you for my name's (character) sake, because they know not him that sent me.*" Then finally in the Garden of Gethsemane in 17:3, which is his prayer on His way to the garden. Actually, it is just before he got to the vineyard when he said I am the true vine. 17:25 *"O righteous Father, the world hath not known thee: but I have known thee, and these have known that thou hast sent me. And I have declared unto them thy name, and will declare it: that the love wherewith thou hast loved me may be in them, and I in them."*

Now I want to point out another word that makes such references obscure by the way they are translated. The word "name" is another word that is critical for your understanding of the New Testament. There are 171 instances when the word "name" is translated in your New Testament. Only one of them comes from the Greek word "name; 170 come from another word that doesn't mean name. The word "<u>onoma</u>" #3686 means "*a personality*" or "*your character*" or what you are like. That's what 170 of them should be saying. Another word "<u>onomazo</u>", which is #3587 means "*an appellation*" or "*what someone is called*" and is used only once. So when they translate the word "name" all the way through the New Testament, 170 out of the 171 times it doesn't mean "name", it means **character** or what a person is like, it comes from the root word "*to know someone.*" So at the garden prayer when He said, "*I have manifested thy name*" He is really saying **I have manifested to the world your character or what you are like in your personality so they can know you**, which is what he said in other places. So that is something that makes some scriptures obscure. There is no instance where Christ used His Father's name being translated into English.

So character and personality and to know someone is definitely not a title or a name of someone or what someone is called. And the other word onomazo "*an appellation,*" you know what an appellation is, it means a term that something or someone is called. So then when He said I have manifested thy name or have

38

declared thy name, He is actually saying I have manifested thy character, the word manifested means "*to make obvious.*" So Christ was saying I have made obvious what you are like or your character or your personality by the good deeds I have done. And when he says I have declared your name he is actually saying I have not only told the world who you are by my actions I am telling the world who you are by my speech. So that is a very significant way to look at what Jesus said to His Father.

I'm going to explain to you more about the word "name" and why it was so important to the Bible translators to use the word "name" instead of the word "character." They had a very important reason to translate it that way. Heathen religions believe in what may be thought of as magic words. The concept of Christian liturgy springs out of that belief. They wanted the word "Jesus" to be a supernatural force, like a magic word. What if we prayed in His character or as He would pray instead? What He is like is certainly the entire force of spiritual power in the lives of Christians. **Knowing Him** is what releases that power in us, not the Greek version of His Hebrew name.

So Christ was actually purposeful when He manifested His Father's character and personality to the world; He was doing that very intentionally. And it is an interesting study to go look and see exactly what he did. For example, when He raised people from the dead: He raised Jairus' daughter – a child; He raised the man at Nain – the widow's son and a young man; and He raised Lazarus – an old man. So he raised a child, a young man, and an old man; he is not just raising anybody, He is raising a variety of people, both male and female. And everything he did was like that. He loved those who were not loved. He loved the unloving or that is to say those people who didn't love. He loved the woman who was brought before him when he wrote on the ground. He loved Matthew who was a tax collector and he loved Zacchaeus. He loved the Roman soldier who was a man of the people who were occupying His nation whose servant needed healed. He loved Nicodemus a member of the Sanhedrin who were his bitterest enemies. He loved Mary Magdalene, who they thought was so evil she shouldn't be touching His feet. And He loved the thief on the cross beside Him. So it is an interesting study. I don't have time to go into that here but you can see when you study the Book of John that Christ very clearly performed deeds of kindness specifically to show who His Father is in the most complete way that he could.

There is another support for his definition of His Father other than His verbal description of His father in the New Testament, not just in John. Matthew is very supportive of Christ's view of His Father. And there is one very good reference in Luke that stands out from all the others. There are not any references to Christ describing His Father in the Book of Mark, in any form. The Book of Mark is actually presenting the idea that Christ is the **destination** rather than **the one taking you to His Father**. So what is His Father like from the point of view of Jesus?

I am going to read a few references starting at Matthew 7:11 to give you a good feel for his writings about this matter. I am going to read you some of Jesus describing His Father in Matthew; this is what His Father is like. So he did it by raising the dead, by showing forth His Father's love, and now He is doing it here with His speech and describing Him with His words in Matthew 7:11, "*If ye then, being evil, know how to give good gifts unto your children, how much more shall your Father which is in heaven give good things to them that ask Him?*" He is saying His Father is a better father than any of us. That was news to a lot of Jews. They often thought of God as vengeful, distant, and jealous.

I will be telling you how that came to be startling news. In Matt 6:8 He says, "*Your Father knoweth what things you have need of, before you ask Him.*" He is so intimate in His love for you and so personally involved in your life that He knows what you need before you even ask Him, maybe even before you know yourself. Aren't fathers like that? You see a little kid struggling he's got his cookie in the sand he isn't saying dad clean the sand off my cookie a dad just knows it must be done and dad just says whoa here let me help you fix your cookie. This kind of character of God is all news to the Jews. Is it news to you? This is really a profound departure to what they are used to hearing. I'm sure they were scratching their heads when they heard Him describing His Father in Matt 10:29-30. I told you I was going to give you a lot of information. "*Are not two sparrows sold for 2 farthings and one of them shall not fall without your father knowing. But the very hairs of your head are all numbered.*" So he is really getting serious about how intimate His Father is in His love for us and with the people he is talking to.

And in Matt 5:43-45 - you will note this is to be a very important scripture, I want you to remember this. "*Ye have heard it and it hath been said thou shalt love thy neighbor and hate thine enemy.*" And where it says that is in Deuteronomy 23:6 it says you shall hate your enemy forever. "*But I say unto you love your enemies and bless them that curse you, do good to them who hate you and pray for them who despitefully use you and persecute you.*" Now as I read this, remember these points because then he is going to say why. He is going to say why you should love your enemies. Why do you bless them that curse you, why you do good to them that hate you, why do you pray for them which despitefully use you and persecute you? He will say **why** to all this: "*That ye may be the children of your Father which is in heaven for he maketh His sun to rise on the evil and on the good and sendeth rain on the just and the unjust. For if ye love them only which love you what reward have ye.*" It is hard to see you with tears in my eyes. "*Do not even the publicans the same. And if ye salute your brethren only what do you do more than others? Do not even the publicans so? Be ye therefore perfect even as your Father in heaven is perfect.*" This is Matthew 5:45-48. His Father is always, only, and ever love. So He is saying every person would like to take after their father, of course those who have good fathers. And if you want to take after Jesus' Father and your heavenly Father, love your enemies and so forth all things that were listed because He is perfect in love. This very teaching is important because that was a load for the Jews; they were aghast because He had just denied Deuteronomy 23:6. He just denied a portion of their Torah, in fact He is denying all the portions of it that describe the character of their God to be other than love.

So then Luke is also supportive. This scripture in Luke is so profound that later authors of the New Testament couldn't grasp it. It is in Luke 6:27-36. This is another account of the same incident which I just cited from Matthew but it adds some things to it that are vitally important. "*But I say unto you which hear, Love your enemies, do good to them which hate you, Bless them that curse you, and pray for them which despitefully use you. And unto him that smiteth thee on the one cheek offer also the other; and him that taketh away thy cloak forbid not to take thy coat also. Give to every*

41

man that asketh of thee; and of him that taketh away thy goods ask them not again. And as ye would that men should do to you, do ye also to them likewise. For if ye love them which love you, what thank have ye? for sinners also love those that love them. And if ye do good to them which do good to you, what thank have ye? for sinners also do even the same. And if ye lend to them of whom ye hope to receive, what thank have ye? for sinners also lend to sinners, to receive as much again. But love ye your enemies, and do good, and lend, hoping for nothing again; and your reward shall be great, and ye shall be the children of the Highest: for he is kind unto the unthankful and to the evil.

Wow. He is kind to those who are evil and to the unthankful. *"Be ye therefore merciful as your Father in heaven is merciful."* I wonder if Jesus would agree with that which says, *"Vengeance is mine sayeth the Lord?"* So that was the ultimate blow to those that were hearing Him. He is kind even to those who are evil.

At this point I would also add some interesting insights given by Jesus about His Father. Did you know Jesus indicates that the Holy Ghost/Comforter is in fact the Spirit of His Father? You will find this in Matthew 10:19-20 and 16:17; and in John 14:16-17, 14:26 and 15:26. In John 14:26 it says His Father will send the Holy Spirit. Which Father do you want to be your source of the Holy Spirit: the one depicted in Numbers 31 or the one described in Luke 6:35 Who is kind and loving to absolutely everybody?

In Matthew 5:16 Jesus shows that He expects us to consider that the kindness we show others will directly affect that person's view of His Father. In this matter do we think the way He expects us to? And Matthew 20:50 Jesus says we will obtain kinship with Him if we do the will of His Father. Whose will do we seek to follow?

Now only John says God is love; that was said nowhere else in the Bible. He says it in I John in 4:7-8 *"Beloved, let us love one another: for love is of God; and every one that loveth is born of God, and knoweth God. He that loveth not knoweth not God; for God is love."* And again in verse16 it reads *"And we have known and believed the love that God hath to us. God is love; and he that* *dwelleth in love dwelleth in God, and God in him.*" You will notice in this scripture that how one is born again is well defined.

So here we come to the Lord's definition of salvation. And I want to read these to you. This is John 5:24. Christ is going to tell you His definition of salvation. I can't seem to find it. Ok, I'm in Luke oops. If I would have lost this scripture I would have just gone home. This is one of my prize scriptures. This is **Christ's definition of salvation,** one of them. "*Verily, verily I say unto you, he that heareth my word and believeth on Him that sent me has everlasting life. And shall not come to condemnation but is passed from death unto life*"; passed unto life means born again. Knowing the Father then is foundational for being born again. "*He that heareth my word and believeth on Him that sent me has everlasting life.*" Everlasting life is salvation.

Then read John 17:3, which is the other place where Christ defines salvation. Boy I'm glad she helped me find 5:24. "*And this is life eternal that they might know Thee the only true God and he whom Thou hast sent.*" So Christ is clearly saying **to know His Father is salvation**. That goes along with everything else that He has been doing and saying. And then there is another one I want to read that is found at John 6:45. It says "*Every man therefore that hath heard and hath learned of the Father cometh unto me.*" And again in I John 5:20 (This is John's words) "*And we know that the Son of God is come, and hath given us an understanding, that we may know Him that is true, and we are in Him that is true, even by his Son Jesus Christ. This is the true God, and eternal life.*" So here are some words that are very essential. It says understanding, knowing, learning, and believing; "Believeth on him that sent me." **So knowing, believing, learning and understanding are the words he used in terms of his definition of salvation**.

When they crucified Christ, when you read in the Bible about that event, you get the impression that they were jealous of His popularity. You get used to the impression that they were upset that He didn't keep the Sabbath. But all the Jews knew that the Nazarenes, those who historians called the Essenes, had a different calendar. They all knew that. This is clearly demonstrated when Jesus and the Apostles did the Passover on what we call the Last Supper on one day and the Jews did their Passover after the crucifixion. The Passover is a Sabbath and Jesus would never have done it on some other day. And this Sabbath business didn't come up at His trials because the Romans knew too that Jesus had a different Sabbath and the matter would have been redundant. Why would you condemn someone for keeping their own Sabbath? Also we often think it was because He said He was the Son of God. Those three things give you the impression that they are the reasons why they crucified Him. But there are records and histories of other people who claimed to be a Son of God and they didn't get crucified. The underlying problem that was facing the temple religion leadership was the Torah. Christ didn't teach or preach **against** their God. He just told them they didn't know Him. He preached **for** His Father. And by preaching for His Father many people believed Him. Had the religious leaders believed Him they would have had to deny their entire religion.

Now I want to show you what I mean by that. When Jesus said they don't know Him what kind of God did they know? Now you need to listen really good here because we are in a time when this topic is very urgent because this kind of god has emerged again in our world. A year before now I could have read this and it wouldn't have meant the same thing. The prophecies are coming true so clearly that I want you to understand Numbers Chapter 31. I'm just going to read selected verses. I don't want you to be too sad when you hear this. It is going to be describing the God they believed in. This is the God they would have had to deny in order to follow Christ and acknowledge His deeds as representing the nature of God. I'm going to read you two such instances so you will get a clear picture of the God they believed in. This is what prompted the Lord to so often tell them that they did not know His Father. This is the God they knew instead. This is written in their Torah and in your Bible. "*And the Lord spoke unto Moses saying, Avenge the children of Israel of the Midianites afterwards thou shall be gathered unto thy people.*"

Now the setting for this chapter is Moses' wife is a Midianite, and I want you to remember Christ said in the New Testament, "*My Father judges no man but gives all judgment unto the Son.*" So now here you are going to have God avenge and judge them. This is the setting for it, just so you will understand this reading. Midian was a son of Abraham, a legitimate son by his wife

44

Ketturah. Isaac was a legitimate son by his wife Sarah. Ishmael was not a legitimate son in the eyes of the Jews because he came from Sarah's handmaiden who was not his wife, even though Ishmael was his first born. Isaac was the second born and Midian was born of Ketturah after Sarah died. So there was a conflict over who was going to be the rightful heir of the Abrahamic Covenant, because the covenant included owning land and controlling vast areas and it encompassed all their world view and religion and legitimacy as a people.

So here is a story of God telling Moses to avenge the children of Israel of the Midianites because the men were following Moses' example in marrying Midianite women. And if they married too many of them and they began to have too many of the Midianite people involved in their culture and lives it could change the balance of power in determining who was the rightful heirs. And then the Midianites would have a primary place in the Abrahamic Covenant.

And even in the time of Jesus it was a sore spot with the Jews for centuries because Moses learned his religion from the Midianites. When he left Egypt he went to the Land of Midian and he was taught by Jethro the high priest of Midian. Jethro then came while Moses was in the desert and gave him advice about how to leave Israel and be replaced by 70 elders. So the men started marrying Midianite women and then this story is told in Numbers 31. "*And Moses spake unto the people saying arm some of yourselves unto the war and let them go against the Midianites and avenge the Lord of Midian. So there were delivered out of the thousands of Israel a thousand of every tribe twelve_thousand armed for war. And Moses sent them to the war a thousand for every tribe, them and Phineas the son of Eliezer the priest, to the war with the holy instruments*" He went with the Arc of the Covenant with them and the trumpets to blow in his hand. "*And they warred against the Midianites as the Lord commanded Moses, And they slew all the males.*" It turns out there were 200,000Midianites.

"*And the children of Israel took all the women of Midian captives and their little ones and took the spoil of all their cattle and all their flocks and all their goods. And they burnt all their cities wherever they dwelt and all their goodly castles with fire. And they took all the spoil and all the prey both of men and of beasts. And they brought the captives and the prey and the spoil unto Moses... And Moses and Eliezer the priest and all the princes of the congregation went forth to meet them without the camp.* Princes of the congregation is a reference to what was later called the Sanhedrin. *And Moses was wroth with the officers of the Host, with the captains over thousands and with the captains over hundreds which came from the battle. And Moses said unto them* **have ye saved all the women alive?** *Now therefore* **kill every male among the little ones.**" The children. "*And kill every woman that hath known man by lying with him. But all the women and children that have not known a man by lying with him keep alive for yourselves.*" Here in verses 26-30 the priests get to have virgin slaves. "*And the booty being the rest of the prey which the men of war had caught.*" It goes on the list how many. "*And thirty and two thousand persons in all of women that had not known man by lying with him.*" 32,000. "*And the persons were sixteen thousand of which the Lord's tribute was thirty and two persons.*" I don't know if that means human sacrifice or not. They gave 32 of these young women to God. "*And the officers which were over the thousands of the host, the captains of thousands and captains of hundreds came near unto Moses. And they said unto Moses thy servants have taken the sum of the men of war which are under our charge and there lacketh not one man of us.*"

So, 12,000 Israelites fought 200,000 Midianite men and all the women and children that they killed and they didn't lose a single soldier. "*For the men of war had taken spoil every man for himself. And Moses and Eliezer the priest took the gold of the captains of thousands and of hundreds and brought it unto the tabernacle of the congregation for a memorial for the children of Israel before the Lord.*" It was so exciting that they killed all those people men, women, and children and sold them as slaves that they made a memorial to put in the temple. That is the god they believed in.

Just so you know, according to Acts 7:39, Moses was not even present with Israel when the events described here happened. In all probability it is not an actual historical account. Think about this for a moment. Moses was a very holy prophet. He stood in the presence of God and he did many wonderful miracles. If this

46

Chapter 31 is actually a valid account, Moses, the founder of the Jewish religion, would have been one of the world's worst criminals with crimes against humanity, war crimes, and genocide. Can you see now for the people who believe that places like Numbers 31 and I Samuel 15 are a part of the whole flowing truth of the Bible that their salvation is compromised? Jesus said knowing His Father is salvation. How would loving your enemies and turning the other cheek make you a true child of such a God as described above? This view of God is at this moment strongly embedded in Christianity and Judaism. Malachi 3:6 says "*I am the Lord, I change not.*" And in Luke it says "*God is kind to those who are evil.*" And in John it says, "*God is love.*" Jesus says "*my Father judges no man.*" Places like the account in Numbers 31 need to be viewed in light of these other statements.

ISIS is doing this as we speak. The BBC reports that at this time they are killing seven people per hour around the clock in the name of God; up to that time in Nov. 2014, 5770 people had been killed. They had sold so far over 5000 young girls as sex slaves in Iraq at a slave market. They sell them every day. They go starting from 12 dollars and up to a thousand. In Nigeria, where terrorism is growing, they stole hundreds of school girls and it is reported that they sold them all for 12 dollars apiece. This is the god they believed in and has emerged again. And it is here now in our world. And it is spreading. Now ISIS isn't the only one doing it. Now in this latest Wall Street Journal I read just yesterday the Iraqi army has the same tactic.

Never before has it been so urgent for Christians to embrace Jesus' descriptions of His Father. So when Jesus told them you don't know My Father they really did not know His Father. Do you know His Father? This is why it was so shocking that they should love their enemies so they could be like God their Father. It was so startling to hear that God is kind to those that are evil let alone the children of the people of Moses' wife.

Now I want to read a little bit more about the kind of God they believed in. This is not going to be pleasant either. But it is important to have more than one example. It is important for you to know this. You have all heard that Samuel was a prophet and he anointed Saul as king of Israel. And, if you studied your Bible, it is in the back of your mind that the kingdom of Saul was taken away from him because he was disobedient, remember that? So Samuel went to anoint David instead. David didn't want to take the kingdom and he went in and took Saul's possessions while he was asleep and then gave them back to him to show him he could have killed him but he didn't because David considered Saul as the Lord's anointed. I'll read what Saul did to lose the kingdom. This is the background for what is recorded in I Samuel chapter 15.

Have you ever known just what Saul did to disobey the Lord so the kingdom was taken from him? *"Samuel also said unto Saul, the Lord sent me to anoint thee to be king over his people Israel. Now therefore hearken thou unto the voice of the words of the Lord. Thus saith the Lord of hosts I remember that which Amalek did to Israel, how he laid wait for him in the way when he came up from Egypt."* This is avenging a wrong that happened about 500 years before. Who could hold a grudge that long? *"Now go and smite Amalek, and utterly destroy all that they have and spare them not, but slay both man and woman, infant and suckling, ox and sheep, camel and ass."* So they went to do that. I just don't have the stomach to read this horrible account here in church before you gentle loving people. There are parts of the Bible that are too gross to be read in church. The short of it is Saul did not do enough killing and that is the reason why the kingdom was taken from him. I just do not have the heart to read it to you. But for those of you who are reading this I will include this information here from portions of I Samuel 15, *"And Saul smote the Amalekites from Havilah until thou comest to Shur, that is over against Egypt. And he took Agag the king of the Amalekites alive, and utterly destroyed all the people with the edge of the sword. But Saul and the people spared Agag, and the best of the sheep, and of the oxen, and of the fatlings, and the lambs, and all that was good, and would not utterly destroy them: but every thing that was vile and refuse, that they destroyed utterly.*

Then came the word of the LORD unto Samuel, saying, It repenteth me that I have set up Saul to be king: for he is turned back from following me, and hath not performed my commandments. And it grieved Samuel; and he cried unto the LORD all night.

And Samuel came to Saul: and Saul said unto him, Blessed be thou of the LORD: I have performed the commandment of the LORD. And Samuel said, What meaneth then this bleating of the sheep in mine ears, and the lowing of the oxen which I hear? And Saul said, They have brought them from the Amalekites: for the people spared the best of the sheep and of the oxen, to sacrifice unto the LORD thy God; and the rest we have utterly destroyed.

Then Samuel said unto Saul, Stay, and I will tell thee what the LORD hath said to me this night. And he said unto him, Say on. And Samuel said, When thou wast little in thine own sight, wast thou not made the head of the tribes of Israel, and the LORD anointed thee king over Israel? And the LORD sent thee on a journey, and said, Go and utterly destroy the sinners the Amalekites, and fight against them until they be consumed. Wherefore then didst thou not obey the voice of the LORD, but didst fly upon the spoil, and didst evil in the sight of the LORD? And Saul said unto Samuel, Yea, I have obeyed the voice of the LORD, and have gone the way which the LORD sent me, and have brought Agag the king of Amalek, and have utterly destroyed the Amalekites. But the people took of the spoil, sheep and oxen, the chief of the things which should have been utterly destroyed, to sacrifice unto the LORD thy God in Gilgal.

And Saul said unto Samuel, I have sinned: for I have transgressed the commandment of the LORD, and thy words: because I feared the people, and obeyed their voice. Now therefore, I pray thee, pardon my sin, and turn again with me, that I may worship the LORD.

And Samuel said unto Saul, I will not return with thee: for thou hast rejected the word of the LORD, and the LORD hath rejected thee from being king over Israel. Then said Samuel, Bring ye hither to me Agag the king of the Amalekites. And Agag came unto him delicately. And Agag said, Surely the bitterness of death is past. And Samuel said, As thy sword hath made women childless, so shall thy mother be childless among women. And Samuel hewed Agag in pieces before the LORD in Gilgal.

Samuel the prophet dismembered a man in the name of God. A man who came delicately to him and asked to live and would not even forgive Saul when he asked for it! And this is a major prophet of Israel who was dedicated to God from his birth. Certainly Samuel was a true prophet, so this account must be an overwrite.

Now continuing on let me just quote one bit more. I Samuel 15:10 *"Then came the word of the Lord unto Samuel saying, it repenteth me that I have set up Saul to become King for he is turned back from following me and hath not performed my commandments."* He did not kill as many as God wanted. Because he did not kill all the animals and people, the kingdom was taken away from him is the short of it. So Christ had a tough job: to show them Who his Father was and to demonstrate what He is like, so they could know who His Father is and find salvation.

Now what does all this have to do with us? I John says in 4:8 *"He that loveth not knoweth not God for God is love."* In the communities of the world right now, where this kind of God that these reading have described is believed, there is murder and chaos; there is every kind of awful thing you could ever think of and more happening. Christ's view of His Father is what it takes to be a people that can pass through these tribulation times. Christians need to love like Him. They need to be the true children of His Father.

I am going to read you some of that but first I want to tell you my experience of being born again. I want to tell you about my experience with the love of God that changed my life forever in a moment, when I was 14, one year after my grandfather died. My grandmother had woods with big trees behind her house on their property in Oregon. The big woods were Douglas fir and western red cedar. And they were all 3 and 4 feet on the stump; big huge trees and a very wonderful place to be with the Lord. And I decided I was going to go there and spend the summer with the Lord.

And being 14 years old, I built a little grass hut and it leaked right over my bed. And I just spent every day walking around the woods speaking to the Lord and reading the scriptures and talking out loud to the Lord. I was delighted because his spirit was with me all the time. I spent the whole summer doing that. In fact my grandma was always worried because I wasn't eating very often and then only a little bit. I was only a couple hundred yards from her house. But I did not come much to eat. I would just get an orange or something and go back. I was really little. I weighed 72 pounds when I was 14. I could close my fingers around my biceps. I used to do it to show the kids how skinny I was. So I was really little and skinny.

So one night as the summer was ending and I was getting ready to return home, I had to write to my mother to tell her to send me a bus ticket to come back home. I lived near the Oregon ocean beach. And I was trying to describe to her what kind of summer I had and it was hard to find the words. After dealing with the bus tickets, I wrote on the paper "God is here." When I wrote that it was long after darkness fell. And I had a double mantle white gas lantern that you have to pump up; and they are usually so bright that you can't look at them. As I wrote those words, "God is here" the forest began to get light. My first thought was there was something wrong with my lantern. I looked at it and it looked dim. I thought there is something wrong with it. And when I went to reach for it I realized that it wasn't the lantern. And I stood up and I went over by a tree and I started looking at this awesome light. It was so brilliant. It was more brilliant than a welders' arc or anything I am familiar with. But it did not hurt my eyes.

And I walked up to this tree, and I knew the Lord was there and I said, "Lord there are no shadows in the bark." I had never seen a tree that didn't have shadows in the bark. The cracks in the bark can't get light in them. There was light coming from my side. I looked at the tree on the other side and there was light in all the cracks all the way around the tree. And I said 'Wow Lord your light comes from everywhere' And I looked down there was a big spray of sword ferns. And underneath of them they have tiny globules of spores that look like a little droplet of honey. And I picked them up with my arm like this and I looked underneath and all those little spores were glowing. Then I realized that the Lord was there! He came just to tell me He loved me. That's all. Just that. I didn't think there would ever be anybody who loved me besides my mother and my granddad. Girls didn't like me, because I was skinny and shy. And I couldn't play sports.

But He loved me. And it was just natural. It was not a huge deal. He just came and loved me. And then he began to talk to me. And I would ask Him questions. And He was like right here over my shoulder. I didn't think to turn around to look at Him but I heard his audible voice. And He was just there in the brilliant light. And it was all so utterly natural that I didn't think anything to be extraordinary at the time. How wonderful it was. And I still looked at this tree. And He said to me "that tree is your brother." And I said "Lord how can that be?" And He said "well you are both alive and I have given you both the gift of life. And you both are going to get older. And you both need nourishment. And you both live in the weather when it is cold or hot. When the tree is cold, you are cold. The tree has a spirit and you have a spirit." And He explained to me that kind of thing.

Then He said "quit worrying about your body." He said, "Your body isn't you. It is just what you live in. It is just a servant that I have given you so you can spend time with your gift of life upon the earth. So don't worry about being skinny or how people see you because you are what I love". And He said, "Take good care of your body. If you don't take good care of it then it won't be around as long as I want it to be". And He just told me simple things like that. And it changed everything in my life. I quit being shy. The kids at school the next year when I went into the freshman class in high school were shocked. I was as bold as brass. I could talk to anybody because he loved me.

He loved me. That is where He is taking us. That is where we are all going. God is here. And so I have this testimony. I have never denied it. There is nothing else in my life that is more defining than this experience with the love of the Lord Jesus. And during that year I gained 50 pounds. I weighed that until I got married.

Now one of the sad things about your Bible, and we are all going to go there next time, is the Old Testament view of God was grafted into your New Testament. And it was far and away not the intention of Jesus that this should happen. But this was done by authors who came later who did not know the Lord during His earthly walk and who were unfamiliar with His ministry. They were unfamiliar with His teachings and with what he did. There is a view in Romans 5:9 that says when a Christian is saved they are saved from the wrath of His Father. There is another one in Romans 6:3 which says when you are baptized you are baptized unto death. Even though Christ says *"I am the way the truth and the life"*. He said let the dead bury the dead. I am the living bread. I give you living water. I come that you might have life and have it more abundantly.

So in spite of all those things that He taught, some later authors taught you are baptized unto death. So I want to read one out of Hebrews in closing. This is part of the information so you can know that the Old Testament God, in spite of all Christ did, got grafted into your New Testament. This is Hebrews 10: 30-31 *"For we know him that hath said, Vengeance belongeth unto me, I will recompense, saith the Lord. And again, The Lord shall judge his people. **It is a fearful thing to fall into the hands of the living God.**"*

They knew the god of vengeance. Even though Christ said my father judges no man. Now listen again to this verse 31. *"It is a fearful thing to fall into the hands of the living God."* They are afraid of Jesus' Father in the New Testament after Christ taught all he could about His Father being loving and kind. After all His works of kindness demonstrating the character of His Father they were afraid of Him. After all His times of showing that He knows that His Father is so intimate and personal with you that he knows what you need before you even ask Him. He is kind even to those who are evil and to the wicked and to those who are unthankful. All the things he taught about His Father, the author of Hebrews, whoever he was, said it is a fearful thing to fall into the hand of the Living God.

So here into the Christian life comes the Old Testament view of the Father. And then you get inquisitions, you get the crusades. Now both sides are killing in God's name. Both the terrorists and the armies of the nations are killing in His name. They interviewed a military officer in the paper and he said "I just hope I live long enough to kill as many people as I can in the name of the Lord". And who was he killing? He was killing ISIS terrorists who were also killing in the name of the Lord. So we live in a day when it is no longer going to serve the Christian community to ignore the ministry of Jesus Christ as He demonstrated the character of His Father as expressed and recorded in your writings of the New Testament.

And now to close this session let me say, because it is central in importance to this series, I will now recap in Jesus' own words what He says and demonstrates the character of His Father to be. First, that aspect of Jesus' Father that is in clearest contrast with their Torah, is God is kind to those who are unthankful and evil. If we want to be the true children of Him we must love our enemies, turn the other cheek, pray for those who despitefully use us and so on. Another important point of departure from what the Jews were used to in their concept of God was just how intimately personal and involved in every person's life He is. The hairs of your head being numbered and God's knowing what you need before you even ask being the case in point. God is love was for many a novel idea, but most of all His definition of salvation resonated with a public that was finding their newly developed access to the words of the prophets and the writings of Jeremiah. Being intimately and dearly loved by Him was very comforting in contrast with being afraid of Him and having to watch out for your life if you violated even a minor point of the traditional legal code. Simply put Jesus represented freedom to an oppressed people: oppressed from without and from within. Thank you.

Session 3
Choosing a Pathway to Discovering the One True God
January 11, 2015

Good morning everybody. Hopefully I won't be looking in Luke for a scripture in John this time. I am going to be speaking a lot about the Lord in this series. We are continuing the series called Jesus' View of His Father: a perspective for the Thinking Christian. To start, I want to mention something about His name a little bit. Jacob, in what is written about him by the early church, called Him the many named One. And I think we have found over 30 different names for the Lord Jesus in the scriptures: Son of Man, Lion of Judah, Redeemer of Israel, Son of David, Wonderful Counselor, Emmanuel, Jesus, the mighty God, the everlasting Father, the Prince of Peace, and many more. He preferred to call Himself the Son of Man. And His name in His native language, which was Aramaic, was Yeshua. It is hard to say what His parents called Him when it was time to eat dinner. But "Yeshua" is one way to say it, which is probably the most common. But "Yahoshua" is when you want to put the first syllable of Yahweh onto his name. And I doubt that they used that very much at all because they were hesitant to use the sacred name in a casual way. I don't know how He might have been called in Hebrew. So basically what I am going to do is call Him Jesus. All right? So everybody will know who I'm talking about when I call Him Jesus.

So let's review a little bit about the last two sessions before we get into this one. In the first session we talked about all the I Am's; what Christ said in describing Himself I Am thus and so. I think there are 12 different ones. You remember them: I Am the Good Shepherd, I Am the Bread of Life, I Am the Living Water, and so forth. And we talked about knowing Him and His Father and keeping the First Commandment and loving Him with all your heart and all your soul and all your might as it says in Deut. 6:4-5. So the question is **will you love Jesus**? Will you have excuses why you can't keep and live by the First Commandment? Are you going to have all those excuses ready for Him when you meet Him? Oh Lord I couldn't keep the First Commandment because I had too many bills. My job just took too much of my heart and soul and most of my attention. I liked scary movies after which it took

55

some time to feel you near me again so I couldn't think of you all the time. What will He feel when He hears all such excuses? What excuses will they have when they haven't loved Him with all their heart? That of course means loved Him with all of their feelings. Is He going to weep when He encounters how the world took from His very own loved ones, who the Father has given Him, their ability and opportunity to love Him with all their feelings and all their soul and all their might? Will you be one who makes Him cry? Those who must face Him in this way did not decide to create the environment in their life to keep His sayings. And they will find the importance of that decision will be before them as they contemplate the meaning they put to their gift of life.

We also talked in the first session about not walking in the way of the people so we can better keep the First Commandment. And the Lord said *"come out of her my people that you partake not of her sins that you receive not of her plagues."* Will you reject even the idea that He wants you to withdraw from Babylon? Will you say He wants you there? He could've said "stay there but don't partake of her sins," but He said "come out of her." Will you have all those excuses, too, or are you going to be found faithful in keeping His request? That raises the next question, **are you going to obey Jesus**? Are you going to say, well Jesus I couldn't come out of the world's sinful society because I had to put my kid through college? And everybody would have thought ill of me if I didn't use my college education to pursue a career. I had to earn money; there was so much I wanted. Are you going to have all those excuses ready for when you meet Him? What will His poor heart think to hear those excuses from you when He was so diligent to try to guide you? So will you obey Him when he says come out of her my people?

In session two; I cited many of the descriptions Jesus said about His Father. And I have a list here that we will post of all the different scriptures that I cited, (there are many more,) concerning when Christ actually defines and identifies what His Father is like, His Father's character, and His personality. I also have another list to post of all the times He told people that they did not know His Father.

Will you believe Jesus? Will you believe that His Father loves His enemies? Will you believe that in order to be like His Father, you must turn the other cheek? And you must pray for those who despitefully use you and really believe Him when He says that it makes you kindred to His Father? Will you believe Jesus when doing so requires you to set aside those places in your scripture that describe His Father otherwise? That may be hard in view of the traditions that have come down to you. Will you believe Him no matter what else that means? Will you believe Him when your family and friends oppose such belief? Or when your pastor takes the position that it is a fearful thing to fall into the hands of the living God? Will you tell him that in the hands and arms of the living God is the rightful destination of every living human soul, so that they can experience salvation and come home finally to their loving Father? Will you believe Him when He touches your heart with the Spirit to guide you into paths that you have not known? Will you be humble enough to follow the Lamb withersoever He goes? Will you believe Him in His discourse called the Sermon on the Mount?

If you will believe Him and believe Him as recorded in your New Testament with His own words, then you will benefit from this series. That's where we are headed from here on. I am going to take you on a journey. We are going to where Christ says He will take us. Where does it take you when you believe Jesus, specifically in what He says in your Bible's New Testament **about His Father**? Where does one go when they believe His description of His Father? When you believe that He said the people didn't know Him and they had never heard His voice at any time nor seen His shape, where will that take you? Where does it take you when you believe Him, when you love Him, and when you obey Him?

So we are going on a journey through the Scriptures. I am going to be giving you hundreds of scriptures. And our journey is going to be to discover the Lord Jesus' One True God and the same One True God that is cited in John 17:3. I am going to read this to you again. *"And this is life eternal, that they might know thee the only true God, and he whom thou hast sent."* And then in the 5:24, *"Verily, verily, I say unto you, he that heareth my word, and believeth on him that sent me, hath everlasting life, and shall not come into condemnation; but is passed from death unto life."* So

Jesus here, Christ, Himself defined salvation in His own terms and, spoke about the One True God in the writings of John more than any other place. The Bible uses the phrase the true God fourteen times and all but four are in the writing of John, with two in the Old Testament and twelve in the New Testament.

So the Scriptures say they didn't know Him but there is a One True God which means there is also another god that isn't the One True God. So your Bible is a treasure. I just love the Bible. Your Bible has in it the One True God in your Old Testament in spite of Numbers 31; and in your New Testament in spite of Hebrews 10:30-31. So the prophets knew of Him and the One True God is in the New Testament as well. Now all the apostles who walked with Him knew the One True God; and He said they did in John 17:7-8. *"Now they have known that all things whatsoever thou hast given me are of thee. For I have given unto them the words which thou gavest me; and they have received them, and have known surely that I came out from thee, and they have believed that thou didst send me."*

And so if you will follow Jesus and believe Him, we can go on a journey through your Bible and we can find His One True God. May the Lord bless you as you do this, here we go!

This is an account of a discourse given by Stephen when he was forcibly taken to stand before the Sanhedrin to be judged. And it is absolutely true that without Stephen you could not find the real pathway in your Bible to the One True God. This is a pretty big statement. One can safely assume by the way Stephen is described in your Bible that his views are indeed the views of all the early church and of Jesus. And so I want to read to you this account in Acts. I want to read it in its entirety. I want to give you a general outline of what this reading is about. And you are going to find out in here that there are four different places that we will take off from in our journey. Four different statements that Stephen makes that can lead you, very clearly, through the Scriptures to many references that open up the One True God to you who is the Father of Jesus and the One Who sent Him.

So here we go. I have a few notes on different verses as we go through this reading. I first want to give you a little background for this reading. The first five books of your Bible are called the Torah in Hebrew; called in the Pentateuch in Greek, which of course are cited as written by Moses. The Decalogue is what they call the Ten Commandments. And as we go on this journey you will find that there are two Torahs. The one was "the original Torah" written by Moses in the Egyptian language because he couldn't speak Hebrew and there was no written Hebrew in his day. And the other one is what I call "the imposed Torah." And as I read this reading in chapters 6 and 7 of the Book of Acts, Stephen is referencing the original Torah. And those in the Sanhedrin who were listening to him are the ones that are bound to the imposed Torah. So you are going to begin to be able to distinguish the difference. And I am going to go through it all very carefully. There are four points in his address that are central to defining and finding and knowing how to distinguish the One True God, who is Jesus' Father in your Bible.

We will go over those four points. The implications of each one is simply too vast to go over them quickly in only one session, so we will spend a session on each of the four points. I am now going to take you through this chapter and identify these points. Then we will address each one.

All right, now I am going to start with the Acts 6:7. "*And the word of God increased; and the number of the disciples multiplied in Jerusalem greatly; and a great company of the priests were obedient to the faith.*" So the background here is that Stephen is a threat to the Sanhedrin because of the numbers of people who followed and supported what he was teaching; and he was teaching from the original Torah and numbers of followers were multiplying every day. So there was a great groundswell of them. "*And Stephen, full of faith and power, did great wonders and miracles among the people.*"

Now I have to say to you that in all probability Stephen was James the Lord's brother. And there are volumes written supporting that idea. But that is not an issue for us today, I just thought you would like to know this. But for it to say that he was full of faith and power and did great wonders and miracles among the people, shows the threat felt by the Sanhedrin and that it was real to them. Stephen, in this writing, was just a deacon who was ordered to serve food to the elderly. As a result of the events described in this chapter, what happened after this event of Stephen appearing before the council was they killed him, then all the church people in Jerusalem were scattered. Most of them went to Pella. That wouldn't have happened if a deacon was killed. That happened because the church's high priest with the Urim and Thummim was killed. But anyway, I bring this up just so you kind of get the idea Stephen is likely more than a deacon.

"Then there arose certain of the synagogue, which is called the synagogue of the Libertines, and Cyrenians, and Alexandrians, and of them of Cilicia and of Asia, disputing with Stephen. And they were not able to resist the wisdom and the spirit by which he spake." And it just keeps saying how powerful this man is. And of course he was citing authoritative sources widely respected by the people. *"Then they suborned men,"* suborned men means they paid them to lie, *"which said, we have heard him speak blasphemous words against Moses, and against God."* There is our first and second point; against Moses and against God. *"And they stirred up the people, and the elders, and the scribes, and came upon him, and caught him, and brought him to the council,"* of the Sanhedrin, *"And set up false witnesses, which said, This man ceaseth not to speak blasphemous words against this holy place,"* the third point *"and the law:"* the fourth point. *"For we have heard him say, that this Jesus of Nazareth shall destroy this place, and shall change the customs which Moses delivered us."* This is a reference to the original Torah that Stephen was teaching. *"And all that sat in the council, looking stedfastly on him, saw his face as it had been the face of an angel."*

So they have him charged with four counts of blasphemy. There is a little clarification that is needed here. He did blaspheme God, Moses, the temple, and the law in their view coming from the imposed Torah, but they did not have to suborn false witnesses. They did not have to have people who were suborned to run and tell lies about him, because he *did* blaspheme in their eyes. He didn't blaspheme anything about the One True God, or what really happened with Moses, or the real law, or what they should have had instead of a temple. He was just expressing the original Torah.

So *"then said the high priest, are these things so?"* And I want you to understand that many people do not grasp the significance of what follows this in the seventh chapter. That was the first verse; the high priest said to Stephen, Are these things so? Did you in fact blaspheme these four things? And Stephen then is going to rehearse the Jewish history to 70 men who were like Jewish history professors. They were the most learned Jewish history experts in Israel. Doesn't that seem remarkable to you? And you would think they are going to say why do we have to hear all this when we know all this already; that wasn't the case. This was life and death. They listened to every word intently. They were going to kill this man for what he would say. They were listening to every word of his rendition of Jewish history. They were listening to see and ascertain the source of this huge ground swell of threat that was coming from the sect of the Nazarenes, or as historians of the period called them Essenes. This is what his words meant to them because his version of history was in large part why there was a great company of priests who were faithful to this other Torah. And his version of history was what those who could not counter his power and wisdom were so threatened by. And this issue of history wasn't small because killing the central representative of his version of history caused all the church people to be scattered, and the apostles to go into hiding. So this is not just a man coming and speaking to them about history, which they already know better than anybody, at least in their own minds, this is more than that. He is rehearsing the original Torah.

In Stephen's narration in the first verses of Chapter 7 the history is basically the same down to verse 20. *"And he said, Men, brethren, and fathers, hearken; The God of glory appeared unto our father Abraham, when he was in Mesopotamia, before he dwelt in Charran, And said unto him, Get thee out of thy country, and from thy kindred, and come into the land which I shall shew thee. Then came he out of the land of the Chaldaeans, and dwelt in Charran: and from thence, when his father was dead, he removed him into this land, wherein ye now dwell."*

And I have checked all of this history he is citing to make sure it is exactly what the Bible says up to verse 20. Here are verses 5-6: *"And he gave him none inheritance in it, no, not so much as to set his foot on: yet he promised that he would give it to him for a possession, and to his seed after him, when as yet he had no child. And God spake on this wise, That his seed should sojourn in a strange land; and that they should bring them into bondage, and entreat them evil four hundred years. "* And that is actually what God said to him.

7:7-13 *And the nation to whom they shall be in bondage will I judge, said God: and after that shall they come forth, and serve me in this place. And he gave him the covenant of circumcision: and so Abraham begat Isaac, and circumcised him the eighth day; and Isaac begat Jacob; and Jacob begat the twelve patriarchs. And the patriarchs, moved with envy, sold Joseph into Egypt: but God was with him, And delivered him out of all his afflictions, and gave him favour and wisdom in the sight of Pharaoh king of Egypt; and he made him governor over Egypt and all his house.*

Now there came a dearth over all the land of Egypt and Canaan, and great affliction: and our fathers found no sustenance. But when Jacob heard that there was corn in Egypt, he sent out our fathers first. And at the second time Joseph was made known to his brethren; and Joseph's kindred was made known unto Pharaoh" So he is rehearsing this history which they all knew by heart.

7:13-14 *"And at the second time Joseph was made known to his brethren; and Joseph's kindred was made known unto Pharaoh. Then sent Joseph, and called his father Jacob to him, and all his kindred, threescore and fifteen souls"* How many is that, 75?

7:15-19 *"So Jacob went down into Egypt, and died, he, and our fathers, And were carried over into Sychem, and laid in the sepulchre that Abraham bought for a sum of money of the sons of Emmor the father of Sychem. But when the time of the promise drew nigh, which God had sworn to Abraham, the people grew and multiplied in Egypt, Till another king arose, which knew not Joseph. The same dealt subtilly with our kindred, and evil entreated our fathers, so that they cast out their young children, to the end they might not live.* " All the ears of the Sanhedrin are listening very carefully now.

Verse 20 through 22 is the first blaspheme – it is against Moses. *"In which time Moses was born, and was exceeding fair, and nourished up in his father's house three months: And when he was cast out, Pharaoh's daughter took him up, and nourished him for her own son. And Moses was learned in all the wisdom of the Egyptians, and was mighty in words and in deeds"*

That was the first blaspheme, those three verses, that the council is hearing. I imagine that many of them were shaken and were offended and very alarmed at these sayings of Stephen. I can just see them learning forward to hear him better.

"And when he was full forty years old, " which is the only place in the scriptures that tells us Moses' age at this point, it isn't in the Old Testament, *"it came into his heart to visit his brethren the children of Israel. And seeing one of them suffering wrong, he defended him, and avenged him that was oppressed, and smote the Egyptian."* Verse 25 is continuing with more information of blasphemy against **Moses**. *"...for he supposed that his brethren would have understood how that God by his hand would deliver them, but they understood not."*

So you have verses 20 through 22 and verse 25 as the source for the blasphemy charge against **Moses**. And by this time, rage is growing with his listeners. They didn't like at all where this was going.

"And the next day he shewed himself unto them as they strove, and would have set them at one again, saying, Sirs, ye are brethren; why do ye wrong one to another? But he that did his neighbor wrong thrust him away," which suggests something physical, which is rather remarkable. Here is a slave and one raised in the courts of Pharaoh which is obvious by his dress, manner and language that intervened politely and yet he is so handily and perhaps physically rebuffed. *"Saying, Who made thee a ruler and a judge over us? Wilt thou kill me, as thou didest the Egyptian yesterday? Then fled Moses at this saying, and was a stranger in the land of Midian, where he begat two sons."*

63

Now in verse 30 we move into the blasphemy against the **law**. And you are going to find the first mention out of four mentions of an angel in this reading. *"And when forty years were expired, there appeared to him in the wilderness of Mount Sinai an **angel of the Lord** in a flame of fire in a bush."* In those other references in the Bible it says of this incident in the Old Testament that it was an angel. There are three other references where he mentions an angel. The Bible, or the imposed Torah, does not say it was an angel but rather says it was God. *"When Moses saw it, he wondered at the sight."* So now there you have the second blasphemy starting with verse 30. And now verse 31-34, *"And as he drew near to behold it, the voice of the Lord came unto him, Saying, I am the God of thy fathers, the God of Abraham, and the God of Isaac, and the God of Jacob. Then Moses trembled, and durst not behold. Then said the Lord to him, Put off thy shoes from thy feet: for the place where thou standest is holy ground. I have seen, I have seen the affliction of my people which is in Egypt, and I have heard their groaning, and am come down to deliver them. And now come, I will send thee into Egypt."*

Now verses 35 through 36 is the rest of the blasphemy against the **law**. And you are going to hear the word angel again. *"This Moses whom they refused, saying, Who made thee a ruler and a judge? The same did God send to be a ruler and a deliverer **by the hand of the angel** which appeared to him in the bush. He brought them out, after that he had shewed wonders and signs in the land of Egypt, and in the Red sea, and in the wilderness forty years."* OK that is the second section of blasphemy against the **law** and it is of critical importance as it continues!

"This is that Moses, which said unto the children of Israel, A prophet shall the Lord your God raise up unto you of your brethren, like unto me; him shall ye hear." Verse 38 through 39 is the first section of blasphemy against **God** in the eyes of the Sanhedrin. Verse 38, *"This is he, that was in the church in the wilderness **with the angel which spake to him in the Mount Sinai**, and with our fathers: who received the lively oracles* (which means "the living word") *to give unto us."* He is saying the Angel gave the law to Moses, not God. *"To **whom our fathers would not obey**, but **thrust him** (Moses) **from them**, and in their hearts turned back again into Egypt."* Again, "thrust him" is used. So there is the first

64

part of the blasphemy against **God**. Because he is saying that it was not God who gave them the law but an angel. "*And in their hearts turned back again into Egypt, Saying unto Aaron, Make us gods to go before us: for as for this Moses, which brought us out of the land of Egypt, we wot not what is become of him.*"

Verses 41-42 are the second section of the blasphemy against **God**. There are two groups of verses for each accusation. "*And they made a calf in those days, and offered sacrifice unto the idol.*" This was the very first instance of blood sacrifice that Israel ever performed and it was to an idol, "*And rejoiced in the works of their own hands.*" Here is a very important and far reaching statement in verse 42. "***Then God turned***, *and gave them up to worship the host of heaven; as it is written in the book of the prophets.*" God gave them up before they even got started. Moses had not even come down from the mountain yet. "God turned," there is only one other place in the Bible that says God turned. It is in Isaiah 63 and we are going to be reading it later on. Now we are moving on into the fourth blasphemy which is against the **temple**.

"*O ye house of Israel, have ye offered to me slain beasts and sacrifices by the space of forty years in the wilderness? Yea, ye took up the tabernacle of Moloch.*" Moloch is the god of human sacrifice where they burn little children alive. "*and the star of your god Remphan, figures which ye made to worship them: and I will carry you away beyond Babylon.*" He mentioned Remphan and Moloch because their temple was made after the pattern of the Canaanites and these were the gods of the Canaanites in their temple.

Now versus 44-47 are more blasphemy against the **temple**. The rage is almost uncontainable with the Sanhedrin by now but their intention at this point is to allow Stephen to finish speaking. At this point his death is already assured by them. "*Our fathers had the tabernacle of witness in the wilderness, as he had appointed, speaking unto Moses, that he should make it according to the fashion that he had seen. Which also our fathers that came after **brought in with Jesus into the possession of the Gentiles**, whom God drave out before the face of our fathers, unto the days of David; Who found favour before God, and desired to find a tabernacle for the God of Jacob.*" This is blasphemy against the **temple** as there are 7 chapters in the imposed Torah in I Chronicles that describe David designing their temple: not a tabernacle after the fashion Moses saw. And he is saying that David only desired to have a tabernacle not their temple. *"But Solomon built him an house. Howbeit the most High dwelleth not in temples made with hands; as saith the prophet, Heaven is my throne, and earth is my footstool: what house will ye build me? saith the Lord: or what is the place of my rest? Hath not my hand made all these things?"*

Versus 51-52 is the additional section on blasphemy that summarizes all four blasphemies. *"Ye stiffnecked and uncircumcised in heart and ears, ye do always resist the Holy Ghost: as your fathers did, so do ye."* Now remember that all the prophets were against the temple. We are going to go through this very carefully in future sessions. So he says, *"Which of the prophets have not your fathers persecuted? and they have slain them which shewed before of the coming of the Just One."* The Just One is their Messiah. "Just One" can be translated as the "Righteous One," *"of whom ye have been now the **betrayers and murderers.**"* Remember, he is saying, those specific words betrayers and murderers. He is saying they, the Sanhedrin, betrayed and murdered their Messiah; remember it just said *"the coming forth of the just one."* It gets now even more graphic. ***"Who have received the law by the disposition of angels, and have not kept it."***

So again he is reiterating that angels gave them the law. And he is telling these men, who are the most meticulous men there are in the world at keeping the law, that they have never kept it. An example of how diligent they were would be if you were a tailor and you had a needle in your shirt on the Sabbath, you could be killed for carrying a tool on the Sabbath. They were radical at keeping the law of the imposed Torah; they kept it to an absurd extent. So Stephen is saying you received the law from angels and have not kept it. Here is Stephen telling the Sanhedrin who are radical at keeping the law. Rage at this point was about to spill over.

"When they heard these things, they were cut to the heart." So this history is not just a history and they are not just mad because he said the temple was unto Moloch, he has just demonstrated, with His own words, the accuracy of their claim that he is blaspheming those four things: Moses, God, the temple and the law. At this, they can't resist their rage and do not allow him to finish. *"When they*

*heard these things, they were cut to the heart, and they gnashed on him with their teeth. But he, being full of the Holy Ghost, looked up steadfastly into heaven, and saw the glory of God, and Jesus standing on the right hand of God, And said, **Behold, I see the heavens opened, and the Son of Man standing on the right hand of God**. Then they cried out with a loud voice, and stopped their ears, and ran upon him with one accord, And cast him out of the city, and stoned him: and the witnesses laid down their clothes at a young man's feet, whose name was Saul* (of Tarsus.)"

Why do you suppose they stopped their ears? And that they could not listen to another word? It was because they all knew that *their* Messiah stood on the right hand of God. And he was telling them you have betrayed and murdered your Messiah who was the angel who gave Moses the law. You have murdered the Angel of the Presence. You have murdered the angel Moses used to bring your fathers out of Egypt. They all knew Jesus called himself the Son of Man. And they were very familiar with Daniel's writings and the original Torah that call him that.

Now I want to read a couple of more things to you. Why was that the deciding factor? Why was it intolerable when Stephen said he saw Jesus standing on the right hand of God? This is because they were all familiar with Psalms 110. Every one of them knew this by heart. Let me read it to you. *"The Lord said unto my Lord, **Sit thou at my right hand**, until I make thine enemies thy footstool. The Lord shall send the rod of thy strength out of Zion: rule thou in the midst of thine enemies. Thy people shall be willing in the day of thy power, in the beauties of holiness from the womb of the morning: thou hast the dew of thy youth. The Lord hath sworn, and will not repent, **Thou art a priest for ever after the order of Melchizedek.**"*

They are all very aware of that scripture in their Torah. They were also all aware of another very profound scripture. And boy do I love Isaiah. Wait until you hear this one. When Stephen said *"God turned,"* the only other place in the Bible where the Bible says that God turned is Isaiah 63:10. Now I want you to notice that Stephen is saying that God gave up on Israel at the time of the golden calf. That was very early on. The scene here is Moses had led them through the Red Sea. We are going through all this in a

67

separate session. It is going to be fun. There are hundreds of scriptures that you just will love and think they are great. I can hardly wait. He led them through the Red Sea. The first thing he did after that, remember Stephen said, the Lord said to Moses after you bring them out of Egypt bring them to this place. OK, he brought them to that place. When he got there and told the Lord they were there, the first thing he did was ask God what to do now. God was ready with what is known as the Mosaic Covenant. We will go over this in detail when we follow where Stephens blasphemies takes us. The Lord will lead us into this part of our journey by us hanging on to this ministry about the law.

So the Lord gave them the covenant, you'll remember it: "*If you will obey my voice indeed you will be my people and I will be your God. You will be a treasure to me and a holy nation.*" God said to Moses go and tell the people this and see what they will say. So Moses went back and told them all the Lord had said. And the people answered and said "*All that God has said we will do.*" They made a covenant as a people with God. God said this is what the covenant is - will you do it? And they said we will do it all. They agreed. They entered into the covenant. That was the very first thing that happened after their arrival at Sinai. This of course was before the golden calf. So then Moses went up the mountain to get the law. And Stephen is saying that this is the time when God turned and gave them up when they built the golden calf while Moses was up on the mountain the second time. God wrote them off as a people at that time, according to Stephen. Stephen is actually telling the Sanhedrin they had not been relevant since the golden calf.

Now this scripture, you guys, I hope that you memorize Isaiah 63:7-19. It is one of the most marvelous Scriptures you will find. We were led here by Stephen saying God turned, when he spoke about the angel. Now in this reading you are going to have every word that Christians use in relation to salvation. You are going to hear the terms saved, redeemed, a Savior, Holy Spirit, the Good Shepherd, the right hand, and the Angel of the Presence which is Christ, the arm of the Lord and loving kindness. All those words are in this little reading. All have to do with Christ. Isaiah is fabulous. OK I'm going to read this to you. And I'm going to explain a little bit about it as we go through.

68

Now this is what the Sanhedrin knew and had on their minds as they were listening to Stephen. And they knew very well that Stephen was referencing this scripture in Isaiah. And they are all very familiar with this scripture. And when he said God turned, when he is talking about the angel, they knew what he was doing. Isaiah was held in such high esteem that they couldn't stand to have the people take Stephen's view. It was too threatening and impossible to counter or dispute effectively. *" I will mention the loving kindnesses of the Lord, and the praises of the Lord, according to all that the Lord hath bestowed on us, and the great goodness toward the house of Israel, which he hath bestowed on them according to his mercies, and according to the multitude of his lovingkindnesses. For he said, Surely they are my people, children that will not lie: so he was their Saviour."*

Now probably the most important phrase in your entire Old Testament starts with verse 9. *"In all their affliction he was afflicted,"* past tense, it is not talking about Jesus being afflicted on the cross or with stripes if they beat him. But it is talking about in all their affliction in Egypt He was afflicted. Remember that. We are going into that deeper later. *"**and the angel of his presence saved them in his love and in his pity he redeemed them;** and he bare them, and carried them all the days of old. But they rebelled, and vexed his Holy Spirit: **therefore he was turned*** (there is the phrase) *to be their enemy, and he fought against them. Then he remembered the days of old, Moses, and his people, saying, Where is he that brought them up out of the sea with the shepherd of his flock?"* Where is Moses? What did you do with Moses? *"where is he (Jesus) that put his Holy Spirit within him?"* Where is the shepherd of his flock?

What did you do with the shepherd? I'm sorry Lord. You have been through so much. Oh, your poor, poor heart! What did you do with the shepherd? *"That led them by the right hand of Moses with his glorious arm, dividing the water before them, to make himself an everlasting name? That led them through the deep, as an horse in the wilderness, that they should not stumble? As a beast goeth down into the valley, the Spirit of the Lord caused him to rest: so didst thou lead thy people, to make thyself a glorious name. Look down from heaven, and behold from the habitation of thy holiness and of thy glory: where is thy zeal and thy strength, the sounding of thy bowels and of thy mercies toward me? saith the Lord are they restrained? Doubtless thou art our father, though Abraham be ignorant of us, and Israel acknowledge us not: thou, O Lord, art our father, our redeemer; thy name is from everlasting.*" So what has happened? What did you do with Moses and the Shepherd? Doubtless you are our father even though Abraham would not even know us because we have gone so far astray. And we are so departed from the way Israel will not even acknowledge us.

All right. *"O Lord, why hast thou made us to err from thy ways, and hardened our heart from thy fear? Return for thy servants' sake, the tribes of thine inheritance. The people of thy holiness have possessed it (the inheritance) but a little while."* They possessed it until they made the golden calf and abandoned the covenant, according to Stephen, which was a very short time. *"...our adversaries have trodden down thy sanctuary. **We are thine: thou never barest rule over them; they were not called by thy name**."* The Lord never was able to rule Israel. They were not known by His character. The temple religion represented this falling away.

OK everything that Stephen is speaking about is in this reading. He is reproving the Sanhedrin in an astonishing fashion by quoting Isaiah 63. And the church people knew that Christ was the Angel of the Presence. Other scriptures witness of it in your Bible. Let me read something to you here. In Corinthians 10:1 the author of Corinthians knew that Christ was the Angel of the Presence that led them through the Red Sea as a shepherd. *"Moreover, brethren, I would not that ye should be ignorant, how that all our fathers were under the cloud, and all passed through the sea; And were all baptized unto Moses in the cloud and in the sea; And did all eat the same spiritual meat; And did all drink the same spiritual drink: for they drank of that spiritual Rock that followed them: and **that Rock was Christ**."*

So they knew that Christ was the Angel of the Presence who sat on the right hand of God. That is why Stephen's words stung so hard the ears of those of the Sanhedrin when he said he saw the Son of Man standing on the right hand of God. They betrayed and murdered the Angel of the Presence that gave Moses

70

the law. And there are many references affirming that Jesus is in fact the Angel of the Presence. We are going to get into that in a future session in our journey as we use Stephen's message and we use it as a guide to lead us in finding and identifying the One True God in your Bible.

We are going to find that Christ was completely active in the Old Testament exactly the same way that He is today. You will find that Jacob says that the angel he wrestled with during his vision "redeemed him from all evil." And the angel that spoke to Hagar told her that He, the angel, *would make a great nation of her child.* It has to be Christ. So we are going to go through all that and I am going to give you a host of scriptures. When I have a list of scriptures on a certain topic I will read some and note the rest on a handout. We are going to take these blasphemies one at a time. And we are going to start with blasphemy against Moses in our next session. We are going to examine just what that means and its implication to the Jewish and Christian religions. We are going to read what the imposed Torah says and about what Stephen says. And show the evidence that the Bible has in it. Stephen's version is the right one for both Christians and Jews. Thank you.

Session 4
Opening up the Truth about Moses and the High Priesthood
January 18, 2015

I hope you guys aren't tired of me by now. We are at a point now in this series where I want to clarify some things before we start out exploring the four blasphemies that Stephen was accused of by the Sanhedrin. I want to read two scriptures to bring them back to your mind. One is John 5:24. This is Christ defining salvation. *"Verily, verily, I say unto you, He that heareth my word, and believeth on him that sent me, hath everlasting life, and shall not come into condemnation; but is passed from death unto life."* Whoever hears his word and believes on the one who sent him has salvation; speaking of his Father. Then in John 17:3 he says it another way. *"And this is life eternal, that they might know thee the only true God, and he, whom thou hast sent."* I just wanted to have you recall those two readings because remember I am here today and you are basically here today to take the Lord's side.

And throughout your Scriptures there are two perspectives that have been threaded through your Bible from Genesis to the Book of Revelation. One perspective is Jesus's description and demonstration of his Father. He loves you so much the hairs of your head are numbered. He knows what you need before you even ask Him. He is kind to those who are unthankful and those who are evil and so forth. The other perspective is He is seen to be one who is very vindictive, who is murderous, who demands the slaughter of innocent men, women and children; completely the opposite of Jesus's Father. We are not nitpicking the words when we look for these two contrasting perspectives which portray the character of God. They are very clear in their expressions and are dynamically demonstrated in the Bible; obviously in direct contrast and contradiction.

So there are a couple of things I want to clarify for you. One is that I am not going to, in this series; try to indicate what part of your Bible portrays Jesus's Father correctly and what part portrays someone else. What I want to do is to help you recognize His Father by learning what the other perspective means and how to identify the difference between the two, and to help you to discern

73

the meaning they represent and the influence that they have had in the lives of people. If you learn that, then you can read anywhere in the Bible and you will know which parts of the Bible are referencing Jesus's Father and which parts are referencing somebody else. So your Bible is very precious. You will be very well justified spending time seeking to know Jesus's Father, seeing that Jesus said knowing Him is life eternal. And it is so precious, what is right in your Bible is so precious, so infinitely important to everyone that we really do not have a lot of time to pursue that which may be wrong with it. **Jesus is what is right about your Bible. And His Father is what is right about Jesus.**

So it is very beneficial for you to know the difference. And I want to be brave enough to tell you that if you as a Christian believe that the whole Bible is the word of God and accurately represents Jesus's Father then your salvation is compromised; because Christ said to know His Father is salvation. Either God is love or God owns violence and vengeance. How can he do both? James says in 3:10-11 *"Out of the same mouth proceedeth blessing and cursing. My brethren, these things ought not so to be. Doth a fountain send forth at the same place sweet water and bitter."* And if you think that Numbers chapter 31, and I Samuel chapter 15, and like places, Hebrews 10:30-31, and Romans 5:9, and all like Scriptures represent Jesus's Father to you, and if knowing the Father is salvation, then your salvation is compromised.

So let me then continue on and give you a little more background before we begin the section on the blasphemy on Moses. We are going to do Moses today. We are going to do the temple blasphemy next. And then we will do the law, which may be a long session, and finally the accusation of blasphemy against Stephen about God will be last.

So at this point I would like to clarify also why we are using Stephen's message as our point of departure in our journey. What happened was throughout your Bible the prophets generally had the correct perspective that supported the character of Jesus's Father. This generally is so because every once in a while some of them threaded into their narrative the wrath of God, the fury of God, the sword of God. That view is sometimes included in the writings of the prophets even though they knew God. I find this dynamic is present in the Bible because of the tendency on the part of the prophets to attribute natural calamities to God that wicked people brought upon themselves by the evil one presiding over those who choose his influence. And they perceive those events as acts of God. So it is a mixed bag sometimes. It was hard for the prophets sometimes to understand just who God is and for us to sort out the many cultural influences impacting their view.

However, there are some serious difficulties in translation that add to this dilemma. For example, in Isaiah in all except for two places throughout the book he uses the word #639 in Strong's "af" which is always translated there to be "anger;" God's anger. But the word "af" can mean *to be long suffering*. The translators could have translated it that way, but they chose *anger* which is a more obscure meaning of the word "af." I doubt that Isaiah ever intended to communicate that God was angry. Anger is a lot different than long suffering. But as we go along you will see that under such depictions the prophets generally knew the One True God that Jesus lived his earthly life to demonstrate. John says in 1:18 *"No man hath seen God at any time: the only Begotten Son which is in the bosom of the Father He hath declared Him."* He demonstrated Him. It is obvious that prophets knew Him as is clearly demonstrated by such references as Isaiah 63rd chapter. We will get into that later, in more depth. Here in Isaiah 63 are both kinds of expressions made evident. In this Isaiah reading one verse describes God carrying them like a loving Father and the next verse says His wrath will be poured out. The word translated as *wrath* is another word that is not properly meant to mean wrath. It means *an outburst*. It could be an outburst of joy. The word *wrath* is assumed; it does not appear in the definition. At times, such translations can be perplexing.

This dynamic in Scripture is very difficult and Jesus addressed this with His life and ministry. He came to dissolve all doubts about the character of His Father. He came to demonstrate with His life, with His words, with His compassion, with everything in His soul, who the Father actually is. If we really listen to Him we can, as it might be said, decontaminate cultural perspectives that are in this way very perplexing.

So He demonstrated with His life, beyond all doubt who His Father is. And I hope you can come to understand in the session when we do the blasphemy on God what a genius Christ was. He addresses the very same issues that Stephen did and He did it in such a way that they could not accuse Him the way they did Stephen. Christ was in total control of His behavior. He did not confront their religion. In a masterly way, He simply demonstrated His Father. We are going to get to that because that is really important for our last session on Stephen's blasphemies.

Now what happened was Stephen picked up and firmly stood for Christ's clarification on who the Father is. The whole church did; the whole Nazarene, or Essene movement. That is what you see in Stephen, this is why we are using his discourse as a launching place to discover the One True God throughout the whole Bible; Old and New Testaments. What you will see is that Stephen actually defined the core issues. And he defined them very clearly and very simply in terms of just four issues. It is obvious to me that the Holy Spirit helped him to know what to say. Where did he get those issues? He got them from the teaching and influence of Christ but he also got them from the original Torah. And it is good for you to know that there are two Torahs. The battle of the Torahs is what was happening in Stephen's confrontation with the Sanhedrin. And it had already happened between them and Christ resulting in His death and resurrection. And again you will notice they didn't kill Stephen for what a false witness said. They killed him for what he said to them in person. They killed him over the same issues that were underlying their actions toward Jesus. So Stephen had access to the original Torah, so did Christ and so did the people of the early church. And I think we will be getting into that when we go over the section on the law.

Now this battle of the Torahs with Stephen, happened, according to scholars in AD 66. And the temple was destroyed four years later. It was about 40 years after the resurrection. And it is very probable that the murder of Stephen, who was so powerfully prominent in the church, was involved with the rebellions that resulted in the destruction of the temple and Israel as a nation. This is not the first time a battle of the Torahs happened in history. It simply happened again. This was a repeat of history; because Jeremiah had the original Torah and his dispute with the princes of

Jerusalem also was the cause of the first temple being destroyed about 40 years after Josiah. This example in the early church was exactly the same dynamic that was repeating itself.

So the people of the early church had a version of the original Torah. And we will be getting into that later; I think the church first came across the original Torah around 150 BC; that's when it came to them with the kind of information Stephen recited to the Sanhedrin. So there was this dramatic repeat of history. The incident in Jeremiah's time turned out to be only a foreshadow. The temple and the Jews were restored after Jeremiah but not after Jesus and Stephen, clear even into our times.

So we have then Stephen's discourse and it is central to our journey because of the four foundational issues that he identified and paid for with his life. These were foundational differences between Christ, Stephen, the early church on the one hand and the Sanhedrin on the other. And it all could be said that it centered on the character of God which Jesus addresses so squarely. And the forms these issues outlined in the biblical writings, inform us as to what to look for as we seek the One True God and seek to know and how to identify Him when we find Him because knowing these central definitions and issues illuminates the Bible and allows it to shine forth in glorious purity. The Bible is not precious because it is infallible, but it is precious because it has in it the truth of Jesus' Father.

So let us begin our investigation of these blasphemies. What I want to do is read a verse in Stephen's discourse and then I want to read the other version of that information in the Old Testament. I want to compare the two Torahs. I want you to see what they say in the imposed Torah that is in your Bible and from the original Torah, parts of which is also found in your Bible. They are intertwined together. I will call what Stephen says, and that which supports it in the Old Testament, the original Torah. We will look at these things together verse by verse. We will probably use this same format throughout our whole investigation during the rest of this part of the series.

So I want to read Acts 7:20-22 where Stephen is quoting from the original Torah, "*In which time Moses was born, and was exceeding fair, and nourished up in his father's house three months.*" All these words are very important facts. "*And when he was cast out*" that means into the river, "*Pharaoh's daughter took him up, and nourished him for her own son. And Moses was learned in all the wisdom of the Egyptians, and was mighty in words and in deeds.*"

Ok, now in this reading he was raised in his father's house only three months. The Egyptian woman nourished him like he was her own son. Moses was learned in wisdom and mighty in words and deeds. Keep these essential facts in mind. Now let's go to the imposed Torah in the Old Testament and we will find the same account in Exodus 2:5-10, but from the other perspective. Ok, I will start with verse 5. "*And the daughter of Pharaoh came down to wash herself at the river; and her maidens walked along by the river's side; and when she saw the ark among the flags, she sent her maid to fetch it. And when she had opened it, she saw the child: and, behold, the babe wept. And she had compassion on him, and said, This is one of the Hebrews' children. Then said his sister to Pharaoh's daughter,*" This was Moses' older sister. "*Shall I go and call to thee a nurse of the Hebrew women, that she may nurse the child for thee? And Pharaoh's daughter said to her, Go. And the maid went and called the child's mother. And Pharaoh's daughter said unto her, Take this child away, and nurse it for me, and I will give thee thy wages. And the woman took the child, and nursed it. And the child grew, and she brought him unto Pharaoh's daughter, and he became her son.*"

This is saying that Pharaoh's daughter didn't nourish him and raise him up in the early part of his life. In Stephen's discourse, there was no nursing mother at all. In Exodus 2, Pharaoh's daughter says take this child away and nurse it for me. It says Moses's mother nourished him and the child grew, indicating a passage of time. After the child grew she brought him to Pharaoh's house. Why is this different? What is it that is going on here? Why is there a different version? Stephen says he was raised in his father's house only three months. Why would these seemingly small differences in detail so inflame the Sanhedrin?

What is happening here is this is the battle of the Torahs and in these subtle differences lays a threat to the very heart of Judaism. Aaron's supremacy in the high priesthood depended on this issue. If Moses **could** speak Hebrew, he needed Aaron to be his mouthpiece to Pharaoh, because the imposed Torah says he was slow of speech. If Moses **could not** speak Hebrew and was mighty in words and deeds, he only needed Aaron as a spokesman to the Hebrews as a translator. If Moses **could** speak Hebrew and he needed Aaron to stand with his staff before Pharaoh, and in effect perform the Exodus miracles, then Aaron, not Moses, was the central figure of power in the Exodus narrative.

All those involved in this confrontation between the Sanhedrin and Stephen knew full well the far reaching implications of these seemingly small differences between the imposed Torah's version of history and that which was being presented by Stephen. The high priest who sat before Stephen at that very moment traced his priesthood directly back to Aaron. The entire structure of Jewish religious authority came down from Aaron. So it was essential that Aaron be the central figure of the Exodus.

But Stephen and the church saw their authority in priesthood tracing back to Melchizedek through Moses. Christ was a high priest after the order of Melchizedek. Moses said, speaking of Christ in Deuteronomy 18:15, *"The Lord thy God will raise up unto thee a Prophet from the midst of thee, of thy brethren, like unto me; unto him ye shall hearken."* So those who held the original Torah's view like Stephen, saw priesthood authority coming down through Moses. But those who held the views of the imposed Torah saw their priesthood coming down from Aaron. Stephen's version of history was in fact denying the entire legitimacy of the Jewish priesthood authority.

This is exactly why Stephen in Acts 7:37 quotes Deut. 18:15. He is directly confronting the Sanhedrin's priesthood authority. So let me make it clear what the ramifications of the seemingly small historical differences are. If Moses stayed in his father's house for an extended period beyond the three months referred to by Stephen, then he would have had opportunity to learn Hebrew; he would not have had this opportunity if after he was discovered in the water, Pharaoh's daughter nourished him up as her own son and did not say take him away and nourish him for me. **The issue here is whether Moses could speak Hebrew.** If Moses could not speak Hebrew, how did the imposed Torah come to be written in Hebrew, especially considering there was no written Hebrew language in Moses's day? On the face of it, it is entirely unreasonable to think Moses, who was raised in the courts of Pharaoh, and who was mighty in words and deeds, should need a Hebrew slave to speak and act for him before Pharaoh.

It seems to me also that it should be a point of wonderment to all Christians why priesthood authority should be directly and exclusively linked to Aaron, coming down through his sons, seeing he was an idol maker, but ignore the priesthood authority of Moses who stood in the presence of God. Also isn't it curious that Moses's sons are completely written out of history but Aaron's two oldest sons, who were seen to be the first in line for the role of the succeeding high priesthood office, were killed because they brought a strange fire, one tied to sorcery, to the altar? Perhaps in these things now you can grasp a little of why the Sanhedrin was so inflamed by a mere variation in the recitation of their history. The Jewish religion needed for Aaron to be basically the founder of their priesthood authority and that is what shaped the historical narrative found in your Bible.

So now let's move on to the reading of this account starting in Exodus 3:10 through 4:16 in the imposed Torah. I am just going to read parts of it. It would be unnecessary to read the whole thing. So the Lord told him to draw near and take his shoes off. Now verse 10-11. The Lord said, *"Come now therefore, and I will send thee unto Pharaoh, that thou mayest bring forth my people the children of Israel out of Egypt. And Moses said unto God, Who am I, that I should go unto Pharaoh..."* in other words Moses was surprised. And he didn't think he was able to do it. You are going to find in this reading that Moses is hesitant, he is unwilling, he has no self-confidence, he said he is slow of speech, he is not eloquent. He said that he is slow of tongue and he asked God to send somebody else. God was angry and said OK I will give you Aaron. He will be instead of a mouth to you and you shall be instead of God to him.

So Aaron ends up doing all the miracles and is depicted as holding Moses's staff during them. So as we go through this, watch for this vast difference between Stephen's narration and this account. Continuing on, *"Who am I, that I should go unto Pharaoh?"* And God said, *"Certainly I will be with thee"*. And

Moses said unto God, "*Behold, when I come unto the children of Israel, and shall say unto them, The God of your Fathers hath sent me unto you; and they shall say to me, What is his name? what shall I say unto them?*" By the way, if Moses could speak Hebrew wouldn't he already know something as basic as their name for God? "*And God said unto Moses, I Am hath sent me unto you.*" "*Go, and gather the elders of Israel together, and say unto them, The Lord God of your Fathers, …appeared unto me, saying, I have surely visited you, and seen that which is done to you in Egypt….And they shall hearken to thy voice.*" The Lord says in verse 18. "*And thou shalt come, thou and the elders of Israel, unto the king of Egypt, and ye shall say unto him, …let us go, we beseech thee, three days' journey into the wilderness, that we may sacrifice to the Lord our God.*" Remember the word sacrifice here is going to be of central importance later. "*And I am sure that the king of Egypt will not let you go, no, not by a mighty hand. And I will stretch out my hand, and smite Egypt with all my wonders which I will do in the midst thereof: and after that he will let you go.*"

Now verse 18 said that God said they will hearken unto His voice. But Moses in the first verse of chapter 4 says "*And Moses answered and said, But, behold, they will not believe me, nor hearken unto my voice.*" Here Moses is said to be directly contradicting and denying what God told him in person. "*And the Lord said unto him, What is that in thine hand? And he said, A rod. And he said, Cast it on the ground. And he cast it on the ground, and it became a serpent; and Moses fled from before it. And the Lord said unto Moses, Put forth thine hand, and take it by the tail. And he put forth his hand, and caught it, and it became a rod in his hand: And the Lord said, Put now thine hand into thy bosom. And he put his hand into his bosom: and when he took it out, behold, his hand was leprous as snow. And he said, Put thine hand into thy bosom again. And he put his hand into his bosom again; and plucked it out of his bosom, and, behold, it was turned again as his other flesh.*" "*And Moses said unto the Lord, O my Lord, I am not eloquent.*"

The Lord just demonstrated these miracles to him personally. "*And Moses said unto the Lord, O my Lord, I am not eloquent, neither heretofore, nor since thou hast spoken unto thy servant: but I am slow of speech, and of a slow tongue. And the*

81

Lord said unto him, Who hath made man's mouth? or who maketh the dumb, or deaf, or the seeing, or the blind? have not I the Lord? Now therefore go, and I will be with thy mouth, and teach thee what thou shalt say. And he said, O my Lord, send, I pray thee, by the hand of him whom thou wilt send." In other words send somebody else. Don't forget that Stephen is saying from the original Torah that Moses is mighty is words and deeds.

"And the anger of the Lord was kindled against Moses, and he said, Is not Aaron the Levite thy brother?" By the way that makes Moses a Levite also. "I know that he can speak well... And thou shalt speak unto him, and put words in his mouth: and I will be with thy mouth, and with his mouth, and will teach you what ye shall do. And he shall be thy spokesman unto the people: and he shall be, even he shall be to thee instead of a mouth, and thou shalt be to him instead of God."

Now this is exactly the opposite and in sharp contrast to one who is mighty in words and in deeds as Stephen says! It was absolutely essential that Aaron be the leading power in the Exodus story for the reasons I have cited. And you will see that the existence and legitimacy of their temple was on the line in view of Stephen's speech. This is the reason: Aaron established blood sacrifice when he built the golden calf. There are two kinds of sacrifice. There is blood sacrifice and there is a moral sacrifice. Moses used only moral sacrifice. But Aaron established blood sacrifice and the entire ritual and protocol of the temple was centered on blood sacrifice. That's why the Nazarenes or Essenes would not participate in the temple sacrifice and why Jesus would only go into and teach in the court of the Gentiles.

Moral sacrifice is at the root of the Lord's Supper or what some call communion. The blood sacrifice comes from all the decadent and violent societies that lived around Israel. So I want to read an example of a moral sacrifice. This comes from Genesis 31:52-54. I am going to read a little more than that. I am going to start with verse 44 "Now therefore come thou, let us make a covenant, I and thee; and let it be for a witness between me and thee." This is Jacob and Laban his father-in-law. "And Jacob took a stone, and set it up for a pillar. And Jacob said unto his brethren, Gather stones; and they took stones, and made a heap: and they did *eat there upon the heap. Then Jacob offered sacrifice upon the heap, and called his brethren to eat bread: and they did eat bread, and tarried all night in the mount. This heap be witness, and this pillar be witness, that I will not pass over this heap to thee, and that thou shalt not pass over this heap and this pillar unto me, for harm.*" So what it is saying here is they broke bread together to eat a sacred meal **to formulate a covenant**. It was one to ensure that they would not harm each other.

Ok, now Moses' example in Exodus 19:3-8 that he requested of Pharaoh was the very same thing. It was to be a moral sacrifice for Israel to make their covenant with God. What happened was the Lord said go and deliver Israel and **bring them to this place unto me**, which was Sinai. So Moses did. He arrived there with all the people, 3 1/2 months after they passed through the Red Sea. And he went up the mountain and he said Lord I brought them here like you said. Now what should I do? And the Lord told Moses the covenant he wanted to make with Israel. You will remember that I read this to you in a previous session. They thus made a covenant with God. It is called the Mosaic covenant. This was the sacrifice and sacred meal that Moses asked Pharaoh to allow his people to make. This was a moral sacrifice which is always in relation to a covenant.

The Lord's Supper was a moral sacrifice in the same manner to establish what Jesus called a new covenant. Moses' intention was to ask Pharaoh for permission to go to sacrifice to the Lord; it was not to some idol god to appease him with blood, but to make this all important covenant. Aaron's sacrifice was the other kind. I'm going to read this in Exodus 32:1-8 and I have marked it to read only relevant parts. Moses went back upon the mountain after the people made their covenant. "*And when the people saw that Moses delayed to come down out of the mount, the people gathered themselves together unto Aaron, and said unto him, Up, make us gods, which shall go before us; for as for this Moses, the man that brought us up out of the land of Egypt, we wot not what is become of him.*" Now you see Aaron is very much in charge of this. They didn't have to decide who to go to for leadership. And you may note an important reference in Nehemiah 9:17 which says, speaking of Aaron, "*And in their rebellion appointed a captain to return to their bondage…*" This was said as Ezra was quoting the original Torah found by Josiah and dictated to Baruch by Jeremiah. This shows that there was animosity toward Aaron early on by those who held the original Torah clear from Josiah's time.

"*And Aaron said unto them, Break off the golden earrings, which are in the ears of your wives, of your sons, and of your daughters, and bring them unto me. And all the people brake off the golden earrings which were in their ears, and brought them unto Aaron. And he received them at their hand, and fashioned it with a graving tool, after he had made it a molten calf: and they said, These be thy gods, O Israel, which brought thee up out of the land of Egypt. And when Aaron saw it, he built an altar before it; and Aaron made proclamation, and said, Tomorrow is a feast to the Lord.*" Here it is good to point out that this feast indicates an impending attempt to solicit the allegiance of the idol of the golden calf out of an anticipation of the absence of Moses. Idols were often called "the Lord." Now this was a blood sacrifice to an idol to call upon him to turn from its indifference. They did this because they felt abandoned because they thought Moses might not be coming back. They had treated him terribly.

So in effect they replaced the Lord with an idol, and abandoned their covenant with Him; and appealed to the idol to take care of them by going before them. "*And they rose up early on the morrow, and offered burnt offerings, and brought peace offerings; and the people sat down to eat and to drink, and rose up to play.*" The phrases **burnt offerings** and **peace offerings** indicate an appeal to a god to dismiss his apathy towards them and attend to their wants. A peace offering is always an attempt to appease, neither of which have to do with a covenant.

"*And the Lord said unto Moses, Go, get thee down; for thy people, which thou broughtest out of the land of Egypt, have corrupted themselves: They have turned aside quickly out of the way which I commanded them: they have made them a molten calf, and have worshipped it, and have sacrificed thereunto.*"

So Aaron was the one who established blood sacrifice in Israel. You know, Aaron could have said to the people don't worry he will be back. Let us be careful to keep our covenant with the God of our fathers. The fact that he didn't indicates to me that in this instance he was the real leader and did not know the One True God. This blood sacrifice is the very foundation of the temple religion of the Jews and their perceived framework for their religious authority. The entire essence of the temple was based on Aaron establishing blood sacrifice. It was not a moral sacrifice for a covenant. It was a blood sacrifice of appeasement.

Now Jacob also made a moral sacrifice with his brother Esau, so this blood sacrifice was newly introduced by Aaron. It is also very interesting to note that when Stephen said *"God turned and gave them up to the hosts of heaven"* that he did not say gave them up to the god of Hapi which is the Egyptian name of the golden calf. So the corruption God told Moses about was more than worshiping the idol, it was encompassing blood sacrifice itself.

So Stephen said God gave them up to worship the hosts of heaven. And you will see when we get to the accusation concerning the law that all the way through we have at this time and point in history only the first half of an account of the original Torah. It only records events up to the time they passed through the sea. So we do not have an account of all of these events on Sinai in the original Torah. We must rely on Stephen for this vital information. And in that original Torah the word Aaron does not appear even though it is describing events from the burning bush clear through the sea crossing. Between the time of Nehemiah and the rise of the sect of the Nazarenes someone destroyed the rest of it. The narrative ends before they got to Sinai 3 1/2 months later. And Aaron is not mentioned in any of the Exodus events. If he had been the spokesman before Pharaoh he would have been mentioned as playing a prominent role. Stephen knew this. So the Jews had to have Aaron involved because everything they were about depended on him.

There is another thing I want to compare. I want to make sure I have made this point clearly concerning Aaron. The original Torah that has survived does not have Aaron doing anything in Egypt. The first account of Aaron in Stephen's discourse is at the golden calf. And I think that correlates well with the original Torah.

OK, let's read on then in Acts 7:24-27 from the original Torah. Remember we are going to read what Stephen says and then

85

we are going to read what it says in the Old Testament account. *"And seeing one of them suffer wrong, he defended him, and avenged him that was oppressed, and smote the Egyptian: For he supposed his brethren would have understood how that God by his hand would deliver them: but they understood not."* Stephen is saying that Moses knew **before** he left Egypt that he was destined to deliver Israel from bondage. Did you hear that clearly? Listen again. *"For he supposed his brethren would have understood how that God by his hand would deliver them: but they understood not."* This was before he left Egypt. Moses knew already. But what I read to you a while ago indicated he was surprised. He said to the Lord, what? Who me? Who am I that I should go to stand before Pharaoh? So Moses knew according to Stephen and the original Torah.

In that reading Exodus 3:10 - 4:16 when you recall it, you will see how much surprised and taken aback it portrays Moses as being. So the context of verse 25 through 26 in Acts is very interesting. It says Moses would have set them at one again. And he addresses them as sirs. He was being very respectful and polite. He was supporting the value of brotherhood in them when he said ye are brothers why do you wrong one to another? This was because in his mind he was feeling kinship with them. *"But he that did his neighbor wrong thrust him away, saying, Who made thee a ruler and a judge over us?"* What this is indicating is that the Hebrews who strove together also knew he had been identified by someone to be the one who would deliver them or free them in some way.

Think with me a bit about what is really going on here. You have two slaves who are arguing and maybe some physical violence. And here comes an Egyptian looking and acting person raised in Pharaoh's house. He was enough Egyptian looking that when he went to Midian the women there immediately recognized him as an Egyptian when they spoke to their father. Did he walk or did he come in an Egyptian chariot? Now Moses is even more than a slave master. This is one who could be seen to be over the slave masters. And why would they be so bold and assertive to someone with this kind of status? He was very polite and respectful. And they said who made thee a ruler and a judge over us? Where did those two ideas come from? They already looked upon him as a non-Egyptian and did not claim him as a Hebrew. And they said what they did in the context of questioning his authority. And it says they thrust him away indicating to me some form of physical violence. There is no indication of it in any reading but I believe if the Egyptian was killed, Moses did not do it. I believe firmly that a murderer could not be a prophet of God to stand in his presence; especially an unrepentant one. Can you imagine this all happening as it is recorded?

By the way for what it may be worth, Stephen did not say the Egyptian was killed, just smitten. So perhaps it can be deduced through all this that it was common knowledge among the Hebrews that Moses was identified as their deliverer before he left for Midian. All of this variance between Stephen's account and the one in Exodus is focused on writing a history to make Aaron paramount and central to the Exodus for the purpose of legitimizing the blood sacrifice and, as you will see, the temple religion with its priesthood's lineal authority, all coming from Aaron.

Remember that in the early church, Stephen, James the Lord's brother and Jesus saw their entire religion with its priesthood authority as coming down from Melchizedek through Moses. So the task for the Jews was to write Moses and his sons out of history and put Aaron and his sons in, even though Moses was just as much a Levite as Aaron. So in Acts 7:20-27, what we just read, the blasphemy accusation against their view of Moses was threatening their entire temple religion and the culture that had sprung up around it.

So let me read to you some more of the two perspectives that are threaded throughout your Bible. This example which I will now cite is very good in demonstrating the contrast that grew up because of these alterations of Jewish history. In Matthew 22:36-40 Jesus is asked by a lawyer a question saying, "*Master, which is the great commandment in the law?*" And they would have liked for Him to have said to keep the Sabbath day holy. That was in their eyes and in their practice their greatest commandment. But they knew that wasn't the great or first commandment. So Christ quotes the First Commandment, and what He called the Great Commandment.

What He quoted is not in the central law as given in Exodus 20, and you all will remember what He said, which comes from

Deut. 6:5, *"Thou shalt love the Lord thy God with all thy heart, and with all thy soul, and with all thy mind. This is the first and great commandment. And the second is like unto it, Thou shalt love thy neighbor as thyself. On these two commandments hang all the law and the prophets."*

In quoting this passage, Jesus just happened to quote the original Torah version, knowing full well what their imposed Torah said. Christ said in Matthew 22:38, *"This is the first and great commandment."* The word for "great" in this instance in Greek is "mega" with the same meaning as we use it today. And the Greek word for "first" in this reading means *first in **time** and first in **importance**.* I believe that this quotation by Christ was in fact the statement God said to Moses when He brought to them the Mosaic covenant and that these two commandments were the actual First and Second Commandments that should have been stated in the original Ten Commandments in Exodus 20:3-6.

And I believe further that the form of the First Commandment given in the Ten Commandments list as it is stated in Exodus 20:3-6, came directly as a result of the golden calf incident; and in this way the First Commandment that Jesus cited was not found in the Levitical law but in Deuteronomy. By the way, "Deuteronomy" means *the second law* or *the law restated.*

Let me read to you the other one. This is the other version of the First Commandment in the imposed Torah. The difference here is startling. This version of the First Commandment comes from Exodus 20:3-6 and is now the first of the Ten Commandments listed in the imposed Torah. *"Thou shalt have no other gods before me. Thou shalt not make unto thee any graven image, or any likeness of any thing that is in heaven above, or that is in the earth beneath, or that is in the water under the earth. Thou shalt not bow down thyself to them, nor serve them: for I the Lord thy God am a jealous God, visiting (punishing) the iniquity of the Fathers upon the children unto the third and fourth generation of them that hate me; And shewing mercy unto thousands of them that love me, and keep my commandments."* I see the entire wording of this coming exclusively from the golden calf episode. Remember, Moses received the Ten Commandments **before** he knew about the golden calf.

88

According to this reading, God is going to punish people for the sins of someone else. That means you could be punished for what your great grand parents did. So why would you love God according to this reading? Because if you didn't He is going to "visit you." You are in trouble. Not just you, but your future offspring. By the way that word "love" in this reading is the only place where the word love is used in the entire first four books of the Bible in relation to God. The six other places are in relation to food or family. In the first four books of your Bible, the entire account of creation, all the stories about the patriarchs, the Exodus and all the Levitical law does not contain the word love or any expression of people loving God or God loving His children. All the forms of the word love in this context are absent there.

So here you have what Christ could have said. He could have chosen to cite what was written in Exodus 20:3-6. He could have chosen this but He did not. I think it would be helpful now to read the entire text of what Christ quoted to the lawyer. This is Deuteronomy 6:4-9. Look with me now to see if this better expresses Jesus's Father than the Exodus reading. So here are two competing versions of the First Commandment.

"Hear, O Israel: The Lord our God is one Lord: And thou shalt love the Lord thy God with all thine heart, and with all thy soul, and with all thy might. And these words, which I command thee this day, shall be in thine heart," He wants you to deeply feel your love for Him. *"And thou shalt teach them diligently unto thy children,"* So your children will also feel a deep love for Him. *"And shalt talk of them when thou sittest in thine house, and when thou walkest by the way, and when thou liest down, and when thou risest up."* He wants you to think only of God and how much He loves you and how much you love Him all the time. *"And thou shalt bind them for a sign upon thine hand."* Why? So that everything you do with your hands will be thought of as being for Him because you love each other so much.

"And they shall be as frontlets between thine eyes." So everything you see shall be seen through the eyes of your love for each other. *"And thou shalt write them upon the posts of thy house, and on thy gates;"* so that all of your incomings and outgoings will be unto the Lord. And so that which occurs in your home the Lord

89

will be happy to attend. And all that is spoken in your home will warm His heart.

How is that different than the Exodus reading which says if you don't love God He will visit you. Which one best expresses a God who knows what you have need of before you ask? Or the one who loves you so intimately that He was has numbered all the hairs of your head?

So Christ purposely chose to cite this version because it was the original Torah and it best depicted His Father. And in your Bible now, and this is what we are going to be studying, there is this conflict between these two perspectives of God. And Stephen articulated it eloquently and put it in such a way that we could follow that lead to better be able to distinguish between the two.

Now remember the word Deuteronomy means *the law re-spoken*. It is almost a certainty that this reading of the First Commandment is both *first in time and in importance*. It was what was really said by God when He initiated the Mosaic covenant. The other version, "thou shall have no other gods before me," certainly came because of the golden calf after the Mosaic covenant was recited to the Israelites and subsequently abandoned. And you are going to find out that at the end of their 40 years of wandering in the wilderness, that they came across Moses again. They hadn't seen him for 38 years. This is all part of the study that we will cover in the law segment of this series. And he rehearsed to them from memory through a translator everything that happened to them while he was with them. This is the source of the book of Deuteronomy. And he wrote the original Torah in the Egyptian language that was later found by Josiah; and he gave that very book of the law to them at this time. We will explore this whole episode in detail.

Now, in case you get the idea that God was just different in those days, that all this different and contrasting expressions of God are legitimate, that God just kind of became different in New Testament times, let me read to you Malachi 3:6 *"For I am the Lord, I change not."* So just in case anybody thinks that they can harmonize these two different perspectives you can reconsider that thought.

OK, now Christ, as I said before and I am going to get into this during a future session in a big way, dealt with the very same things that Stephen did. He dealt with the temple by cleansing it and prophesying its destruction. He said a greater than the temple is here. He dealt with his Father by saying His Father was kind to those who are evil. He dealt with Moses when He said that He did not need to accuse them as Moses would be their accuser at the last day. He dealt with the law every time He said ye have heard it said but I say unto you etc.

So Christ dealt with the very same things Stephen did, the same four points they accused Stephen of. Christ was such a sweetheart and He was so immaculately in control of Himself and His words and His behavior were so that they could not successfully accuse Him of any of those things. Do you think that the Jews turned Him over to Pilot because it was against the law for them to condemn a man to death? Don't believe that. They condemned Stephen to death and killed him very handily. And any time they picked up rocks to stone Christ they could have done it. And nobody was thinking we better put our rocks down as this is against the law. They just couldn't find a good enough reason to kill Jesus that would seem justified in light of the public groundswell of sympathy for the original Torah.

And in your Bible concerning this incident, as convoluted as it is, you can see that Pilot, who was a really bad nasty guy, was at a loss to know what to do because the Jews really did not have a sound reason to kill Him. That is very remarkable to me. That Christ was so much in control of His behavior and so much in control of what He said and how He said it. Surely He only spoke and did what the Father told Him to say and do. Next time we are going to do the section on the temple and the blasphemy about the temple. We will use Stephen's message as our launching point.

In closing, let me say that the example and teachings of Jesus Christ were the most clear and resonating call to repentance the people of the Jewish religion have ever encountered. The problem they had with Him was not that He was trying to start a new religion among them, but that He was restoring the old. For many, many Christians His teachings and example would be just the

91

same today; *"you don't know my Father."* Do we need the old restored to us, too? Thank you.

Session 5
Transitioning from Tabernacle to Temple:
The Effect of the Knowledge of the One True God
January 25, 2015

Welcome to the fifth session of our Jesus' View series. I would like to say a word about your Bible. First, about the time I was 12 years old I started reading the Scriptures and I found that there were many parts of it that didn't speak to my heart at all. I couldn't feel anything with parts of it. I had to kind of just ignore those parts and concentrate on the parts that spoke meaning to me. I find now that people love their Bible more when they understand it. And they are not as troubled by the parts that don't feel inspired. There is Jesus' Father and then there is "the other guy." Chapter 31 of Numbers is about "the other guy."

So when you understand how these things came about and how "the other guy" got in there you will find that you will study your Bible more and get more out of it. And you will also get more out of it when you understand the One True God. I have had people tell me that after hearing the kind of information that I am presenting in this series they want to read their Bible more and more.

So today we are going to be working on increasing your faith and your love for the truth in your Bible and your joy in your redemption. In the Bible there are two perspectives that are intertwined from beginning to end and they are competing. And so it is hard to know, it is hard to realize what that means and what the effects are of those competing perspectives. They get all jumbled together.

So one of the good things we have found is that Stephen in Acts chapters 6 and 7, outlines a clear expression of the major issues facing the church in Christ's day; issues that the church was confronting in his previous ministry before this present confrontation with the Sanhedrin. Evidently he had been very clearly outlining the differences between these two perspectives. And because Stephen's stance was so well received and effective, he was a real threat to the Sanhedrin. And he presented his point of view and the truth he knew to them. And he outlined those differences in those perspectives to them in the form of a historic narrative. And they had already clearly identified the differences. They accused him of four blasphemies which I have mentioned. They were blasphemy against Moses, against God, against the law and against the temple.

So we will take off from those four points of accusations and see where they will lead us in our scriptures being led by Christ using the same criteria that He did to define His Father and that which He used to define salvation. And by believing what He said and putting that together with Stephen's message, you can find out some very amazing truths in your Bible.

So today we are going to do the accusation of blasphemy against the **temple**. Last time we did the accusation of blasphemy against Moses. And today's verses that are pointed to the matter of the temple are Acts 7:44-52. And I am going to read them right now and then we are going to go on a little journey through your Bible and you will see where these verses lead us.

I will read now. *"Our fathers had the tabernacle of witness in the wilderness as he had appointed,"* (He being God) *"speaking unto Moses that he should make it according to the fashion which he had seen."* In other words God told Moses exactly how to make it, probably in a vision because it uses the words" *he had seen."* *"Which also our fathers that came after brought it with Jesus into the possession of the Gentiles whom God drove out before the face of our fathers unto the days of David."*

So he is saying that they had the proper tabernacle until the days of David. David *"who found favor before God and desired to find a tabernacle for the God of Jacob. But Solomon built him a house."* So he is distinguishing between the tabernacle of David's desires which was after the manner which Moses saw and the temple of Solomon. *"Howbeit the most high dwelleth not in the temples made with hands; as saith the prophet."* And here in verse 49 he is quoting Isaiah 66:1-2. *"Heaven is my throne, and earth is my footstool: what house will you build me saith the Lord? Or what is the place of my rest? Hath not my hand made all these things?"* And Stephen goes on saying *"ye stiff-necked and uncircumcised of heart and ears, ye do always resist the Holy Ghost: as your father's did so do ye."*

By the way, this saying by Stephen indicates the people of the church in Christ's day believed the "Holy Ghost" was operating during the Old Testament period. So he is saying that the Spirit would have told them not to build a temple. And the prophets told them not to build a temple; and in point it was their most illustrious prophet, Isaiah. Their prophets all told them not to build a temple all the way through their history except for possibly two, and that would be Zachariah and Haggai. That is why he says here, *"Which of the prophets have not your father's persecuted? And they have slain them which showed before of the coming of the Just One, of whom ye have been now the betrayers and murderers."* Ok, the two prophets who did not condemn the building of the temple where the ones during the rebuilding of the temple after the Babylonian captivity. They are the only prophets that are said to encourage the building of it. Now let's take off with this. He is saying that David had a different desire than Solomon. David wanted what God showed Moses but Solomon built him a house.

So let's follow through a sequence of events. And this is hard to do because it is complicated and yet I want to shed some light on this temple issue. I am going to read lots of scriptures. So you will need to note this large amount of really good information none of which is off-the-wall but is clearly and plainly stated in your Bible. I am going to start with Exodus 19. We are going to go through a sequence of events in our journey that shed light on this issue of blasphemy against the temple of which they are accusing him.
All the Bible scholars say that three and a half months after the Red Sea crossing they arrived at Sinai. And it says here in Exodus 19:1 *"In the third month when the children of Israel were gone forth out of the land of Egypt, the same day came they into the wilderness of Sinai."* The three and a half months reference comes directly from Jeremiah's Torah.

And Moses went up on the mount first thing to get what is called the Mosaic covenant. You will remember he told the Egyptian Pharaoh, let us go into the wilderness three days journey to sacrifice to our God. That was what he was asking in terms of being let go. What he had in mind, and what the Lord had told him already, was that the Lord was going to give him a covenant to make with the children of Israel. Moses knew this before he left Egypt the first time. So God said when you get the people out from Egypt **"bring them here to me"** to this mountain. So he did. Moses went up to the Lord on the mount and he says, Lord I brought them here to You, now what?

Ok, and the Lord in Exodus 19:3–8 brought them the Mosaic covenant. Bear in mind that this narrative originally most certainly included the first commandment that we covered in Deuteronomy 6:4–9. You want to remember that one point of view is the Mosaic Covenant that I read you and the other point of view is that the Ten Commandments are the Mosaic covenant. Are you hearing this? Those are the two perspectives. Remember the one you better love God or he will come after you? That was the covenant in the eyes of Stephen's accusers. The other perspective is what I have read to you already.

And so the first commandment was indeed first in time and first in importance as the Greek word used in Jesus's recitation of the first commandment indicates. Now it says, obey my voice "indeed." If you look up that word "indeed," you will find it very interesting. It is Strong's #552 "oom – nawn" and it means *of a surety in a very deed, no doubt, truly*. All that is applied to hearing His Spirit.

So what happened was God told Moses His conditions, if you will do this, I will be your God and you will be my people. Go tell them. He went and told them. They said we will do it. He went back and told God, they said they are going to do it. All this was certainly done with a moral sacrifice of a sacred meal as are all covenants in the culture of Israel, which was the sacrifice Moses was referring to in speaking to pharaoh. Are you with me?

While he was up there, he was instructed by God on how to make a tabernacle, which by definition is a *shepherd's hut*. Moses was a shepherd, as were Jacob and all his children. I am going to read this to you. This is Exodus 33:7 *"And Moses took the [shepherd's hut] and he pitched it without the camp."* Listen to these words now, *"Afar off from the camp, and called it the [shepherd's hut] of the congregation. And it came to pass, that*

96

*everyone which sought the Lord went out unto the [shepherd's hut]
of the congregation, which was without the camp."*

The word tabernacle means shepherd's hut. It is Strong's
#4908 and is said "mish-kan" *a shepherd's hut, a lair for animals.*
Israel has been so ashamed of the word "mishkan" that when they
have their Feast of Tabernacles they call it the Feast of Booths,
rather than calling it Feast of the Shepherd's Hut. And they liked the
word temple better. They couldn't stand to call the house Solomon
built for God an animal den or a shepherd's hut so they named it
with a new name which is "hay-kal", which means *a large public
building.* This can in no way be viewed as a hut.

So Moses established the shepherd's hut. Why? It was a
chapel. That is what it was. It was a place where people of the
congregation **who sought the Lord** went out into the shepherd's
hut of the congregation which was without the camp to be with God
and personally interact with the Spirit of His Presence in
preparation to enter into the covenant.

So Moses wanted people to be able to go and deal with their
covenant that God just gave them; and this was with the use of the
element of righteousness in privacy and in the solitude of worship
with their families. It was a chapel for that very purpose. And it was
15 feet wide and 30 feet long. It wasn't half as wide as this room.
And in the back there was what was called the holy place,
15'x15'. You had to enter the chapel from the east. And in the back
of it, it had a 15 foot square room with curtains with a little table
upon which sat the small little Ark of the Covenant. I will be
reading you this in a minute. Those dimensions come from the
descriptions of the scriptures told in cubits.

And people would go there and they would do a moral
sacrifice. And they all would eat a sacred meal, which is the
forerunner of your Lord 's Supper. And they would either make
their covenant or renew it. There were items of furniture to facilitate
this in this little shepherd's hut. There was a menorah that you could
use to **seven yourself.** The Hebrew word for sevening yourself is
"Shabuwa." You could light a section of it every time you renewed
your covenant. It is also called the Feast of Weeks, which in Greek
is "Pentecost."

Since ancient times, it was held that when a person made and renewed a covenant seven times it made it permanent. This is the original purpose and use of the menorah and the tabernacle. And when a person had reaffirmed or made their covenant every year for seven years, it was then complete and irrevocable and they had lighted all seven candles. There was also a little altar for incense. And there was a table for the sacred meal. So people could break "the bread of the presence" with God and their family in this private chapel. Everybody could do it. The bread of the presence is called "shewbread;" which is Strong's #6440 and #3899.

So people would go there when they would have some young member of their family ready to begin the covenant process and they would break the bread of the presence and they would eat together as families or as individuals. And they could eat a holy meal there and they could make their covenant with God in privacy outside the camp in this little shepherd's hut that was 15' x 30'. The holy place was the little room at the back, so called because of the divine worship of its people.

All right. Moses viewed all this when he went up to establish the covenant. He must have had a vision of how to make the shepherd's hut because Stephen uses the words *after the manner which Moses saw.* And those items of furniture were all that was in it. By the way, I found the dimensions for the tabernacle in the Smiths Bible dictionary under temple in the description of the tabernacle.

Now I want to talk to you about Shabuwa. What the Lord was doing when he instructed Moses concerning the shepherd's hut was laying the groundwork for Shabuwa. God was restoring Shabuwa that came under the leadership of Melchizedek. This would have been Israel's pinnacle of spiritual accomplishment. Remember another word for Shabuwa is Pentecost, which is referring to the same event. Please note that Shabuwa was central to the spiritual power also for the early church as described in the second chapter of Acts. So when you read in Acts about Pentecost, and all the Pentecostal religions do this and they put a lot of emphasis on that reading, the Spirit came to them, remember, in great abundance because they were doing Shabuwa.

When you look up Shabuwa in your Strong's Concordance # 7620, the Feast of Weeks, Pentecost and Shabuwa are all the same thing. You will find in #7620 and #7651 the meaning of those words is that the covenant is completed by repeating it seven times. It is said that a person is **sevening oneself** by doing this.

And so the seven candles on the menorah were precisely for Shabuwa or Pentecost. It was specifically for people to seven themselves privately with their covenant in the shepherd's hut or the tabernacle. So Moses had this idealistic expectation. And he fully expected the people to be able to do it. Moses was really an innocent and sweet man. How wonderful and how much like a loving father to provide a little place for prayer and dedication outside the camp for people to go and break the bread of the presence and make their personal covenant with the Lord to love Him according to the First Commandment.

In Exodus 32:7–8 Moses went up to the mountain. *"And the Lord said unto Moses, Go, get thee down, for thy people, which thou broughtest out of the land of Egypt, have corrupted themselves: They have turned aside quickly out of the way which I commanded them."* That is, they turned away from the covenant that God had just given them. And the Lord said, *"They have made them a molten calf, and have worshiped it, and have sacrificed thereunto."*

So here you have the establishment of blood sacrifice, I want to read to you Deuteronomy 10:1–3. This is real important to take note of this. This is one of those perspectives you will not want to forget. *"At that time the Lord said unto Moses, hew thee two tables of stone like unto the first, and come up unto me into the mount and make thee an arc of wood."* This is after he found out they had done blood sacrifice and worshiped the golden calf. *"And I will write on the tables the words that were in the first tables which thou breakest, and thou shall put them in the ark. And I made an ark of shittim wood, and hewed two tables of stone like unto the first, and went up unto the mount, **having the two in my hand**."* One hand - the Ark of the Covenant and the two tables of stone in one hand. Remember that. Remember these were small objects on a little table in the back of the shepherd's hut that could be held in one hand.

Now you notice that when they worshipped the golden calf that Stephen said, *"God turned and gave them up."* It wasn't when they built the temple. It was when they established blood sacrifice with the golden calf. So Moses came down and he found corruption.

So let me tell you a story of Moses that few people understand and most are not even aware of. His own brother and sister corrupted the covenant for the people that he brought out of Egypt to Sinai unto the Lord. They corrupted them with the blood sacrifice of the golden calf who the Egyptians called Hapi. What did Moses do? Go to Exodus 32:30-33. *"And it came to pass on the morrow that Moses said unto the people, ye have sinned a great sin, and now I will go up unto the Lord, peradventure I shall make an atonement for your sin. And Moses returned unto the Lord, and said,"* now listen to this folks this is amazing, *"Oh, this people have sinned a great sin and have made them gods of gold. Yet now, if thou wilt forgive their sin -; and if not, blot me, I pray thee, out of thy book which thou hast written. And the Lord said unto Moses, Whosoever hath sinned against me, him will I blot out my book. Therefore now go, lead the people unto the place which I have spoken unto thee."*

Here is clear evidence that God did not support the theology that one man, other than Jesus, could intercede for other people's sins to be forgiven. This is a denial of the central function of the Aaronic priesthood and of Western Christian priestly expression. What has been said here is critical for you to understand. In the temple religion, the High Priest is supposed to go into the Holy of Holies and simply ask for God to forgive the sins of all the people. But Moses was willing to trade his very soul for God to forgive all the people, and He said, no I will forgive whoever I will. So it seems to me unreasonable to assume that any ministerial ritual could do more to obtain forgiveness than Moses offering his soul. This calls into question the entire function of ministerial intersession in the Christian or Jewish traditions.

Do you see? Moses was willing to give his soul to undo what his brother and sister had done - mostly his brother. He was willing to say blot me out of the book of life. I will trade my soul if you will forgive my brother and the people. And the Lord said no I will forgive whoever I will. There is no evidence that Aaron or his sister repented. So was the founder of the Israelite priesthood and their temple religion with all its blood sacrifice blotted out? Ask Stephen.

And so Moses was hated even more after that by the children of Israel in the desert. Did the one who established the covenant love his enemies? I just read where Moses prayed for those who despitefully used him. Who between Moses and Aaron represents the One True God and which one represents "the other guy?"

In Exodus 17:4, it says these people were angry because they were tired of manna. And they spoke against Moses. And it reads, *"And Moses cried unto the Lord, saying, What shall I do unto this people? they be almost ready to stone me."* They were ready to kill him. And they were heavily against him no matter what he did. Also they were against his wife. They were racist against her. I will read you some of that. They were racist against her because of her dark skin. So Moses sent his family back to the land of Midian. He didn't want his wife and children to be involved with the people who were willing to murder him and who were racist and who would do blood sacrifice and worship idols. His family lived sacred and dedicated lives to the Lord.

And when you read in Exodus 18:2 and 5, *"Then Jethro, Moses's father-in-law, took Zipporah, Moses's wife, after he had sent her back."* Zipporah means *a happy little bird that skips about.* It is Strong's #6855. Isn't that a sweet name for a wife? *"And Jethro, Moses's father-in-law, came with his sons and his wife unto Moses into the wilderness, where he encamped at the Mount of God."* This is evidence that he had sent his wife and family back. And Moses's father-in-law Jethro heard of Moses's troubles, of course from his daughter. He heard of what all he had been going through. And so he came to see what he could do to help Moses. He was a very kind man. And in Exodus 18:9–12, you will find that Jethro the high priest of Midian did a moral sacrifice with Moses and Aaron and all of the elders of Israel. This is very critical for you to note because Jethro established the Sanhedrin, with the elders of Israel using this moral sacrificial meal to make a covenant, in order to establish the leadership of Israel's religion.

Now remember he was a Midianite, the very high priest of the people of Numbers 31, which is an account that presents God ordering the genocide of the Midianites. And this man established the leadership structure of Israel that stood until 425 A.D.; the Sanhedrin, the ones who killed Stephen. Let me read this to you. *"And Jethro rejoiced for all the goodness which the Lord had done to Israel, whom he had delivered out of the hand of the Egyptians. And Jethro said, Blessed be the Lord, who hath delivered you out of the hand of the Egyptians, and out of the hands of pharaoh, who hath delivered the people from under the hand of the Egyptians. Now I know that the Lord is greater than all Gods (of the Egyptians): for in the thing wherein they dealt proudly he was above them. And Jethro, Moses's father-in-law, took a burnt offering and sacrificed for God: and Aaron came, and all the elders of Israel, to eat bread with Moses's father-in-law before God."*

Remember the bread of the presence is actually what your communion bread is. And it is said that Aaron came. Why did they so carefully designate that Aaron came? Why did they have to say Aaron came? It was because he was the questionable interpreter communicating Moses's words to the people. His attendance was singled out. So Moses's father-in-law made this agreement with them or acknowledged with them his faith in their God. And upon this foundation he continues to speak.

Exodus 18:13–24 *"and it came to pass on the morrow that Moses sat to judge the people: and the people stood by Moses from the morning until the evening. And when Moses's father-in-law saw all that he did to the people, he said, What is this thing that thou doest to the people? Why sittest down thyself alone and all the people stand by thee from morning unto even? And Moses's father-in-law said unto him, the thing that thou doest is not good. Thou wilt surely wear away, both thou, and this people that is with thee: for this thing is too heavy for thee; thou art not able to perform it thyself alone. Moreover thou shalt provide out of all the people able men, such as [reverence] God, men of truth, hating covetousness; and place such over them, to be rulers of thousands, and rulers of hundreds, rulers of fifties and rulers of tens: and let them judge the people at all seasons. So Moses hearkened to the voice of his father-in-law, and did all that he had said."*

You will notice Jethro carefully outlined the necessary traits of holiness needed in the members of the Sanhedrin. Did they still have those qualities in Stephen's day? So Moses's father in law departed. And he went his way into his own land. And so Jethro, after making the sacred meal to affirm his faith in the God of Israel with the people, established the seventy elders of the Sanhedrin. And **they replaced Moses in his temporal duties** and responsibilities in terms of leadership.

But now remember Aaron didn't repent. I want to turn to Numbers 12:1–2 *"And Miriam and Aaron spake against Moses because of the Ethiopian woman whom he had married: for he had married an Ethiopian woman. And they said, Hath the LORD indeed spoken only by Moses? hath he not spoken also by us? And the LORD heard it."*

Miriam is the Hebrew name for Mary. To this day the name means *to be rebellious* because of Moses' sister's doings. In your Strong's it is the only meaning it has. I'm sure it had a different meaning in old times because Christ's mother also had that name.

Moses didn't marry an Ethiopian woman. The Midianites would never have had an Ethiopian for a high priest. She was a Midianite. Her name Zipporah is clearly a Hebrew name that comes from the Hebrew root word #6852. Her name is not Ethiopian. Zipporah was dark skinned and Ethiopians are also. And Aaron and Miriam were against Zipporah. Do you know why? Because she brought her dad and her dad set up 70 elders to lead Israel and Miriam and her brother had their positions and their ambitions stifled. They wanted to lead Israel. They wanted to be in charge.

So they were against her. *"And they said hath the Lord indeed spoken only by Moses? Hath he not spoken also by us? And the Lord heard it. And the Lord spake suddenly unto Moses, and unto Aaron, and unto Miriam, Come out ye three unto the tabernacle of the congregation."* To the shepherd's hut. The Lord came down and He was angry with them for what they were speaking against Moses and Zipporah. Just a side note, the Bible says that Miriam contracted leprosy because of her sin in this matter. So Aaron and his sister did not repent. And when Moses offered to trade his soul, blot me out of your book, when he asked God to forgive them, God said he would forgive whomever he would. They were jealous and ambitious for power and the new Sanhedrin was an obstacle to them. They called Zipporah an Ethiopian woman evidently because she was dark skinned. Midian is thousands of miles away from Ethiopia by traveling through Egypt. Remember Aaron, and perhaps Miriam, were in a position to be translators for Moses to the Israelites. Were they altering what Moses said to their people? Was that what made them think God was speaking also through them? Good question. God knows the answer.

OK now, in Numbers 11:10–17 I want to read more that is a significant part of this continuing story. The people were distressed and angry because they were tired of manna and they wanted meat. I want you to listen to this because first we have Moses being replaced in his leadership by 70 elders, he doesn't have to administratively lead them anymore. *"Then Moses heard the people weep throughout their families, every man in the door of his tent: and the anger of the Lord was kindled greatly; Moses also was displeased,"* because they are crying because they wanted meat instead of manna. *"And Moses said unto the Lord, Wherefore hast thou inflicted thy servant? and wherefore have I not found favor in thy sight, that thou layest the burden of all this people upon me? have I conceived all this people? Have I begotten them, that thou shouldest say unto me, Carry them in thy bosom, as a nursing father beareth the suckling child, unto the land wherein thou swearest unto their fathers? Whence should I have flesh to give all this people? For they weep unto me saying, Give us flesh that we may eat. I am not able to bear all this people alone, because it is too heavy for me. And **if thou will deal thus with me, kill me, I pray thee, out of hand, if I have found favor in thy sight; and let me not see my wretchedness.***" Moses was at his wits end. He couldn't go any further.

"And the Lord said to Moses, Gather unto me (these) seventy men of the elders of Israel, whom thou knowest to be the elders of the people, and officers over them; and bring them unto the [shepherd's hut] of the congregation, that they may stand there with thee. And I will come down and talk with thee there: and I will take of the spirit which is upon thee, and put it upon them; and they

shall bear the burden of the people with thee, that thou beareth not thyself alone... And Moses went out, and told the people the words of the Lord, and gathered the seventy men of the elders of the people, and set them round about the [shepherd's hut]. And the Lord came down in a cloud, and spake unto him, and took the spirit that was upon [Moses,] and gave it unto the seventy elders: and it came to pass, that, when the spirit rested upon them, they prophesied, and did not cease."

So now Moses is replaced spiritually. He was replaced as a leader and as a judge. Now the spirit that was on Moses is shared by these seventy men of the Sanhedrin. Now they are responsible for their spiritual leadership over the people. Men of truth remember? Was it men of truth who were judging Stephen in regards to the truth concerning their charge of blasphemy against Moses? Or was it those who following Aaron were attracted to power? Perhaps some of them were just victims of their traditions.

And Moses left with Jethro and his family. At this time Moses went back with his wife and children. And Stephen says he did. Stephen says in Acts 7:38-39, you remember, *"This is he, that was in the church in the wilderness with the angel which spake unto him in the Mount Sinai, and with our fathers: who received the lively oracles to give to us: To whom our fathers would not obey, but **thrust him from them**, and in their hearts turned back into Egypt."* Moses left, he wasn't even there for the events of the Numbers 31 narrative.

All right, now I want you to understand the response of Aaron to Moses leaving. Remember, as translator he was to the people the voice of Moses. Their entire view of God was subject to Aaron's transfer of the words of Moses. So we are going to go to Exodus chapter 37 and 38. And I am going to skip around through these two chapters to help it go quicker. I have certain verses marked to shorten it. And I want you to notice Aaron's response to Moses's leaving.

"And Bezaleel made the ark of shittim wood: two cubits and a half was the length of it, and a cubit and a half the breath of it, and a cubit and a half the height of it." A cubit is about 18 inches. So it was about 45" long, 27" wide and high. Remember now,

105

Moses carried the original Ark in one hand. Now all of a sudden it is a chest. *"And he overlaid it with pure gold within and without, and made a crown of gold to it around about. And he made staves of shittim wood, and overlaid them with gold. And he made the mercy seat of pure gold. And he made two cherubims of gold, beaten out of one piece made he them on the two ends of the mercy seat. And the cherubims spread out their wings... over the mercy seat. And he made the table of shittim wood. And he overlaid it with pure gold. And he cast on it four rings of gold. And he made the stones of shittim wood and overlaid them with gold to bear the table. And he made the candle stick of pure gold, of beaten work made he the candle stick."* It took six men to carry the Ark and six men to carry the table. And the Ark in Solomon's temple was much, much bigger. The cherubim on Solomon's Ark spread 15 feet wide and were 15 feet tall. Remember all this evolved away from that which Moses carried in one hand through Aaron's leadership. The original stone tablets were about the size of playing card.

In order for a person to take power in a national setting they must be seen by the people to have exclusive access to, in this case, ecclesiastical iconic wealth. After this Aaron was the only one, being the high priest, who had access to see and be in the presence of the Ark of the Covenant. Much like Queen Elizabeth of England is the only one who can ride in the gold plated royal carriage and wear the golden crown.

So that which Aaron did was typical of that dynamic. First he created the icon, and then he established himself as the only one to have access to it. In this way he co-opted power over the Sanhedrin. And this icon over time with Solomon became massive. What happened to the little table in the shepherd's hut, in the back, that those who sought the Lord could use as they broke the bread of the presence? By the way, after Aaron, only priests were supposed to eat the bread of the presence but David did and his men also.

"And he made the candlestick of pure gold: of beaten work made he the candlestick. And he made his seven lamps, and his snuffers, and his snuff-dishes, of pure gold. Of a talent of pure gold made he it." A talent is 96 pounds. *"And he made the incense altar of shittim wood. And he overlaid it with pure gold. And he made the staves of shittim wood and overlaid them with gold."* Now it takes

six men to carry the incense altar. *"And he made the altar of burnt-offering of shittim wood. And he made the horns thereof on the four corners of it… and he overlaid it with brass. And he made all the vessels of the altar, the pots, and the shovels, and the basins, and the flesh hooks, and the firepans, all the vessels thereof made he of brass."*

All this paraphernalia indicates Aaron introduced blood sacrifice into what the shepherd's hut became. And what it became was what the lives of the Sanhedrin were immersed in who were judging Stephen. So Aaron clearly established the temple religion, not Moses. Moses had very little, if anything, to do with establishing what the Jewish religion became. So Aaron changed the entire tabernacle. He moved it to the center of the camp. Numbers 1:50 *"Thou shall appoint the Levites over the tabernacle of testimony,* (called of testimony because of the little covenant tablet)*… and they shall minister unto it, and **shall encamp round about the tabernacle**."* So it is no longer a chapel outside the camp where anyone could go to worship with their families. *"When the tabernacle setteth forward, the Levites shall take it down: and when the tabernacle is pitched, the Levites shall set it up: **and the stranger that cometh nigh shall be put to death**."* Remember that. Only Aaron could enter the holy place now.

Now in 2:1–25, he goes on to make the tabernacle, which is no longer a shepherd's hut, the center of all the nation's political power and all of Israel's ecclesiastical power. And he sets in motion that only his offspring can be high priests with this exclusive access. He grabs power. When the 70 elders were now leading spiritually and socially which could eliminate him, he moved to empower himself to rule over the Sanhedrin. Basically he established the temple religion.

So you see why Stephen was such a dire threat with his ability to inspire the masses? *"Every man of the children of Israel shall pitch his own standard, with the ensign of their fathers house: far off about the tabernacle of the congregation shall they pitch."* And the tribes were assigned one of the directions. So Aaron positioned himself in the center of the camp. The shepherd's hut was no more. And the back room was now called the Holy of Holies. And he could go in there only one day a year.

Now I want to take a moment here and explain something very important that is a central component of the Christian experience for hundreds of millions of Christians around the world. The full impact of this seemingly innocent change in the use of the shepherd's hut is far reaching indeed. As Moses established it, the shepherd's hut was not for ritual. It was, as it says, *"for those who sought the Lord."* To take away people's contact with the Ark of the Covenant and exclusivize the breaking of the Bread of the Presence changed the course of the religious world.

You remember Isaiah says *"the angel of the presence saved them in His love and in His compassion He redeemed them."* Love and compassion are not a ritual; they are personal interaction that brings salvation. They are interaction specifically with **the angel of the presence who is Jesus.** When Moses tried to intercede by trading his soul for their sins, God would not allow it, but He said, "I will forgive whomever I will." The idea of one man bringing atonement for the sins of all people **through ritual** on the Day of Atonement was that which was established by Aaron here. This led to the concept that Jesus could enter into the ritual of human blood sacrifice to atone for the sins of all people. But Jesus clearly demonstrated that **He forgave with love and compassion**, which was always in the midst of **a real relationship** being mutually experienced when He said, *"Your sins be forgiven you. Go and sin no more."* His forgiveness simply does not come through ritual.

So here we come to see that the temple is the centerpiece of the failure of the Jewish religion and Shabuwa of the Tabernacle is the pinnacle of the success of the religion of the One True God. This is saying that bringing one's covenant of living the First Commandment into a state of permanence in one's daily life is the high point of man's experience in salvation. On the other hand the temple is the clearest expression of absolute denial of that commandment. God became so impersonal with the use of blood sacrifice that when He came to live with us as a Man, the temple religion was the framework that produced the ultimate expression of how extreme wickedness could become, and still not compromise God's willingness to love us in spite of our sins – absolutely God is love.

By the way, it may come as a big surprise to you when you look up the word "atonement." It is Strong's #3722 Kaw-far which means *to cover with bitumen.* Bitumen is a pitch-like substance used to waterproof cisterns and waterways. You may have thought it meant shedding blood, but it is directly associated with the living water that Jesus talked about which is reproval, repentance, and forgiveness. The idea of atonement is squarely aimed at your ability to hold in your souls the Living Water. Can that be ritualized? The one Man, Jesus, does it all right, but not by ritual. And when you further add that the high priest of the seed of Aaron was viewed as head of government, seeing he had oversight of the ruling body called the Sanhedrin, you naturally connect this ritual with government. So when Isaiah prophesied about the coming of the Lord, he said, *"the government shall be upon his shoulders."*

The ritualization of the spiritual role of the kingdom of God was that which was anticipated by the Jews. And it was a huge factor in the Israelites not recognizing their Messiah when He came. This seemingly obscure change in the use of the shepherd's hut has actually defined the nature and function of ministerial authority for millennia, for both Christians and Jews. The "other guy" has so effectively cut off personal interaction with the Angel of the Presence that he changed bitumen into blood; and he changed a personal experience into a ritual that is done in secret by a high priest who is beyond the average person's ability to know. Is your salvation compromised?

Liturgies are a part of this ritual. Even the Lord's Supper became a ritual. Does your salvation come to you through ritual? Or does it come to you when you feel reproved and you humbly repent and experience the exhilaration of the newness that forgiveness brings; a direct and personal relationship with your Redeemer. You are born again. Does your soul need covered with bitumen, so you can have the Living Water springing up inside of you? Job says, *"Happy is the man who God reproves in any manner."* Aaron's sins were very far reaching indeed. His offspring for perpetual generations were in the position now to control the focus of the Jewish religion and from there all of Christianity.

Now remember that there are two kinds of sacrifices. Blood sacrifice serves two purposes: **to appease** an angry god, or to appeal

109

to god **to amend his indifference**. In a burnt offering the smoke was intended to get his attention. This is what I mean. Let's take Baal the storm god for example - you are used to seeing his name and hearing about him in your Bible. If you were to see a huge big storm coming and it was going to blow your house away you would quickly kill something, put blood on the altar to say I have given you this life to pacify you oh Baal today, and sprinkle blood on the people to identify them to the god to say, please do not be angry at us but be kind to us because we have given you the gift of this life. And they would burn it so the smoke would go to Baal. Put the blood on the door of your house and say, please don't be mad and blow my house away, and spare all in my house and take care of us. That is an example of blood sacrifice.

But if you want to only appeal to him for being indifferent, you are having a drought and you will just get rain by chance because the rain god is indifferent towards you, then you must deal with his indifference. So when you go and you kill and give blood to the storm god Baal and you say, please be aware of us and think about our need and give us rain when we need it, you are making a peace offering. So when there was a big drought and the king's horses were dying and all the people were distressed for water, and Elijah was trying to prove who God was, he said, perhaps your god Baal is off on a journey or he is asleep and needs awakened. He is indifferent. He is not paying attention to you. Do you understand? Elijah didn't do blood sacrifices. Elijah's sacrifice was to reinstitute the Mosaic Covenant.

OK, so when Aaron established blood sacrifice, I want you to understand this, he moved away from the golden calf, and we know this because he never used it again, he had created a monster. He established blood sacrifice for the God of Israel as if He were an idol. A God who loves his enemies, who turns the other cheek, who is kind to people who are evil, who judges no man: why would you need to appease a God like that away from His anger, when He clearly doesn't have anger? How can you ask a God to quit being indifferent when He has the hairs of your head numbered and He knows what you want before you even ask it? Do you understand? And further your infirmities are His infirmities, and your tragedies and triumphs are His tragedies and triumphs, and your joys are His joys. A God like that cannot be viewed as indifferent.

Aaron's established ways actually built into Israel's religious life a wall between the people and the God that called them to Sinai unto Himself because He had so much love for them. Now do you understand why Christ was so intently focused on revealing who His Father is and how He could define salvation as knowing him? Aaron effectively created a religion that had no God. No wonder the children of Israel perpetually strayed and adopted the religions around them. Solomon's temple was to Molec, remember? Jesus' Father was not the god of this religion. He doesn't need or want grandiose gold things. He wants hearts and minds that feel sweet and dedicated love for Him and all men. And yet Aaron was applying blood sacrifice to Jesus's Father. Was there a broken heart in heaven?

All right, Acts 7:46, I want you to understand this, that this is a huge thing for Jesus. He loved David and indicated it in the New Testament many times. He liked to be called Son of David. He didn't say, why do you call me son of David like He said when they called Him good. Acts 7:46, "*And [David] found favor before God, and desired to find a [shepherd's hut] for the God of Jacob.*" David was a shepherd. David knew the difference between blood sacrifice and moral sacrifice. Let me read to you Psalms 50:5, this may be a surprise for you folks, it was for me. "***Gather my saints together unto me; those that have made a covenant with me by sacrifice.***" He knew what moral sacrifice was. He also knew what it wasn't. Psalms 51:14, "*Deliver me from blood guiltiness, O God, thou God of my salvation: and my tongue shall sing aloud of thy righteousness. O Lord, open my lips; **for thou desirest not sacrifice;** else I would give it: thou **delightest not in burnt-offerings. The sacrifices of God are a broken spirit... and a contrite heart.***" After saying all this, why would David be the one to design a temple for sacrifice?

The reason those readings are surprising to me is Israel put so much emphasis on David yet they do not take to heart what he is saying in those two readings. David knew the difference. He knows the difference between a shepherd's hut and Solomon's temple. What does your Bible have? Your Bible has David doing the whole design and establishment intricately for the temple of Solomon. It is in your Bible in I Chronicles, let me read this now. By the way, David was called the shepherd king and he had a special love for the

111

shepherd's hut of Moses. He knew what Moses wanted. Let's turn to I Chronicles 22-28 chapters. This is a lot. What happens in these chapters is they are blaming David for Solomon's temple.

It was very important for the Jews, remember, to have Aaron as their founder. And so they diminished the role of Moses and gave Moses's rod to Aaron and Aaron put the rod down over the river to turn it to blood and Aaron did everything with the rod because Moses was viewed as insecure, instead of being *"mighty in words and in deeds."* It was real important for the one who established blood sacrifice to be their founder because that was what their whole religion depended on. It was also very important that they have David be the founder of their temple because his role as king tied the religion to the state. So chapters 22–28 are a description of all the long and tedious things that David did to establish the temple. *"And David commanded to gather together the strangers that were in the land of Israel; and he set masons to hew wrought stones to build the house of God."* There are no rocks in a shepherd's hut. *"David prepared iron in abundance for the nails for the doors of the gates, and for the joining; and brass in abundance without weight."* And it goes on and on of everything David did to design all the aspects of the temple of Solomon. *"And David said, Solomon my son is young and tender, and the house that is to be builded for the Lord must be exceedingly magnificent, of fame and of glory throughout all countries."* What happened to the shepherd's hut? *"I will therefore make preparations for it."* So David prepared abundantly before his death. So all these chapters describe what he did. *"David divided the courses of all the sons of Levi. I have prepared for the house of the Lord a hundred thousand talents of gold."* You know how much that is when a talent is 94 pounds? Talent is described as much as a man could carry. Eighteen million, eight-hundred thousand pounds of gold. Certainly the number is exaggerated! It just goes on and on clear through chapter 28. David does it all.

Now I want to tell you something. There are two threads of perspective as you know. Remember? There is one thread of perspective that says God forgave Solomon for all his wickedness and he was known to be a man of great wisdom. Here is the other one. This is in I Chronicles 28:9, part of those chapters I just cited. *"And thou, Solomon my son, know thou the God of thy father, and serve him with a perfect heart and with a willing mind: for the* LORD *searcheth all hearts, and understandeth all the imaginations of the thoughts: if thou seek him, he will be found of thee; but if thou forsake him, he will **cast thee off for ever**.*"

Now we have in all the Bible stories the wisdom of Solomon. And we have all the archaeologists saying Solomon's reign was the best in all of Israel's history. It was the highest point in their nation. And he is the one who did some terrible things and he forsook God. I want to read to you from I Kings 11:5–7 *"For Solomon went after Ashtoreth the goddess of the Zidonians, and after Milcom the abomination of the Ammonites. And Solomon did evil in the sight of the* LORD, *and went not fully after the* LORD, *as did David his father. Then did Solomon build an high place for Chemosh, the abomination of Moab, in the hill that is before Jerusalem, and for Molec, the abomination of the children of Ammon."*

Molec and Chemosh both required **human blood sacrifice,** specifically the blood of little children. They were burned alive. Solomon did it. Ashtoreth is the goddess of sexuality. Terrible orgies were done in worship for her. Who knows how bad and perverted they were. Solomon is said to have had 700 wives. Milcom is a name for Molec when you make a covenant with him. And the Lord was angry with Solomon because his heart was turned from the Lord God of Israel. Is he cast off forever? Should we be reading stories of his wisdom to our children? Or is he forgiven as in the other perspective? Were the Jews rightly inclined to bend history to put David in a central role for the temple of Solomon because of his gross wickedness?

Now I want to read to you another very important scripture. The scripture was written 787 years before Christ, which is at least 800 years before Stephen. This is one of the prophets. Amos 5:21–27 is a very important reading. *"I hate, I despise your feast days, and I will not smell in your solemn assembly."* This is God talking. *"Though you offer me burnt-offerings and your meat-offerings, I will not accept them: neither will I regard the peace-offerings of your fat beasts. Take away thou from me the noise of thy songs, for I will not hear the melody of thy viols. But let judgement run down as waters, and righteousness as a mighty*

113

*stream. Have you offered unto me sacrifice and offerings in the wilderness for forty years, O house of Israel? But ye have **born the tabernacle of your Molec and Chiun** your images, the star of your god ,which ye made to yourselves, Therefore will I cause you to go into captivity."* He had already defined the temple as a tabernacle of Molec. This was about 200 years after Solomon and 800 years before Stephen. So it was a very well-known thing among the prophets and the early church that Solomon's temple represented apostasy on a grand scale.

Ok, the tabernacle also became under Aaron a place for God to dwell that only Aaron and the Levites had access to giving them supreme directional control. And remember God said - I dwell not in tabernacles made with hands. So that carried all the way from Aaron to Solomon and beyond until the time of Christ; and it is lying in wait even for us today. Many of the Hebrew people long for the return of the temple.

Before we leave this topic of Stephen's blasphemy against the temple, I want to deal with a far reaching bit of information that comes from Acts 7:45 in regards to the temple. There is a word in verse 45 that is extremely perplexing to Bible translators and scholars are also stumped by it. That word is "Jesus." My Schofield Bible has the word "Jesus" there but footnotes it to say "Joshua" which is the Hebrew form of "Jesus." My Nelson's Bible just says "Joshua" and my Dickson Analytical Bible says just "Jesus." The Life Application Study Bible, New International Version simply changed this verse and eliminated the whole idea surrounding the word "Jesus."

Let me read the KJV verse 45 to you. I will start with verse 44 so you have the word Jesus in context. *"Our fathers had the tabernacle of witness in the wilderness, as he had appointed, speaking unto Moses, that he should make it according to the fashion that he had seen. Which also our fathers that came after **brought in with Jesus into the possession of the Gentiles**, whom God drave out before the face of our fathers, unto the days of David."*

Scholars are boxed in with this word "Jesus." If they say Joshua in reference to Joshua who was contemporary with Moses and Aaron (Joshua was born in Egypt and succeeded Moses,) it won't work because Aaron established that when the tabernacle is pitched any "*stranger that cometh neigh shall be put to death*" (Num. 1:51.) Strangers was the name for Gentiles during that period. So it just won't work to have the verse say Joshua in reference to the Joshua at the time of Moses. Joshua would never on his life bring the tabernacle into the possession of the Gentiles.

And then again if you leave the verse as is found in all the manuscripts, the word "Jesus" points in a direction that makes them squirm. They simply cannot conceive of Jesus having any association with a tabernacle, let alone with Jesus bringing it into the possession of the Gentiles.

At the heart of this dilemma are two erroneous assumptions. The first one being that Jesus and the early church would not have that kind of acceptance of Gentiles. The idea of the exclusivity of the gospel for Israel is promoted strongly in the New Testament. However, there are many contradictions to that assumption, principally what James, the Lord's brother who succeeded Jesus in the high priesthood of the early church, declared in his decree in Acts 15:13-21. Here pay particular attention to verses 16-17; which is James quoting Amos 9:11-12. "*After this I will return, and will build again the tabernacle of David, which is fallen down; and I will build again the ruins thereof, and I will set it up: That the residue of men might seek after the Lord, and **all the Gentiles, upon whom my name is called**, saith the Lord, who doeth all these things.*" James here is affirming Stephen's use of the word "Jesus" in 7:45, and, I might add, so is the prophet Amos. You will remember Moses actually established the shepherd's hut to include Gentiles.

The context of this statement by James is very important. His high priest decree is directly addressing the Gentile role in the church. James and Peter in this dialog of Acts 15 are stating their complete acceptance of the inclusion of the Gentiles. In addition to that, he is saying what he said directly in relation to the tabernacle as did Stephen. So Jesus really is the right word there.

The other assumption that makes all this problematic for scholars is they cannot comprehend that Jesus had anything to do with any tabernacle. They want to think at Jesus' time there was no tabernacle in Israel, it having been replaced with the temple. But there was a tabernacle in Israel during Christ's ministry and life. It was found at a place called by the church Secacah, which in our day is called Qumran. Qumran is Arabic for *the unbelievers*. They call it that because the eleven hundred or so graves there do not face Mecca. But Secacah was the name for the place in Hebrew. You will find Secacah listed in Joshua 15:61 and it also is listed in the Copper Scroll. It is the Copper Scroll that identifies Qumran as Secacah.

Let me explain some of the undercurrents here that define this issue. Christian scholars just do not want the sect of the Nazarenes to be one and the same as those around Jesus' time who were called Essenes. The prospect of that simply calls into question too many of their traditionally held positions in regards to what Christianity has become. We know the early church was called the sect of the Nazarenes: see Matt 2:23 and Acts 24:5. It is universally accepted that John the Baptist was an Essene. And John's relationship with Jesus was very close and well documented in the New Testament.

John, you see, can be an Essene without bringing into question what Christianity has become. So they are comfortable with John the Baptist having a relationship with Christ. But John also had a relationship with the early church. Now this is really an amazing and little known fact. John's grandfather, who is named Honi, who of course was Elizabeth's father, gave the property of Secacah/Qumran to the church. Isn't that interesting? We know this because a clay contract has been found at Qumran describing this transaction and naming Honi. This shard is cited on pages 596-597 of G. Vermes book <u>The Complete Dead Sea Scrolls in English</u>. John and Jesus were relatives. The tabernacle in Qumran was the place where the Essenes went to take their covenant. It was the very tabernacle that was established by God through Moses to promote the covenant. On top of all this, Robert Eisenman posits that James the Lord's brother actually functioned as an "opposition" high priest with the evidence that he functioned with the duties for one with what he supposes to be the temple in Jerusalem. But it could in fact be with the tabernacle at Qumran instead. It is hard to imagine the temple establishment allowing him to practice as a high priest there. The temple, especially the inner areas, was heavily guarded around the clock. You will carefully note that it says the tabernacle was brought into the possession of the Gentiles by Jesus. It doesn't say by the Church.

Those who do not want Jesus to be an Essene point out the differences between what Jesus did and how scholars describe the Essenes. But Jesus changed the sect of the Nazarenes/Essenes dramatically with His ministry among them. As an Essene, John the Baptist would never have baptized in public. Before Christ that was a closely held private practice among the Essenes. So when it says Jesus brought it into the possession of the Gentiles, it is because Jesus influenced the church to openly accept Gentiles into their covenant which was done in the tabernacle. He discarded the exclusivity of the gospel for the Jews. Jesus, as an Essene, is a whole other topic than what is intended in this series. But I just could not allow the significance of the word "Jesus" in verse 45 to go unaddressed.

But I have just one more comment about this word "Jesus." The context of verse 45 is an inflammatory moment for the Sanhedrin. Stephen just told them in verse 43 that because they had the temple of Molec, God would carry them away into captivity. Basically he is saying that the tabernacle would be taken away from them because they turned it into a temple. Then he says Jesus, who they killed, has in effect already done so. This was absolutely outrageous to the Sanhedrin. So when all is said and done with the controversy over the word "Jesus" in verse 45, it just means what it says. The real significance here of Jesus' association with a tabernacle is strong evidence that the sect of the Nazarenes and the Essenes are one and the same. Jesus had no other place to have an association with a tabernacle other than in Qumran/Secacah.

Ok now, I want to finish a little thing yet undone before I end this session. What do you do when you establish a religion like Aaron did, when it doesn't have a god? You establish a religion and apply it to Jesus's Father when it doesn't apply to Him at all. There are two things that happen. In order to make it work, you have to start defining God in different terms. He has to be somebody who is described in Numbers 31. He has to be frightfully angry and indifferent to the people of His creation. You have to

117

describe God and begin to view Him as somebody who constantly needs appeased. So that it says in Romans 5:9 that by the blood of Jesus we are saved from the wrath of God.

And then you have to do something else. You have to use the religion that you established. And the only way they could use it, validly, was with the likes of Molec because the God of Israel, the One True God, did not fit Aaron's religion. So your Bible has in it those kinds of descriptions of God that are actually of "the other guy." Not Jesus's Father as He Himself by His own words and deeds described and demonstrated Him. And they have in the Bible all the strayings of Israel. Time and time again they worshiped the gods of the heathens around them because the God of Moses didn't fit. Their religion was made to fit other gods; all this is because Aaron established blood sacrifice.

So now you understand what Stephen was saying when he said you have killed all the prophets. And in our next session we are going to do the section on the accusation concerning the law. And I am going to read to you many different things the prophets had to say about the law and about sacrifice. So that it is how it happened. That is how they got the temple; because somebody established blood sacrifice instead of doing their repentance. Blood replaced humility and love for Jesus's Father. Somebody in effect replaced the Son of God who forgives sin with love with shed blood. Somebody made it so somebody else has to do something ritually for you to be forgiven instead of being forgiven by the Lord by your mutual love and your own repentance. That has caused untold suffering by mankind and profound grief in heaven. And Shabuwa became a harvest festival and no longer represented man's covenant with the One True God. They created a religion where the Son of God took His life in His hands to be kind and compassionate on the Sabbath. They could have killed Him for representing the kindness of God of Israel on the Sabbath. Which is your God? Thank you.

Session 6
Finding the Truth about Moses and the Law, Part 1
February 1, 2015

Well, here we are on our sixth session of the series. And we are talking about <u>Christ's View of His Father: a Perspective for the thinking Christian</u>. Today our topic is on the blasphemy charges against Stephen concerning the **law**. And we have been finding that it was not by the words of false witnesses that the Sanhedrin that were going to condemn him but it was by his own words. However, in our studies it is certain that Stephen was reciting the truth that can be overwhelmingly substantiated in the Biblical record. In the end his death was the murder of an innocent man. In their view he blasphemed Moses, the temple, the law and God because his views on these topics differed from the accepted norm and was explosive in its ability to influence the public.

So today is kind of a long session because there is so much information. You will receive lots of information and many scriptures references. I will reference them not expecting you to remember all of them. But when they are noted, they are valuable for future inquiry.

I want to give you a little bit of background of Stephen. First, for centuries and centuries there was opposition to the temple and blood sacrifice by nearly all the prophets, major and minor. But their influence was overcome because there was usually only one living at a time. The opposition was sometimes prophets like Isaiah or Elijah who had great sway with many followers. But basically the opposition toward what the tabernacle became, or that is to say the temple and blood sacrifice, was mainly just a single prophet and they were relentlessly persecuted and often killed and in this way the opposition was eliminated.

At about 150 BC there arose the sect of the Nazarenes which are also called the Essenes. And they emerged with an opposition high priest; and there was for the first time in the history of Israel a parallel religious force. And early in that period they began to have a following. Stephen and Jesus were a part of this sect of the Nazarenes, which was the early church clear through the life and ministry of Jesus. And with the ministry and influence of Jesus, this parallel group began to bring a deeper crisis to the temple establishment. Starting about 30 or 40 years after its inception, about 100 BC maybe, it began to be a crisis because since the time of Aaron the Israeli society was primarily illiterate and only a few people could read and write. And because their scriptures were still in the midst of being codified and the knowledge of them was scant and generally in the possession of the elite, the public opposition was more easily subdued.

So the first thing they did, and the method they used in order to put down this opposition, was to kill the parallel high priest which was assumed to have the effect of disbanding this sect. Opposition high priests during this period were targets clear up until the Romans destroyed Israel. While Christ was indeed such a high priest, He was not perceived as such by the authorities. But James the Lord's brother decisively took on the role of opposition high priest and all the evidence points to the account of Stephen's trial and death were in fact that of James. But that is another story and not an issue for this series. These high priests were referred to in the Dead Sea Scrolls as "Teachers of Righteousness." And about the time that Christ emerged on the scene there was a big change within the sect of the Nazarenes, because before that the Essenes, or Nazarenes, were a private group as an act of sanctity and survival. Because of the Sanhedrin, or the leaders of the temple religion, the Essenes were rather secretive and held many things close to themselves. But the ministry of Christ brought about a remarkable change. He started to influence the Essene movement to change many things. And He influenced them to love those who, by tradition, they refrained from loving. One would expect them to follow the lead of their Messiah. Jesus radically changed the interaction the Essenes had with the public. With Jesus being seen by them to be the Messiah of Israel, He moved them to become more loving. John began to baptize people, including Gentiles, in public where baptisms before among the Essenes were carefully kept private.

And so Christ was a high priest to this sect with the corresponding influence to make this radical change, but He didn't present Himself as a high priest to the public. This was carefully observed to allow His ministry to proceed as He determined so as not to be exaggerated or cut short. They hid His priesthood and viewed it as betrayal for anyone to reveal it but Himself. The phrase they used here was that no one should "betray the Man who is worthy."

But His brother James was openly a high priest and he became a huge threat to the temple establishment. And he had a large following of many thousands of people. Remember there was a large company of priests who were obedient to the faith of the Nazarenes? This grew after Christ's resurrection. And James had broad support which caused the issues to be publicly debated. And they began to deal with the Essene's perspectives and positions and because of this many did not believe in the validity of the temple any longer and they only practiced moral sacrifice. Christ would only go into the court of the Gentiles. He would not go where Jews were expected to want to go. So there began to be a vibrant public debate because the Nazarenes were very active scribes and made many copies of the words of the prophets and of Jeremiah's Torah.

And the issues that Stephen raised came to the attention of the public because of Jesus's teachings and through the writings of the church. And Stephen in effect put voice to the central four most pressing issues. And scholars on both sides, those among the Essene group and on the temple side, were very familiar with all the knowledge that these issues involved. The Essenes in the Dead Sea scrolls, and in their community rule, had something that we don't have in our community rule today; they had to study several hours every day. It was mandatory. And the Jews had the same thing. In fact, even to this day there is a group of thousands of Jews who from the time they leave high school get a pension so they can devote their lives entirely to study the Scriptures. What they do for a living is study the Torah. Right at this time the government of Israel is trying to revoke that system and bring them into the workforce and into military service.

So Christ opened up those issues to the public simply and dramatically just by how He presented His Father. Remember that. And He did it in a way that reflected His control of His behavior so that He didn't cause the kind of stir that James or Stephen did. It was hard for the Sanhedrin to pin Him down and the people loved Him. So the temple religion at this time was extremely vulnerable because they had a weak defense in substantiating their points of view because now the words of the prophets who had been long oppressed were openly contributing to the public debate. And they couldn't defend themselves to the public in light of the words of the prophets because they had been able to justify the system they had simply through a public willingness to assume their traditions were correct. And their wealth and their status were on the brink of collapse. And they killed Stephen out of an act of desperation because of the growing threat to their religion and awareness of their high level of vulnerability. So Stephen comes along and then you hear in the seventh chapter of Acts this speech.

Now as I told you before, a central issue facing the Sanhedrin was the issue of their priesthood authority. Remember the Sanhedrin traced their priesthood to Aaron the idol maker and the people of the church traced theirs to Moses coming down from Melchizedek. And Melchizedek was, in fact, Shem, the son of Noah. This knowledge is a part of Jewish tradition that is validated by Kobelski in his work translating material from Cave 11 on page 69 of his book entitled <u>Melchizedek and Melchiresa</u>. Very few, if any, modern scholars have caught on to the importance of this issue of priesthood authority. This subject of priesthood authority was a major influence in the willingness of the Sanhedrin to destroy Jesus. Jesus even identified it as an issue to the temple authorities. In John 5:45-47, He said, *"Do not think that I will accuse you to the Father. There is one that accuseth you, even Moses, in whom ye trust. For had ye believed Moses, ye would have believed me: for he wrote of me. But if ye believe not his writings, how shall ye believe my words?"*

When Jesus said these words, He was speaking to people who were in that very moment ready to kill Him with stones. Why was this such a hot topic? Because the only thing Moses wrote about Jesus was precisely this issue of legitimate priesthood authority. It is found in Deut. 18: 15 & 18. This is what it says: *"The Lord thy God will raise up unto thee a prophet from the midst of thee, of thy brethren, like unto me, unto him shall ye hearken."* And again in verse 18 God is saying much the same thing. *"I will raise them up a prophet from among their brethren, like unto thee (Moses), and will put my words in his mouth, and he will speak unto them all that I shall **command him**."* Christ said to them that He only spoke the words His Father commanded Him to speak. He used the "command" language. And to add to this in the time of Christ there was a Messianic fervor. And the public, especially the church people who are the sect of the Nazarenes, knew full well to look for a Messiah who conformed to this prophecy of Moses. You can read an indication of this in John 1:45 where it says *"Philip findeth Nathaniel, and saith unto him, We have found him, of whom Moses in the law, and the Prophets did write, Jesus of Nazareth, the son of Joseph."* So the people of the church were well aware of who they were looking for, specifically in regard to this issue of priesthood authority coming down from Moses not Aaron.

Let me give you some further information of just how severe this issue between the church and the temple authorities was in Christ's day. In a fragment of a scroll written by the church scribes that was found in Cave #4, the fragment called #265 on a piece #7, in column #2 it says: *"Let no man from the seed of Aaron sprinkle water for cleansing on the Sabbath day."* Now this was a part of an expression of the community rule for those living in cities, but apparently not the rule used by most of them in Secacah. Here they are countering, in no uncertain terms, the lineal authority of the priesthood of Aaron; a very bold and provocative position to take that would to this day provoke Jews. This statement probably applied to both literal descendants of Aaron and those who claimed to be.

More of this acrimony is described on another fragment from Cave #4, fragment #266, column 2. Here are some quotes: *"Any of the Aaronites who are taken in* (the word used here is sometimes "captured") *by the Gentiles may not come to profane the temple by their impiety; he may not approach the worship."* Astonishingly, this is directly addressing temple high priests appointed by Rome. As you can see here, they had what could be seen as a derogatory term for those who adhered to the temple religion; they called them Aaronites. The sect of the Nazarenes did not think the high priest selected by Rome had authority to even approach the worship let alone perform it.

By the way, the sect of the Nazarenes defined the temple as the body of those who worshiped the One True God. Let me go on to quote more from this fragment. *"He* (the Aaronite) *may not go*

123

within the curtain (the Holy of Holies) *or eat the holy food.*" All of this was precisely the traditional role of the high priest of the seed of Aaron. Let me read some more, "*Any Aaronite who befouls the worship of God [you shall not associate] with him in the foundation of the people.*" This is saying that all their religious influence is to be censored, isn't that amazing?

And again let me read further, "*Any of the Aaronites whose name is dropped from the truth [and he intends] in his willful heart to eat any of the holy food [during the worship] of Israel, the council of Aaronites*" (here there occurs a hole in the writing) "*if he has eaten any of the food and become guilty of consuming blood [they must have no friendly interaction] in their relationship. This is the rule for those living in the cities.*" Here is cited a reference of just how strict the blood issue was for the sect. The use of blood brought shunning from them – no friendly relationships. The phrase "*the council of the Aaronites*" undoubtedly is referring directly to the Sanhedrin who were aware of these views held by the Essenes. And I'm sure when they killed Christ, they thought they were eliminating this view of one who was like unto Moses that should be listened to. It is entirely possible that the crisis in Israel that brought their nation to an abrupt end was not in the outset promulgated by their rebellion against Rome, but it was divisions in Israel's religious factions that made their society ungovernable. Can you now better understand the events surrounding this confrontation the Sanhedrin had with Stephen?

Another bit of evidence is in Nehemiah 9:17. It reads that the rebellious Israelites "*appointed a captain to return to their bondage,*" referring to Aaron. And Nehemiah was rehearsing the Book of the Law found in Josiah's time about 100 years earlier. And one can know for a certainty that the sect of the Nazarenes knew of this important scripture as they quote and recite from the verses just prior to it every time they take the covenant or renew it. You will find this written in the Community Rule. So this view of Aaron, which led to the title of Aaronites, was seen very early in Israel. At least 500 years B.C. So now can you see that this issue of legitimate priesthood authority in the context of the temple was front and center?

So this time we are going to follow the Bible trail of the information that Stephen supplies concerning the law. And these people, the Essenes and Sanhedrin, had available to them all the information that I will give to you today. I am getting it out of just the Bible. So this information is not new. This is why the Sanhedrin was so alarmed, because this information was now public. And it was part of the public debate. So here we go. Let us get into the law. I want to go through and acquaint you with the situation of how they viewed their law.

Remember I said there are intertwined parts of scripture presenting Jesus' Father and parts of scripture presenting "the other guy." I want to tell you about founders of religions a little bit to give you a feel for the contrast between Moses as the founder of Judaism and founders of other religions. And this is important because they hold to what they say is the Law of Moses. The Lutherans love Martin Luther so much they are called by his name. We had a Lutheran pastor visit us out here. He gave us a book on Luther's life. He also gave us a video on Luther's life and they were very proud of Luther. He told us that Martin Luther used to live in a boarding house and eat at a large table with all the other people in the boarding house. And he would speak of things while he was eating. They were so intent on that which he would say that during the discussions at the meals they would write down what he said. And they hung on his words even in this casual setting. And those comments are preserved and studied and viewed by the conservative side of Lutheranism as a valid guide for behavior. And ministers familiarize themselves with this information. Menno Simons was so loved by his people that they called them Mennonites after him. Charles and John Westley are viewed very highly, also.

But Moses was entirely different. I want to give you some background information that comes from your Bible about Moses and about his situation as a founder of a religion that has vast implications concerning the law. Stephen said Pharaoh's daughter raised Moses. There was a strict protocol for slaves who worked in the presence of royalty in Egypt. And because of that, it is almost certain that if his mother would have nursed him in the courts of the Pharaoh, she would have had no opportunity to teach him to speak Hebrew as his first language. That would have had to be an intimate kind of relationship that would take lots of exposure and repetition

125

and lots of time. And so it is almost certain that Moses's first language was Egyptian. And his second language was Midianite because he left Egypt and married a Midianite woman named Zipporah and was there for 40 years. And the spokesman dynamic regarding Moses needing Aaron as a spokesman probably was so he could translate for him to the Hebrews. And I've told you this before.

So you have a founder of a religion who doesn't speak the language of the people with whom he is engaged. Martin Luther spoke German and all the people could listen to him first hand; and the same for Menno Simons and all the rest. But Moses was different. Here you have a man who couldn't speak the language of the people whom he is leading. Moses had to know the Lord God in Egypt. For one thing Stephen says that Moses knew that he was called of God to deliver Israel before he left Egypt for Midian. And a person doesn't go into the presence of God like Moses did at the burning bush without knowing Him with background in that knowledge, especially in their youth. So God must have had an open relationship with Moses during his early days while he was in the courts of Pharaoh. And there are indications also that the Hebrews knew it. I read those to you last week that Moses was designated by God to deliver Israel while he still lived in Egypt. That rumor had spread. But by the long time that had passed after he left Egypt this idea of him being a deliverer was forgotten among the Hebrews. And a new generation had come along.

And the Hebrew people had no opportunity to practice a religion or to develop a religion in Egypt. They only had collective memory from their fathers. And there certainly was no writing in Hebrew at the time of Moses. Remember they were slaves. They were subjected to the Egyptian religion to some degree. They wrote religious symbols on the walls as an occupation. They were artisans and when they built religious buildings they would be exposed to their function. They may even have had direct exposure as slaves during religious gatherings. So they knew about the religion of the Egyptians. They knew that they worshipped, among other things, a calf called Hapi.

Ok, when Moses came back he was a shepherd. He wasn't a shepherd when he was in Egypt. He was in royal circles. He came back as a shepherd. Shepherds in Egypt were seen to be the lowest form of human being. Egyptians were forbidden to eat with a shepherd. So contrast this with Martin Luther as the founder of a church; he was a high-class priest in the Roman Church with intelligence enough to effectively protest, but Moses was a shepherd of the lowest caste. And people there were ashamed to associate with shepherds. Bedouins fit the stereotype perfectly.

Not only that, but Moses learned his expression of religion in Midian. While he had a relationship with God in Egypt, the aspects of what he learned about religion that he practiced in the land came from his father-in-law whose lineage can be traced directly back to Abraham. And Jethro was in the situation to practice his religious tradition of his people's collective memory. So here is the man in the lowest caste, who doesn't speak Hebrew, and learned his religion among a people who would historically be the avowed enemies of Israel, and he is coming to establish their religion. And on top of that, because he was raised in the house of Pharaoh; he represented to the Hebrews their oppressors. Many of them saw him as interfering in their lives, rather than coming there to deliver them, especially when what he did resulted in their having to work harder. And many were not even looking for a deliverer because in Egypt rebellion was treated very severely. And it was very risky to rebel as slaves in Egypt.

So here is this man who comes there with a foreign wife; they were suspicious of him. They didn't trust that he could do it, after all Egypt was the most powerful nation on the earth at that time. Once they were delivered suddenly the whole delivery issue became Moses' idea when they faced the reality of desert survival. It was no longer their idea. And, in short, they hated Moses. At the burning bush Moses didn't even know the Hebrew name for their God. What if Martin Luther had to ask how do you say God in German? There is now evidence that the name Yahweh did not come into existence for some 200 years after Moses. And then it was borrowed from the Edomites.

I know of no other founder of any other religion that was so hated as the Hebrews hated Moses. And this is not a small point. Their attitude towards Moses was a pivotal foundation to that which the Jewish religious expression became, starting even during his life time. From the very first contact when Moses was very polite he said, brethren why do you do harm to one another, and they cast him from them and said, who made thee a prince and a judge over us? So I want to read to you a list of references that indicate the Hebrews had hatred for Moses. In this part of the dynamic of this day's topic, I will be giving you lots of scripture references. So bear with me because it is important for you to get a feel for Moses as the one that established their religion. So today the Jews say they believe in the Law of Moses. Here is the history. I am going to give you references starting at the beginning and running through Moses's time with the Israelites. You can read these references yourselves and get the entire context.

Exodus 2:14 "who made thee a prince and a judge over us?"
Exodus 5:20–32 "the Lord look upon you" (scorned him)
Exodus 6:9 "they hearkened not unto Moses"
Exodus 14:11–12 "taken us away to die in the wilderness"
Exodus 15:24 (three days after Red Sea) "what shall we drink?"
Exodus 16:2-3 "would to God we had died in the land of Egypt."
Exodus 16:20 "they hearkened not unto Moses."
Exodus 16:27 "there went out some of the people" (against Moses)
Exodus 17:2 "people did chide with Moses."
Exodus 17:3 "[Moses will] kill us and our children"
Exodus 17:4 "they be almost ready to stone me"
Exodus 17:7 "is the Lord among us, or not?"
Exodus 18:2 wife visited "after he had sent her back"
Exodus 32:21 Aaron went against Moses pridefully.
Numbers 11:1 "the people complained" (angered the Lord)
Numbers 11:4 "who shall give us flesh to eat?"
Numbers 12:1–16 they called Moses' wife an "Ethiopian woman"
Numbers 14:2-5 "Murmured against Moses."
Numbers 14:10 stoned Moses' supporters
Numbers 14:22 "tempted me now these ten times"
Numbers 14:36 "all congregation to murmur against" (Moses)
Numbers 14:27 "murmur against me."
Numbers 14:41 "[the people] transgress the commandment"
Numbers 16:3 "and they gathered... against Moses"
Numbers 16:41 "murmured against Moses."
Numbers 20:3 "people chide with Moses."
Numbers 21:5 "and the people spake against God, and against Moses."

Numbers 25:1–3 people rebelled and did idols
Numbers 17:5 "cease from me the murmurings of the children of Israel"
Nehemiah 8:17 the people had not kept Passover since Joshua

There is more that I will bring up in later sessions that are not on this list. And this list is just what is recorded in the Bible. How many more such instances could have occurred that weren't recorded? So these are just some indications of how severely Moses was treated. No wonder Moses reached his limit. Remember him saying, If I have found favor in thy sight kill me out of hand? He couldn't bear the burden of the hatred of this people any longer. What if Martin Luther would have said that? Remember when Moses said Lord if you will forgive them I will trade my soul? He surely knew Jesus' Father.

So here is this man who was unbearably and cruelly treated by the people he is supposed to be leading to the One True God, and he stayed behind when his family had to be sent away because of the ill treatment. They simply did not want what Moses was establishing. And in the end, they did not embrace it or carry it forward. They wanted a religious state, a religious elite like Egypt. One can understand how slaves would aspire to live the life like those they served.

Now there is another aspect of this that I want you to understand. Moses wrote a testimony; it is called a testimony thirty-two times in your Old Testament and one time in the New Testament. But **Moses's writings were specifically a testimony against Israel.** Did you hear that? He wrote a testimony against Israel. Did Luther write a testimony against Lutherans? This is a very clear sign of how severe the relationship between Moses and Israel became. So I want to read this to you. I know of no other founder who this could be said about. Read Deuteronomy 31 starting at verse 9. "*And Moses wrote this law, and delivered it unto the priests, the sons of Levi, which bear the ark of the covenant of the Lord, and unto the elders of Israel. And Moses commanded them, saying, At the end of every seven years, in the solemnity of the year of release,*" in the feast of booths (shepherd's huts) "*when all Israel is come to appear before the Lord thy God in the place which he shall choose,*" (in the first place was outside the camp, remember) *"thou shalt read this law before all Israel in their hearing.*

*Gather the people together, men, and women, and children and **thy stranger that is within thy gates,** that they may hear, and that they may learn; and [reverence] the Lord your God, and observe to do all of the words of this law: And that their children, which have not known anything, may hear, and learn to [remember] the Lord your God, as long as ye live in the land whither ye go over Jordan to possess it.*

*And it came to pass, that when Moses had made an end of writing the words of this law in a book, until they were finished, that Moses commanded the Levites, that bear the ark of the covenant of the Lord, saying, Take this book of the law, and, put it in the side of the ark of the covenant of the Lord your God, **that it may be there for a witness against thee.** Gather unto me all the elders of your tribes, and your officers, that I may speak these words in their ears, and **call heaven and earth to record against them."***

So the book of the law that Moses wrote was written against Israel. I think he wrote it after they kicked him out as Stephen says. I think he wrote it after he knew that they were going to go with Aaron's blood sacrifice and the temple instead of a shepherd's hut. I think he wrote this just before they went over Jordan at the time Deuteronomy was recited to them.

Ok, so calling heaven and earth as a witness against them is a very strong statement, maybe the strongest one possible in the context of Hebrew culture. It is hard for us to know just what Moses established. I don't think even those in the early church knew for sure. The last half of the Book of Jubilees is lost. It represents our only version of the original Torah at this time. The Book of Jubilees is a part of the Dead Sea Scrolls. It represents one of the more numerous copies found there and were written by different scribes. If I remember right there are ten or twelve different recensions. It was a major source of scripture for the sect of the Nazarenes. And it undoubtedly is the source of Stephen's information.

So we don't know what Moses in fact established, but we do know what he did not establish. Moses did not write the first five books of the Bible in Hebrew. The Hebrew written language did not come into existence or develop for five or six hundred years after Moses. And in Solomon's time, the written Hebrew language was just beginning. It was not standardized yet in Solomon's time. I would recommend that you read an article in <u>Biblical Archaeological Review</u> entitled *How the Alphabet was Born,* by Orly Goldwasser. She is a professor in Israel. The evidence she presents is good, outstanding scholarship. And the picture on the front of this article I'm holding shows a little statue with Hebrew writing on it. And the next article following hers discusses the oldest Hebrew writing ever found in Israel and it comes from Solomon's time. The letters could read up or down or sideways. The individual letters had no right side up. So that is what I mean by it not being standardized yet. Solomon lived 500 years after Moses. So Moses could not have written in Hebrew. But he did indeed write and it had to be in Egyptian. Remember he was learned in all the wisdom of the Egyptians in word and deed as Stephen said. So it was probably sometime after Solomon that written Hebrew began to be used to record a rendition of an oral history.

However, you will see that Moses's actual writings were discovered. The best account of what they contained was dictated by Jeremiah to Baruch his scribe and is in fact the Book of Jubilees. But remember, everything in this document after the crossing of the Red Sea has been destroyed. The Book of Jubilees covers a period from creation through the stories of the Patriarchs, down to Moses' birth and his fleeing from Egypt, through the episode of the burning bush and on through the miracles before Pharaoh and the crossing of the Red Sea. Aaron's name does not appear in the Book of Jubilees. He is not mentioned there in the account of Moses' conversation with God at the burning bush. Pretty amazing don't you think?

This paper is important for you to read. This article was voted best of the year for BAR Magazine. It traces the development of the alphabet starting in southern Egypt in the turquoise mines where workers first experimented with symbols that represented sounds not words. The Hebrew alphabet was the world's first alphabet. A good read! This all happen 500 years after Moses. There is strong evidence that the Torah was originally written in Egyptian. What if Martin Luther had written all his writings in

Russian? How would that have affected his role as a founder of a German church?

Now I want to go through the Bible and I will give you some of this evidence. And we will look at this seriously. I am going to read in II Kings, chapter 22. This is a story of King Josiah finding the very book of the law that Moses wrote. Israel had no contact with his writings until this time. This is the first time, 863 years after Moses, according to the dates in my Bible. So what Moses wrote could not be that which influenced the development of the temple religion. In this account, they first found his writings. Now they had them before that but they didn't give them value because they were not written in Hebrew and because of where they were kept. It is also certain according to this II Kings reference, that before this time, no one even knew what they were because they were not in the format that their writings of sacred things usually had taken. They couldn't read them and had they been aware of them they would have treated them simply as a curiosity.

So what you are going to see as we go through this is that the entire Jewish religion was developed without Moses's writings. During those 863 years, their religion developed without Moses's writings. Think of what a long a time that is. The reality is probably Moses had little or nothing to do with establishing what Judaism became. Is it any surprise he wrote a testimony against them? It was written against them because his writings represented what their religion ought to have been instead of what he knew it would become.

II Kings 22: "*Josiah was eight years old when he began to reign. And he reigned thirty and one years in Jerusalem. And his mother's name was Jedidiah, the daughter of Adziah of Boscath. And he did that which was right in the sight of the Lord, and walked in all the ways of David his father, and turned not aside to the right hand or to the left.*" This is a little witness of what I was telling you about the other day how David, with regards to the tabernacle, or the shepherd's hut, would not turn to make it all gold and glory. "*And it came to pass in the eighteenth year of king Josiah, that the king sent Shaphan the son of Azaliah, the son of Meshallum the scribe, to the house of the Lord, saying:…*" Now this is interesting because Meshallum means *an immigrant* (from Egypt?) or *to be allied with us for his safety* (see Strongs #4918 and #7999). So Meshallum was a scribe, and his grandson was a scribe, which was common in those days.

So again saying, "*Go up to Hilkiah the high priest, that he may sum the silver which is brought into the house of the Lord, which the keepers of the door have gathered of the people.*" The keeper of the door was a special position that received offerings of the people who passed through the door. People would give something they thought would be of value and the keepers would put what they received in the treasury. It was a room just stacked with these offerings and seldom looked at. And he said count the silver, in other words there was to be expected that other things of value were there. "*And let them deliver it into the hand of the doers of the work that have the oversight of the house of the Lord.... Howbeit there was no reckoning made with them of the money that was delivered into their hand, because they dealt faithfully.*" The silver was called money. "*And Hilkiah the high priest said unto Shaphan the scribe, I have found the book of the law in the house of the Lord. And Hilkiah gave the book to Shaphan and he read it.*"

Right there is an indication that it was not written in Hebrew, because if it was in Hebrew the high priest himself would have read it. Shaphan the scribe, whose father was an immigrant, had to read it; because the typical high priest was the most learned of anyone anybody in reading Hebrew Scriptures, albeit there was not yet written Hebrew at this time. "*And Shaphan the scribe came to the king, and brought the king word again. And Shaphan the scribe showed the king, saying,*" he had the book, he showed it to the king, "*saying, Hilkiah the priest has delivered me a book.*" And Shaphan read it before the king.

"*And it came to pass, when the king had heard the words of book of the law, that he rent his clothes. And the king commanded Hilkiah the priest... and Shaphan the scribe... saying, Go you inquire of the Lord for me, and for the people, and for all Judah, concerning the words of this book that is found: for great is the wrath of the Lord that is kindled against us, because our fathers have hearkened not unto the words of this book, to do according unto that which is written concerning us. So Hilkiah the priest, and Ahikam, and Achbor, and Shaphan, and Asahiah, went unto Huldah*

133

the prophetess... And she said onto them, Thus saith the Lord God of Israel, Tell the man who sent you to me, Thus saith the Lord, Behold I will bring evil upon this place, and upon the inhabitants thereof, even all the words of the book which the king of Judah hath read." It was written against them.

"*Because they have forsaken me, and have burned incense unto other gods, that they might provoke me. But to the king of Judah which sent you to inquire of the Lord, thus shall you say to him, Thus saith the Lord God of Israel, As touching the words which thou hast heard; Because thine heart was tender, and thou hast humbled thyself before the Lord, when thou heardest what I spake **against this place**, and against the inhabitants thereof, that they should become a desolation and a curse, and hast rent thy clothes, and wept before me, I also have heard thee saith the Lord.*" It is a constant theme that Moses wrote against Israel. The king sent for all the people.

Now chapter 23 "*And the King sent, and they gathered unto him all the elders of Judah and of Jerusalem. And the King went up into the house of the Lord, and all the men of Judah and all the inhabitants of Jerusalem with him, and the priests, and the prophets* (which included Jeremiah), *and all the people, both small and great: and he read in their ears all the words of the book of the covenant which was found in the house of the Lord. And the King stood by a pillar, and made a covenant before the Lord, to walk after the Lord, and to keep his commandments and his testimonies and his statutes with all their heart and all their soul, to perform the words of this covenant that were written in this book. And all the people stood to the covenant.*" In this instance the writings of Moses are called the book of the covenant –the Mosaic Covenant. You will also note that Josiah is referencing the first commandment with the words of all their heart and all their soul.

Now I want to read about three verses to show you and let you feel for how Josiah responded to the original book of the law written by Moses himself. He changed the entire religious culture of Israel. "*And the king commanded Hilkiah the high priest, and the priests of the second order, and the keepers of the door, to bring forth out of the temple of the Lord all the vessels that were made for Baal, and for the grove* (Grove is for Ashtoreth the Goddess of sexual activity), *and for all the host of heaven* (the gods of the Assyrians): *and he burned them without Jerusalem in the fields of Kidron, and carried the ashes of them unto Bethel."* Bethel means the house of El. And I think he did that because El is "the other guy."

Ok, now I want you to understand the importance of what we just read, and I want you to understand that no writing in Hebrew would ever be found in the treasury. They won't even throw sacred writings away when they were worn out. Their scriptures are seen to be very sacred. They have what is called a genizah, which is a repository for old worn-out sacred writings. It is usually in an attic or somewhere. No sacred writing would have been put in the treasury. And it was not a scroll because any scroll would not ever have been treated that way. It had to be written on metal plates, probably brass. They would allow no sacred writing to be in the treasury; so just the fact that it was in the treasury tells you that it wasn't written in Hebrew.

So Josiah goes on and he cleanses Israel. *"He defiled Topheth, which is in the valley of the children of Hinnom that no man might make his son or daughter to pass through the fire to Molec."* This is talking about human sacrifice by burning little children alive at the hands of their own fathers. Solomon did it. So the whole thing is very interesting and disgusting. As you study, you can go through the rest of that chapter and learn a lot about the gross sins of Israel founded on blood sacrifice. Josiah did very astute things, that came from a deep understanding of how evil works, to prohibit anyone taking up again their evil and dark ways. This is a very instructive reading indeed.

This was the first battle of the Torahs. This time instead of Christ, James or others bringing it into public debate, Josiah, the King of Israel, brought it. And all the princes of Israel, who were central in the corruption that had come, had to simply wait for Josiah to die before they could carry on their evil traditions. In my opinion, they had something to do with his death using their powers of darkness.

Ok now, since this was about 863 years after Moses, and since this was the very first contact that they had with his writing,

135

you will find that during this long passage of time the perspective of "the other guy" had slowly developed. And this is the case even today as it was in Christ's day. And this is why the last half of Jubilees has been destroyed; because they knew that the book of the law was not found until after their religion was fully and well-established.

I want to read II Kings 17:15–17, *"and they rejected his statutes, and his covenant that he made with their fathers, and his testimonies which he testified against them; and they followed vanity, and became vain, and went after the heathen that were round about them, concerning whom the Lord had charged them, that they should not do like them. And they left all the commandments of the Lord and their God, and made them molten images, even two calves, and made a grove, and worshiped all the hosts of heaven, and served Baal. And they caused their sons and their daughters to pass through the fire, and used divinations and enchantments, and sold themselves to do evil in the sight of the Lord, to provoke him to anger."*

This reading is describing spiritual conditions at the time of Josiah's father. His father did all these things. So Josiah was very brave. And Jedidiah, his mother, was a very holy woman. And she raised him up unto the Lord secretly, without his father knowing.

Now I want to read another scripture to you from Nehemiah 8:17, this is another indication that supports the view that they did not have Moses's writings. *"And all the congregation of them that were come again out of the captivity* (of Babylon) *made booths* (shepherd's huts), *and sat under the booths: for since the days of Joshua the son of Nun unto that day had not the children of Israel done so. And there was very great gladness."*

Remember I read to you when Moses wrote the book of the law and he said every seven years during the feast of tabernacles, which is the shepherd's hut, that they should read this law unto all the children of Israel, including the Gentiles who were among them. They hadn't obeyed Moses to do this in all that time. Isn't that interesting? 1000 years passed without them obeying Moses's explicit instructions in your Bible. Why? Because they simply did not have them! This came about because they lost track of the book

136

of the law because they no longer had someone who could read Egyptian. This is more information to substantiate this dynamic. Now remember that was a thousand years.

This issue of the Israelites not acting on Moses' explicit instructions for so long has in it evidence that is important to note. When you read Numbers 1:50 you will read the decree that a stranger who approaches the shepherd's hut is to be put to death but when you read Deuteronomy 31:9-25 you will see Moses instructed the people specifically to invite the "stranger" to the assembly at the shepherd's hut to hear the law read. What is of interest here is the decree of death to strangers was issued early on during the life time of Moses. This is evidence that, when Stephen said they thrust Moses from them and he left, Stephen was correct. By the way, there is some evidence also to support the idea that Jesus could have brought the shepherd's hut into the possession of the Gentiles as Moses' words here indicate a willingness to include them in what happened there, at the very inception of the shepherd's hut. So we can know that even in Josiah's time and shortly thereafter, because the princes of Jerusalem persecuted Josiah's supporters, like Jeremiah, this was not done until about a hundred years after Josiah. It wasn't long after the death of Josiah that they were taken into captivity in 588 B.C. and returned seventy years later in Nehemiah's time. Ok, are you all tired? By the way history, repeats itself. About 40 years after Josiah brought these same issues as Stephen did, the temple was destroyed. About 40 years after Christ and Stephen the same issues led to the destruction of the temple again. Thank you again.

Session 7
Finding the Truth about Moses and the Law, Part 2
February 1, 2015

Good afternoon, let us continue on again today with our study of the **law.** What did Israel develop as a religion during this long interim that I spoke of? And if they did not have the book of the law, where did their religion come from? What you have learned so far is that they had a temple instead of a shepherd's hut, remember how drastic the differences? I was thinking about the poor Levites who had to dismantle and pack up and carry this exploded version of the tabernacle. They had blood sacrifice instead of moral sacrifice. They had a Levitical law instead of the law of virtue, a part of which Christ enumerated in His Sermon on the Mount. You will find the law of virtue referred to amply in the 5th chapter of Matthew and other places. The parables are particularly noteworthy in expressing the law of virtue.

So all this amounted to what I called the original Torah rather than the imposed one. They had a version of the original Torah that was attributed to Moses starting at the time of Josiah. You will remember in Matthew 5 in the Sermon on the Mount Jesus cites the law of virtue in the Beatitudes. You all remember what they are. He is drawing from the original Torah. He said you have heard it said, but I say to you etc. over and over. These kind of sayings can indicate that Christ's ministry was to the people of the church not a new religion, but a restoration of lost former things. Do you suppose John the Baptist being described as coming to restore all things is acknowledging this fact? Let's look into the coming forth of the original Torah.

First of all, there were many witnesses to the reading of the book of the law in the court of Josiah. One who is of principal interest is Jeremiah. We don't know who the other ones were however. I'm going to read something to you here from one of my several Bible dictionaries; and I want to read something about Deuteronomy, this is the New International Dictionary of the Bible.. *"Students of the Bible are especially interested in the comparison of Hammurabi's code with the mosaic legislation of the Bible. Hammurabi was a king in Babylon about 1800 BC or about 300*

139

years before Moses and Aaron. There are many similarities, both
codes agree in prescribing the death penalty for adultery and other
things. How are the similarities to be explained? It is obvious that
Hammurabi could not have borrowed from Moses for Moses lived
several centuries after Hammurabi. Most scholars today agree that
the similarities are to be explained by a common background of the
Hebrews and the Babylonians. At first this explanation seems to run
counter to the physical claim that Moses's law was given by divine
revelation."

And if I could, I would show you a picture of the obelisk
that is written with the law of Hammurabi, but I forgot to bring it. It
shows the sun god giving this law to him. So scholars are very
aware of that which I am about to read to you. All the Bible
dictionaries have something to say about it but some of them do not
go as far as mentioning that these similarities could call the divine
revelation process of Moses into question. Actually the Jehovah's
Witnesses are the most forthright. Some scholars, when you look up
Deuteronomy, believe that Deuteronomy was written at the time of
Josiah because it is in so much contrast with the other four books of
the Torah. We don't know who wrote Deuteronomy. It wasn't
Moses; because it was written long after Moses. It most likely came
from oral tradition that was cited in a public reading of the book of
the law by Josiah. The word Deuteronomy you remember means *to*
restate the law.

But we do have Jeremiah; he is one of our heroes. I want to
read something about Jeremiah. This might be a surprise to you.
Jeremiah was an eyewitness to the reading of the book of the law by
Josiah. They were both in their early twenties. The first two verses
of Jeremiah chapter 1 read as follows: *"The words of Jeremiah the*
son of Hilkiah, of the priests that were in Anathoth in the land of
Benjamin: to whom the word of the Lord came in the days of Josiah
the son of Amon." Was it the same Hilkiah that found the book of
the law? I think it was but I may be alone in that belief. I can't find
evidence that it was some other Hilkiah yet it would serve the
interests of those who follow the imposed Torah to assert so. Maybe
it was another Hilkiah. So that makes Josiah 21 years old because
he was eight when he began to reign. So Jeremiah was also a young
man; he may have been even younger than Josiah. He refers to
himself as being a child at the time that the book of the law was

found (see Jeremiah 1:6). That could be an indication that it was possible he was the son of the man who found it.

Ok, Jeremiah wrote a scroll that the Sanhedrin of that day destroyed. This was after some years had passed since the book was discovered (the account of which is in Jeremiah 36). And they were threatened by it just like the Sanhedrin was with Stephen. When Jeremiah supported the book of the law under Zedikiah after Josiah's death they imprisoned him. They killed Stephen but they imprisoned Jeremiah (the first battle of the Torahs). This comes from Jeremiah 36, starting at the beginning. I am going to read selected verses to save time. *"And it came to pass in the fourth year of Jehoiakim the son of Josiah king of Judah that this word came unto Jeremiah from the Lord, saying, Take thee a roll of a book, and write therein all the words that I have spoken unto thee against Israel, and against Judah."* He is going to write the words that were on the book of the law that were described as being against Israel. Remember when Moses wrote, he said his writings were against Israel and he would call heaven and earth against them? And remember, Josiah himself described them the same way? This is primary evidence that the original Torah in Hebrew came from Jeremiah.

"Then Jeremiah called Baruch the son of Neriah: and Baruch wrote from the mouth of Jeremiah all the words of the Lord, which he had spoken unto him, upon a roll of a book. And Jeremiah commanded Baruch, saying, I am shut up; I cannot go into the house of the Lord." Some say that Jeremiah was imprisoned in a slime pit with slippery sides so he could not get out. *"Therefore go thou, and read in the roll, which thou hast written from my mouth, the words of the Lord in the ears of the people in the Lord's house upon the fasting day. And Baruch the son of Neriah did according to all that Jeremiah the prophet commanded him, reading in the book the words of the Lord in the Lord's house."*

So here Jeremiah is making this information public from the book of the law. This is a very scary situation for the princes of Jerusalem, or the Sanhedrin. *"Then he went down into the king's house, into the scribe's chamber: and, lo, all the princes sat there... Then Michaiah declared unto them all the words that he had heard, when Baruch read the book in the ears of the*

141

people. Therefore all the princes sent Jehudi ... saying, Take in thine hand the roll wherein thou hast read in the ears of the people, and come. So Baruch ... took the roll in his hand, and came unto them."

He is now in effect standing before the Sanhedrin. I'm saying that because at this point in history I don't know if they called it the Sanhedrin. *"And they said unto him, Sit down now, and read it in our ears. So Baruch read it in their ears. Now it came to pass, when they had heard all the words, they were afraid both one and other, and said unto Baruch, We will surely tell the king of all these words. And they asked Baruch, saying, Tell us now, How didst thou write all these words at his mouth? Then Baruch answered them, He pronounced all these words unto me with his mouth, and I wrote them with ink in the book. Then said the princes unto Baruch, Go, hide thee, thou and Jeremiah; and let no man know where ye be."*

What Jeremiah wrote was very alarming. It certainly elicited the same response then as it did in the days of Stephen. *"And they went in to the king into the court, but they laid up the roll in the chamber of Elishama the scribe, and told all the words in the ears of the king."*

First they hid the book. The original Torah was the words of the law that Hilkiah had found in the treasury written from memory. Then they burnt the scroll. *"Then the word of the LORD came to Jeremiah, after that the king had burned the roll, and the words which Baruch wrote at the mouth of Jeremiah, saying, Take thee again another roll, and write in it all the former words that were in the first roll, which Jehoiakim the king of Judah hath burned.... Then took Jeremiah another roll, and gave it to Baruch the scribe... who wrote therein from the mouth of Jeremiah all the words of the book which Jehoiakim king of Judah had burned in the fire: and there were **added besides unto them many like words**."* This is a very important statement indeed.

Now I think from my studies that the Book of Jubilees is what he wrote. And there was such a fierce opposition to it by state leaders that only the first part, that doesn't include any part of the description of obtaining the law, was able to survive; but the Book of Jubilees in the very beginning section states that the Angel of the Presence gave Moses an account from creation until the establishment of the tabernacle. In Jubilees col. 1 lines 27-28 it says: *"And (God) said to the angel of the presence, write for Moses from the **first creation** until my sanctuary is built in their midst forever and ever."* From this statement we know that the original Torah did not end at the account of the Red Sea crossing because the sanctuary came after Sinai.

Now I want to read to you a little bit of the beginning of the Book of Jubilees. This comes from the Dead Sea Scrolls. And this is another topic I could cover in this series and I could go through and show you all the evidence that is in the Book of Jubilees that verifies this and it would be fun but I can't do it now. But I do want to give you a little feel for the Book of Jubilees. This is the first column starting with line 5. *"The Lord said set your mind on everything which I will tell you on this mountain."* Now this is Moses who is on the mountain.

"And write it in a book so that their descendants might see that I have not abandoned them on account of all their evil which they have done to instigate transgression of the covenant which I am establishing between you and me today on Mount Sinai for their descendants. And you write for yourself all these words which I **have caused you to know**" Isn't that interesting? He caused him to know. *"For I know of the rebelliousness and their stubbornness before I caused them to enter the land which I swore to their fathers I will give to your seed a land flowing with milk and honey. They will eat and be satisfied and they will turn to strange gods and to those who cannot save them from any of their afflictions. And this testimony will be heard as **testimony against them**."*

See it is everywhere written: the writings of Moses were a testimony against Israel. *"For they will forget all the commandments everything which I have commanded them and they will walk after the Gentiles and after their defilement and shame. And they will serve their gods and they will become a scandal for them and an affliction and a torment and a snare. And they may be destroyed in the seas and will fall into the enemy because they have forsaken my ordinances and my commandments and my feasts and*

143

*my covenant and my sabbaths and **my sacred place**. Which I
sanctified for myself among them and my shepherd's hut and my
sanctuary which I sanctified for myself in the midst of the land so I
might set my chamber upon it and might dwell there. And they will
make for themselves high places and groves and idols and each of
them will worship his own idol as to go astray and they will
sacrifice their children to the demons to every work of error that
there art.*"

That is the beginning of the Book of Jubilees. And it
follows the biblical pattern starting with creation and on through the
patriarchs and on to Moses and the crossing of the Red Sea. It
records all the events leading up to Moses going back to Egypt
through the crossing. And Aaron's name is not in the Book of
Jubilees. So if they needed Aaron for anything they forgot it.

Now there is evidence that the Book of Jubilees is a version
of the original Torah or that is to say this record dictated by
Jeremiah. Here is a fun part for me. All the prophets knew the One
True God; Jesus' Father. The only possible exceptions were
Zachariah and Haggai. They were seen to be supportive of the
temple at the time of the return. Whether they were or not we do not
know. Stephen spoke what prophets have your fathers not
persecuted. And they have slain those who showed forth the coming
of the righteous one. This means Christ and he said that in relation
to the temple and their religion. So the prophets knew the One True
God and were a formidable opposition to the temple and its blood
sacrifice. And almost all of them spoke out against it. And the
temple religion of the Jews always hated the prophets because they
represented the other perspective found in the actual writings of
Moses.

So I am going to give you some vital information
illustrating this and this is very startling. Isaiah, I am going to start
with Isaiah. I have to look all these up because there are so many
scriptures related to this topic that I couldn't mark them all in my
Bible. The prophets are such heroes for us. I love them so much.
They were brave and stood up for the truth no matter what the cost.
Isaiah was a young man. He was a teenager, actually, when he first
started. I don't know how old he was when he wrote chapter 1 but
he came in heavily against blood sacrifice at a young age. Let's look

144

at his first chapter, verse 10. This is amazing now. This is a very young prophet. He is coming in on the scene, like the Lord did when He first started His ministry; He cleansed the temple and again just before He ended His ministry He cleansed it again. Isaiah went in and out of his ministry confronting what the shepherd's hut had become. Isaiah came into his ministry against blood sacrifice. *"Hear the word of the LORD, ye rulers of Sodom; give ear unto the law of our God, ye people of Gomorrah.*

To what purpose is the multitude of your sacrifices unto me? saith the LORD: I am full of the burnt offerings of rams, and the fat of fed beasts;" Now listen to this carefully folks. *"And **I delight not in the** blood of bullocks, or of lambs, or of he goats."* He said I delight not in the blood of lambs. What implications does that have for how so many Christians view the Lamb of God?

*"When ye come to appear before me, who hath required this at your hand, to tread my courts? Bring no more vain oblations; incense is an abomination unto me; the new moons and sabbaths, the calling of assemblies, I cannot away with; it is iniquity, even the solemn meeting. Your new moons and your appointed feasts my soul hateth: they are a trouble unto me; I am weary to bear them. And when ye spread forth your hands, I will hide mine eyes from you: yea, when ye make many prayers, I will not hear: **your hands are full of blood**. Wash you, make you clean; put away the evil of your doings from before mine eyes; cease to do evil;"* That's when he continues on to say though your sins be as scarlet they shall be as white as snow. This reference to their hands being full of blood is not referring to military action. Isaiah lived during a period relatively free of war. It was a profound call to repentance; though their sins be as scarlet they could be as white as snow. The Lord Jesus could forgive them. They didn't need blood to be forgiven. Just to back up a bit and say a word about the phrase I am full of *"the fat of fed beasts."* This means an offering asking for fellowship with God.

Now Isaiah goes out the same way he came in. This time as an old man who has seen many spiritual battles. This is Chapter 66:3. I am very moved by this, I love this man so much. Now he is an old man about to be killed for what he is about to say. Manasseh

145

sawed him in half alive, I believe, as may be indicated in Hebrews. *"He that killeth an ox is as if he slew a man; **he that sacrificeth a lamb**, as if he cut off a dog's neck."* Nobody would ever sacrifice a dog. They were the lowest animal on earth. Here it is again. He doesn't want lambs sacrificed. *"He that offereth an oblation, as if he offered swine's blood; he that burneth incense, as if he blessed an idol. Yea, they have chosen their own ways, and their soul delighteth in their abominations."*

So Isaiah came in and went out against blood sacrifices. Remember Isaiah is a very prominent man, perhaps the most influential and deepest thinking prophet Israel ever had. All the Hebrew prophets used his prophetic style of writing as a model clear through John's Book of Revelation. In Isaiah chapter 10: 28-31 you will find what is known as the Rosetta stone of prophetic code. All Hebrew prophets after him used this code in their writings to make them understandable only to their Hebrew readers, thus protecting the sacredness of their writings and safeguarding them to be not destroyed.

You can see now why the Sanhedrin was so dismayed when Stephen referred to Isaiah chapter 63. They had no defense in the public's mind to counter the words of Isaiah. The Sanhedrin in Christ's day knew he said these things. Today these same words are written on the great Isaiah scroll housed in Israel. Today the fundamentalist faction of Jews long for the return of blood sacrifice and the temple. So how can they defend their views? What implications do these writings of Isaiah have in regards to the New Testament when Isaiah so plainly says God abhors the blood of lambs? And what does it say about how people view the term the Lamb of God as they view Him as a human blood sacrifice?

Ok now in Hebrews 11:37 it may indicate that Manasseh sawed Isaiah in half. That is what the tradition is and that is the only reference I know of that may indicate it was so. Now I want to go on to Jeremiah. And Jeremiah was a good old boy too, of course. And remember he was a first-hand witness to hearing the actual Mosaic Law regarding these matters of blood sacrifice. I want to read to you an astonishing scripture. This scripture is so hard for the Jews that they have done some very subtle work to hide it, or at least modern translations have.

So I am going to open this up to you. And I am reading from Jeremiah 7. And what he says is very plain. 7:21–23 *"Thus saith the LORD of hosts, the God of Israel; Put your burnt offerings unto your sacrifices, and eat flesh."* The word "put" is the main deception. The word "put" comes from Strong's #5595. Out of 880 times the word put is translated in your Bible this is the only time #5595 is used to mean *put*. And it does not mean *put*. It means *scatter, cast aside, remove.* The word in Hebrew is **saw-fah**. And also in this sentence, the word "unto" should be the word "and."

So the sentence actually says: *"Thus saith the Lord of hosts, the God of Israel, **scatter, cast aside, remove** your burnt offerings **and** your sacrifices and eat flesh. For I speak not unto your fathers nor commanded them in the day I brought them out of the land of Egypt concerning burnt offerings and sacrifices. But this thing commanded I them saying obey my voice and I will be your God and ye shall be my people and walk ye in all the ways that I have commanded you that it may be well with you."* This quote right here could have been that which led to Jeremiah's imprisonment.

So here is a verse that says **I commanded you not** in the day I brought you out of Egypt concerning burnt offerings and sacrifices. He puts this squarely at the specific time of Moses and Aaron. Jeremiah is clearly positioning himself completely against the Levitical law of burnt sacrifices and offerings. The Levitical law is totally about burnt offerings and sacrifices. And it is held that it came to Israel specifically at the time when God brought Israel out of Egypt. How much plainer could he have said it?

Now can you better grasp why Jeremiah was so persecuted and his writings burned? There is another reading from Jeremiah 6:20, just turn back a little ways here, *"To what purpose cometh there to me incense from Sheba, and sweet cane from a far country? Your burnt offerings are not acceptable, nor your sacrifices sweet unto me."* So Jeremiah was very thoroughly and openly against them. Nearly all the prophets were, as you will see.

I am going now to Amos 5:21-27. I read this one already *"I hate, I despise your feast days, and I will not smell in your solemn assemblies.*" That would be incense to "the other guy." *"Though ye offer me burnt offerings and your meat offerings, I will not accept them: neither will I regard the peace offerings of your fat beasts. Take thou away from me the noise of thy songs; for I will not hear the melody of thy viols. But let judgment run down as waters, and righteousness as a mighty stream. Have ye offered unto me sacrifices and offerings in the wilderness forty years, O house of Israel? But ye **have borne the tabernacle of your Moloch** and Chiun your images, the star of your god, which ye made to yourselves. Therefore will I cause you to go into captivity.* " He is saying that they didn't offer Him sacrifices but they offered it to Molec, which is what they turned the shepherd's hut into according to Stephen. Now that was Amos.

Now let's go to Hosea 6:6–8. I hope you are listening right here because here is one of the key moments of information that can change your entire perspective of the New Testament. *"For I desired mercy and not sacrifice; and **the knowledge of God** more than burnt offerings. But they like men **have transgressed the covenant**: there have they dealt treacherously against me. Giliead is a city of them which work iniquity, and is polluted with blood.*" This is indicating Hosea's displeasure with changing from a moral sacrifice to one of blood. "Gilead" is Strong's #1568, and it comes from #1567, and it means *a heap of testimony* which is a reference to the heap Jacob built to make his moral covenant with his father-in-law (see Genesis 31:21). And the name "Gilead" is named after that very heap. The knowledge of God is seen to be connected with Christ's definition of salvation, which is to know His Father.

Ok now, the reason that is so important is because Christ quotes it in Matthew 9:3. Christ is saying that He will not be a sacrifice. This is saying to **view Him as a blood sacrifice is in fact transgressing the covenant**. So knowing that He is the Lamb of God, do you conceive of him as a sacrificial lamb or do you use the phrase *"the Lamb of God"* to be pointing to the lamb as a likeness of the innocent, gentle and harmless nature of His personality?

Now, I have laid the sufficient groundwork for us to address the most explicit root of Jesus' view of His Father. I am going to read you two scriptures. They are quotes in Matthew by Jesus quoting Hosea 6:6. They are in Jesus' own words. Had those charged with the care and keeping of the Biblical canon among the Gentile Mission, known what these two scriptures meant, they most certainly would have been struck from your Bible. I think there two references got past them because, first, Jesus is quoting a prophet in the Old Testament which suggests only a symbolic meaning; and second, they survived because it was difficult for translators to connect the words of Jesus to the context in which they were spoken.

The first scripture is Matthew 9:9-13. *"And as Jesus passed forth from thence, he saw a man, named Matthew, sitting at the receipt of custom: and he saith unto him, Follow me. And he arose, and followed him. And it came to pass, as Jesus sat at meat in the house, behold, many publicans and sinners came and sat down with him and his disciples. And when the Pharisees saw it, they said unto his disciples, Why eateth your Master with publicans and sinners? But when Jesus heard that, he said unto them, They that be whole need not a physician, but they that are sick. But go ye and learn what that meaneth, I will have mercy, and not sacrifice: for I am not come to call the righteous, but sinners to repentance."*

And the second one is Matthew 12:1-8. *"At that time Jesus went on the sabbath day through the corn; and his disciples were an hungred, and began to pluck the ears of corn and to eat. But when the Pharisees saw it, they said unto him, Behold, thy disciples do that which is not lawful to do upon the sabbath day. But he said unto them, Have ye not read what David did, when he was an hungred, and they that were with him;*

How he entered into the house of God, and did eat the shewbread, which was not lawful for him to eat, neither for them which were with him, but only for the priests? Or have ye not read in the law, how that on the sabbath days the priests in the temple profane the sabbath, and are blameless? But I say unto you, That in this place is one greater than the temple. But if ye had known what this meaneth, I will have mercy, and not sacrifice, ye would not have condemned the guiltless. For the Son of man is Lord even of the sabbath day."

The context for both of these scriptures is that Jesus was doing something that was seen not to be the accepted way. In both cases He was loving somebody. In the first case His disciples were hungry and compassion for them was being shown to them that allowed them to pick corn and eat it on, in all probability, the Jewish Sabbath. I say "in all probability" because the response of the Pharisees was so mild. In all other cases the perception of someone breaking the Sabbath drew extreme reactions. When the same episode is recorded in Luke 6:1-6, it distinguishes between the Essene Sabbath and that of the Jews. It does so both in verse 1 and verse 6.

In the second scripture, Jesus was loving a group of people who did not participate in the Temple sacrifice rituals. It was Matthew, the author of these two records, and his companions. What is mysterious to Bible scholars is the connection between these contexts and Jesus saying, "*I will have mercy and not sacrifice.*" So let me explain. Let's go back to the seemingly subtle changes made in the use of the shepherd's hut. Moses established it so "those who sought the Lord" could go there in privacy. The clear intention was for direct emotional exchange between Jesus' Father and the people. The effect was not ritual but was a personal relationship with God: a mutual feeling of love each one for the other – God and the individual. When Aaron took the privacy away from that chapel and made it the center of power with very limited access for religious leaders and none for the public, and when he brought in ritual, all the personal sharing of emotion between the people and Jesus' Father was lost. Aaron replaced the relationship dynamic with the blood sacrifice ritual. The whole thing became a very cold unemotional undertaking that represented adhering to the letter of the law. The state of a person's salvation was determined by the strict adherence to the letter of the law. There was no joy in forgiveness, just relief to be seen as socially acceptable. There was no living water. The whole dynamic of blood sacrifice cemented into the religious experience a complete lack of anything personal between God and man. When Jesus said, "*I will have mercy and not sacrifice,*" He was clearly saying He was promoting a personal relationship between mankind and His Father. The indication is, Jesus' view was those without that personal contact with the love of God were those He was focusing on. Those who already had that relationship didn't need such an immediate focus. So He said, "*I am not come to call the righteous but sinners to repentance.*"

In the second instance He said, "*But if ye had known what this meaneth, I will have mercy and not sacrifice, ye would not have condemned the guiltless.*" Who He was referring to when He said that is in all probability Nicodemus. He was a member of the Sanhedrin. He came to visit the Lord in the night and desired a personal relationship with Him. Do you remember the whole discussion of being born again? Being born again is exactly what entering into a personal relationship with God is all about. Then later Nicodemus advocated to the Sanhedrin that they should have personal contact with Jesus also. This is in John 7:45-52.

And because of these two activities by Nicodemus he was cast out of the Sanhedrin. And you will find in John 19:39 that it was Nicodemus who came to provide for and assist in the burial of Jesus – a continuing relationship. He was born again. One can also note in the Matthew 12 reading that Jesus gave another example of when someone was loved who was hungry and it was David and his men who, when hungered, ate the shewbread. And also in that reference Jesus said, "*For the son of man is Lord even of the sabbath day,*" meaning He had authority to love over and above cold expressions of the letter of the law. So over all, it is clear that Jesus had absolutely no intention to be a blood sacrifice for anybody. He was not, as the Savior, going to use the ritual of sacrifice to redeem and save people, but it would be by "*His love He would save them and with His compassion He would redeem them.*" I have now just cited for you in the clearest terms ever from Jesus' own mouth, His firm intentions as our Savior. He would settle for nothing less than a personal relationship of love with us. **Will you believe Jesus**? The cross is not that personal relationship with you. It says in Romans 10:9, "*That if thou shalt confess with thy mouth the Lord Jesus, and shalt believe in thine heart that God hath raised him from the dead, thou shalt be saved.*" That is saying that if you only confess with your mouth that you believe that event happened then the ritual of death will apply to you.

All right now, I am going to read again from Hosea, I'm not done with him yet. This will be Hosea 8:12–14, "*I have written to him the great things of my law, but they were counted as a strange*

151

*thing. They sacrifice flesh for the sacrifices of mine offerings, and eat it; but the LORD accepteth them not; now will he remember their iniquity, and visit their sins: they shall return to Egypt. For **Israel hath forgotten his Maker, and buildeth temples**.*" They forgot their maker and what God told Moses in the law and built temples.

Do you know what it says in Revelation 21:22? John saw the New Jerusalem and he said "*And I saw no temple therein: for the Lord God Almighty and the Lamb are the temple of it.*" In what I just read to you it said they forgot that which God revealed to Moses and built temples. Can you see that all of those prophets are against the temple? No wonder Israel has a long history rejecting their prophets, beginning with Moses.

Now I want to go to Isaiah again. He had a little relapse in the middle of his ministry. He couldn't resist so in chapter 43:22–24 he talks about it again. "*But thou hast not called upon **me**, O Jacob; but thou hast been weary of **me**, O Israel. Thou hast not brought **me** the small cattle of thy burnt offerings; neither hast thou honoured **me** with thy sacrifices. I have not caused thee to serve with an offering, nor wearied thee with incense. Thou hast bought **me** no sweet cane with money, neither hast thou filled **me** with the fat of thy sacrifices: but thou hast made **me** to serve with thy sins, thou hast wearied **me** with thine iniquities.*" So Isaiah said it again, here God is saying to Israel you aren't bringing me your sacrifices, you are sacrificing to someone else.

Now here's another really good one. This is another amazing reading. This is going to be the prophet Micah. This is Micah 6:6-8. Wow, this man had a lot of courage to write this. And the Bible translators had a lot of courage to leave it in. "*Wherewith shall I come before the LORD, and bow myself before the high God? shall I come before him with burnt offerings, with calves of a year old? Will the LORD be pleased with thousands of rams, or with ten thousands of rivers of oil? **shall I give my firstborn for my transgression, the fruit of my body for the sin of my soul?** He hath shewed thee, O man, what is good; and what doth the LORD require of thee, but to do justly, and **to love mercy**, and to walk humbly with thy God?*" Here is mercy again not sacrifice.

The people who worship Molec believed that if you offered your first born, and in this case burned them alive, that your **sins would be forgiven by their suffering and death**. That has huge implications as to where the New Testament took Christ's ministry when some of the authors of the Gentile Mission grafted in Old Testament views of God.

Now there are more. I will not read them all, as it would take too long, so I will just cite the references. Read Proverbs 21:3, Malachi 1:10, and Jeremiah 14:12. Those three are more that you can look up to study. They are more of the same. And I don't want to take the time to read but I do want to read to you I Samuel 15:22, *"And Samuel said, hath the Lord as great delight in burnt offerings and sacrifices, as in obeying the voice of the Lord? Behold, to obey is better than sacrifice, and to hearken than the fat rams."* That is pretty clear. Ecclesiastes 5:1, which many people think was written by Solomon because it is so mournful. Ecclesiastics 5:1, *"Keep thy foot when thou goest to the house of God, and be more ready to hear, than to give the sacrifice of fools: for they consider not that they do evil."* I don't know who wrote that, it doesn't sound like Solomon. Then one more, Psalms 40:6, this is David, *"Sacrifice and offering thou didst not desire; mine ears hast thou opened: burnt offering and sin offering hast thou not required."* So all the way through the prophets you can get a clear view of their position on the temple and blood sacrifice. They all want us to be led by the Spirit.

Ok now, they had to pay a price. What did it cost the Israelites? What was the threat to the Sanhedrin? You can already imagine what the threat was; my, how regrettable was the captivity they experienced.

Now I want to read another thing to you. Bear with me a little longer; I'm sorry this is taking so long. The Levitical Law is from Babylon. It is the law that Hammurabi received. The Levitical Law is not from God. You remember I read to you the statement from the Bible dictionary saying how many parallels the Levitical Law has to the Babylonian Law? What happened was the law was copied and adopted directly from the legal code of Hammurabi during the 863 years. There is a stone stele or column that is about 6 or 7 feet tall and it has a picture of Hammurabi receiving the law

153

from the sun god. And covering the column is writing stating the Babylonian Law. You can find it easy in most Bible dictionaries. And there are lots of books written about this obelisk.

The very best translation of the legal code on it was done by the archeologists named Driver and Miles. They did two volumes on it. Volume 1 is the actual translation. Volume 2 is a commentary comparing the law with the laws of other nations, most notably Israel and the Levitical Law. And I am going to read to you some of what they found. And this is important for you to grasp. Allow me to lay some bit of background first tying together what we have covered so far on this topic. 863 years passed between when Moses wrote his book of law and when it was first discovered by Josiah and read. During that long period, men of God, the prophets, were openly against the entire religious structure and function of the Jewish temple religion. The Jewish religion experienced literally centuries of prophetic opposition. Why? Where did the Jewish religion come from? How did it come into being with such continuous opposition from their nation's most holy men and the very ones that were seen to be holy in the eyes of the people and who their own history records as holy prophets? This information I am about to give you has in it many answers.

Here then is a sample of what Driver and Miles found. This is a list of similarities between the Levitical Law in your Bible and the law of Babylon found on the obelisk which Driver has numbered. I will cite the Biblical reference but not the page number in their books. So here goes.

-The Egyptians used the same laws that Babylonians used to adopt Moses into Pharaoh's house as did Israel to adapt Ephraim and Manassah into the house of Jacob.

-Babylon and the Levitical Law have similar laws regulating the sale of slaves.

-As to the sale of animals, Exodus 22:10-13 is essentially the same as Babylonian Law #244.

-Exodus 22:14-15 represents very old Babylonian laws having to do with who will pay for lost or dead animals.

-Exodus 21:22-25 is a law about the loss of children. Babylonian law #209 is almost identical to the Exodus law in your Bible.

-The law of retaliation and vengence that are still in wide use today are found both in the Levitical Law and in the Babylonian law #206, and cited in Exodus 21:24-26 and in Leviticus 24:18-20. Christ referred to these laws in his ministry. They say, "A life for a life, an eye for an eye, a tooth for a tooth, a hand for a hand, a stripe for a stripe" and etc.

-The law concerning murder found in Numbers 35:31 corresponds with Babylonian law #199.

-Genesis 38:24-26 Judah quotes the Babylonian law #110. It is such an exact quote of the Babylonian law that Driver thinks this passage in Genesis was written during the Babylonian captivity in 589-519 BC.

– Exodus 21:1–11 copies accurately Babylonian laws. Driver compares every verse with some specific code of Hammurabi and cites all the Babylonian laws. They deal with a servant's wife and how to free them.

– Exodus 21:15 corresponds to the Babylonian code law #168 and #169. This is dealing with laws regulating parents and children.

– Hammurabi's law #158 describes the offense of Reuben virtually the same as it is listed in Genesis 34:22.

– All Hebrew laws regarding weights and measures and money have close parallels with Hammurabi's laws. Compare laws #108, #26, #33, and #34. All these laws correspond with Exodus 30:13 and 24, Leviticus 5:15, and Numbers 3:47. These Bible references, as well as the Babylonian laws listed, provide for the holy use of money that lets its weight be different. In other words money given to the temple priests that was spent for sacrificial animals doesn't have the same value as it would if it was spent on something else. It is worth less when giving it to God, perhaps to illustrate that the contributor is giving some additional value beyond the money. That way the religious leaders benefit from the difference in the exchange rate.

   – In Levitical Law such as is found in Deuteronomy 21:3 and I Chronicles 5:1–2 the oldest son has preferential right over his father's property. Hammurabi's code #778, #782, #800, #801 and #802 are the same.

   – Hammurabi's law #142 is a law on marriage and it is the same as Deuteronomy 22:13–19 and 28–29.

   – Concerning the murder of a thief, Hammurabi's code #21, #22 and #24 equals Deuteronomy 21:22–23 almost word for word. The laws on this subject are so similar that Driver has from page 315 through 317 devoted to containing footnotes on their comparisons.

   – All the kidnapping laws are the same. Hammurabi's codes #10 through #15 are the same as Exodus 21:16 in Deuteronomy 24:7, an example is found in Genesis 27:28.

   – The law regarding the goring of an animal is just the same in Genesis 21:28–32 as it is in Babylonian law #250.

   – Hammurabi's code #157 involves incest. The entire chapter 18 of Leviticus corresponds to these laws.

   – Exodus 22:9–15 are laws on borrowing and injury to animals. They directly correspond to Hammurabi's code's #244, #249, and #266.

   – Hammurabi's law #131 is a law on jealousy. It corresponds exactly with Numbers 5:11–31. What makes this Babylonian law so interesting is Christ referred to this ceremony when He drank the bitter cup. (See Matthew 20:22-23 & John 18:11)

   – Hammurabi's laws #268, #269 and #270 concern rates of wages of one who is hired. They are just the same as Deuteronomy

25:4. Also the law of "Not muzzling the ox" is the same as those three laws cited above.

– When Jesus had the woman brought to him who had been caught in the very act of adultery he was being asked to respond to the law of Hammurabi #130 and Deuteronomy 22:23–27. This is a very terrible law of stoning a person to death.

– The whole concept of the Hebrews taking of oaths originated in Babylonian laws #266, #106, #126, #23 and #240. All their oaths were sworn before some god. There are no scripture references telling how they did it but Ecclesiastes 9:2 says they did. Jesus spoke against these laws.

– Deuteronomy 22:20 concerns another reference to incest and it is like Hammurabi law #157.

– The law of inheritance for daughters in Numbers 27:8–11 is the same as Babylonian law #163.

– A long list of Babylonian laws covered in #195–208 are about retaliation and revenge. There are too many references to read them all.

Whew! Wasn't that a wearing exercise? I went through that much so you can see how plainly the Levitical law came from Babylon. It did not come through Moses by divine revelation. For one thing, if it had why would Christ so often dispute it? Also remember we are following Stephen's lead in our journey to discover the meaning behind what he was charged with as **blasphemy against the law.** Why this course or method is so important can be seen in light of the influence these Old Testament dynamics had on the way people viewed Christ in the New Testament. One must ask the question: if the religion of Israel had been truly established by divine revelation through Moses, would Jesus have had to declare so often to so many people that they did not know His Father? Would He have come to be viewed as a human sacrifice? Wasn't His Father supposed to be the focus of their entire culture and religion by covenant? These matters have a direct and profound effect on how Christianity has come to view

Christ and God and the whole plan of salvation, which Christ squarely defined as knowing His Father.

In effect, Jesus was born into a society where His own country had the world's forms of economy, religion and politics when God had expressed to them that if they would listen to His voice indeed He would view them as His own peculiar people and a special treasure differing from the corrupt world. Some last things and I will quit. I told you this before and I want to say this again. In Genesis, Exodus, Leviticus, and Numbers combined there is not one reference to somebody loving God, including all forms of the word love.

But in Deuteronomy I have a long list of instances where Moses is pleading with his people to love God. I will list some of the instances below. And I tell you this to illustrate how clearly the feelings of Moses' heart are not expressed in the first four books of the imposed Torah. The content and style are so vastly different that it is only natural to follow that one would conclude that Moses did not bring the Levitical law but did in fact bring a Torah pointing toward Jesus' view of His Father. Knowing Him and loving Him were the only pathway to forgiveness of sins and eternal life. All references are from Deuteronomy.

– 5:10 "mercy unto… them that love me"
– 6:5 "thou shalt love the Lord thy God" (first commandment)
– 7:9 "love him and keep his commandments"
– 7:13 "he will love thee"
– 10:12 "to love him"
– 11:1 "love the Lord thy God "
– 11:13 "love the Lord your God"
– 11:22 "to love the Lord your God"
– 13:3 "proveth you, to know whether ye love the Lord your God"
– 19:9 "to love the Lord thy God"
– 30:6 "love the Lord thy God"
– 30:16 "love the Lord thy God"
– 30:20 "love the Lord thy God"

And references that call to love without using the word love are all in Deuteronomy: 4:9, 4:15, 4:23, 11:8, 11:16, 11:27, 12:13–14, 12:30, 13:4, 24:9–10, 27:10, 28:62, 30:2, 30:8 and more.

I'm just going to sum it up as I continue. There was no blood sacrifice in the temple which would have nullified any sins. God should be revered not feared. And the word for "fear" of God in your Bible comes from the Greek #5399 and it means *to reverence*. And the word "fear" in Hebrew is #3372 it also means *to reverence*. So they changed it from you shall walk in reverence to the Lord your God to you should walk in the fear of the Lord your God. There is a big difference between reverence and fear. It threatened their temple, which was the center of power, their religious taxes, their offerings, their livelihoods; it threatened their private property because fear was necessary in viewing God in a way to support that He needed to be appeased by blood sacrifices.

Stephen and the Lord and the early church under James had all things in common. The high priest owned all the concessions and selling stalls in the temple. He got a take from all the livestock sales. The real true God was a God that didn't have armies, didn't fight any wars. He didn't even judge anyone according to Christ. A God who had no death penalty. He didn't kill anyone or require killing. So the battles of the Torahs raged in the Old Testament and it raged in the New. And the Jewish religion was in the balance.

So where I am going to go next time is I want to go into the New Testament and show the influence of this corruption and this particular perspective of "the other guy" in the Old Testament and how it influenced the Christian view of Christ. There is one other thing I want to tell you about as I close just for your information. Look up Numbers 20:8-13 and 27:14 and Deuteronomy 3:27 and you will find out an amazing story. People were thirsty. The Lord told Moses go and speak to the rock and bring forth water and nourish the people. Moses went and when he spoke to the rock he tapped it twice with his stick. And it brought forth water. The Bible says, in the references I just gave you, that this act of disobedience of tapping the rock with his stick when he was only told to speak to the rock was why he couldn't go over Jordan with the Israelites into the Promised Land. Never mind Numbers 31 where they have Moses ordering genocide. They had to think of some reason why Moses didn't go with them. He was just too corrupted from having tapped the rock. And that was the only thing they could come up with to show his disobedience.

159

If you look at Numbers 20:24, you will see that Aaron also was kept from crossing over Jordan because of this sin of Moses' having tapped the rock with his stick. They actually blamed Moses for Aaron's absence from the people. Actually, he likely died beforehand because it says that they buried him on the mountain. Anyway I just thought I would conclude with how Israel distanced themselves from Moses in their path to make Aaron and what he established permanent. So what you have is 863 years where the Jews formed their religion without Moses' writings. And that left them very vulnerable. They could not explain how they got their religion and the Levitical law in view of the prophets.

Even though this session has been long, and perhaps tedious, I cannot bring it to an end without a personal expression about Israel and the Jewish people, after all that has been said here about their history and the law. My family background has been Essene oriented Christian for many generations. My grandfather taught me about the Essenes when I was a child on his lap. My mother was an Essene and lived out her life and passed away at a ripe old age here in community. My personal world view and inner self since early childhood has been in harmony with that of the sect of the Nazarenes or Essenes.

I know basically nothing about the practice of Judaism in today's world; but from my limited contact in visiting synagogues and listening to rabbis my view is that some of them are now closer to being in harmony with what Moses established than at any time in their history. They do not have blood sacrifice, they do not have a temple, and they love God. I heard from the rabbis that God is love. I love Israel and the Jewish people. It is hard to explain, but in my inner self I am deeply bonded to Israel. I am constantly dismayed at the seemingly complete worldwide bias against them. No matter how many years go by, I can't seem to grasp why in this world everybody is against Israel. I look forward with absolute dread to where things are going for them. It seems that all this hatred for them can only culminate in disaster. I continually pray for them and not a day goes by that they are not on my heart.

Through all the admonitions that I have read from the Bible, I want you to also notice and remember that Christ loved Israel. He always viewed them as His special people and continuously was reaching out to them in His ministry and He longed for them to know His Father. He still does today. Thank you.

Session 8
Unfolding the Deeper Significance of
the Character of Jesus' Father
February 8, 2015

Good morning folks. We are at a point where I need to do a little introduction for this Session 8. So far we have covered Biblical evidence that Moses had little to do with what Judaism has become. This is clear starting very early on at the Sinai experience where blood sacrifice was established with the golden calf under Aaron. We covered how Moses was hated; that his style of expression is not to be found in the first four books of the Torah, and that he could not be the one who wrote the Torah in Hebrew.

And very critical for our investigations is that which he did write was a testimony against what the Jewish religion had become. That dynamic is witnessed throughout. This is evidence that the Jewish religion became something that displeased him during his lifetime. And the Biblical evidence further indicates that what the Jewish religion became when "God turned" was rather founded by Aaron, not Moses. And what the Jewish religion became is the very crucible in which Christianity was born. One must ask what would Christianity be like if what Moses intended to establish would have been that which prevailed throughout history? Those involved in the Gentile Mission clearly steered the development of Christianity in relation to what Judaism became rather than what was intended in the outset.

In light of all this, it seems imperative that in order for us to be able to discover the truth we must rely extensively on the ministry of Jesus and that of Peter, James and John, who were the main players in what Christianity was intended to be, before the shift it made within the influence of the Gentile Mission. So here we come to rely on the critical importance of Jesus' view of His Father and the complete support that Peter, James and John had from the early church as they interpreted that view from their first-hand experience.

So now before I start, I want to say a prayer as we continue in our studies into areas seldom entered into, so that the Spirit of the

163

Lord may guide every heart, so that these untrodden paths can be for our enlightenment and spiritual edification.

A prayer: Dear Lord, thank you for this day that we can come before you to sing of your love. I pray that You will endow me with your Spirit as I speak today. Not for myself but for the dear hearts that will be listening. I pray that You will bless them with your Spirit in these troublous times we have so their faith in you can be strong in them and made more clear and abiding in their hearts. I pray that You will feel welcome with us today and bless all those who are assembled and those who hear this message. May they all seek You for Your guidance when they hear something they never before considered. I pray in Jesus name, Amen.

Well, we are on our final session on the accusations of blasphemy about **God** brought against Stephen. The sessions after this will be on Christ the Creator. I want to clarify something as I begin. I had a couple of comments asking me if I thought Moses was a holy man. I must have given the impression early when we read chapter 31 of Numbers that that story was really an account of his behavior. You found out later in the things that I have been teaching that Moses was not even present during those events. Stephen says he was cast out very early on. And I believe he was, of course, a holy man, one of the holiest prophets God has ever had.

Also, I want to apologize for the lack of organization in the last session, because I did not come prepared to do it all in one day and it was tediously long, being more than one hour each session. So it was not quite as organized as it should have been.

I want to start out by talking about the Bible a little bit. I love the Bible. And in the Bible, I find the guidance that is essential for my life. It is not just for inspiration but my view of world events is clarified by the prophets, especially the books of Revelation, Isaiah, Daniel and Malachi. The biblical description of Jesus's Father is the center of my life, because of the writings of John especially, and the support of other of the gospels and apostolic writings. The reason I mention this is because many times people who talk about conflicting perspectives in the Bible are liberal, people without a strong faith, but this is different with what you have encountered in this series because I am a man of faith. You are hearing things now in the series that are off the beaten track of Western Christian traditions. So I want to assure you that what I am intending here and what I am prepared for is to increase your faith, your personal love for God and His Son.

I have chosen the path of bringing understanding concerning the character of the God that you worship and the very being of Jesus and the personal effort He made so we can find salvation by knowing His Father. Today we are studying the blasphemy accusation against Stephen about **God**. And I want you to understand that people who criticize the Bible, most of the time, are not usually people of faith. I am a man of strong faith. Let me give you a really short statement: in my view what you have with the Bible is this: The Church in Rome replaced Jesus with a Pope. The Pope has all authority. He was in the early stages even a war lord. He controlled vast sums of money and had an army. He has a national government and is treated as a head of state. The church still has an ambassador to the United States. The Protestants replaced the Pope with a book. The Pope gives authority to his ministers and the Bible gives authority to Protestant ministers. Because the Pope was infallible, in order to compete effectively the Bible had to be infallible. They had to have an equal source of authority. That's the short version, but here is a more complex reason.

So there has been a huge ongoing effort to cover up the inconsistencies of the Bible and people have ignored certain perspectives in it. And the conflicts center between the perspectives focusing on Jesus's Father and that of "the other guy." For me it is not about doctrine, it is about the character of God.

There can be no divergence between perspectives tolerated otherwise Protestant authority would be seen to be diluted. And they have made a giant effort for the last six hundred years, since they started printing the Bible for public consumption, to harmonize everything in it, so that it speaks with one voice and doesn't have any conflicting perspectives, especially about salvation and the nature of the character of God; these are the two urgent aspects of Christ's personal ministry that often stand out in contrast with parts of the Biblical record.

And you read over and over in all the Bible commentaries, and the Bible study guides, and all the footnotes are efforts to harmonize everything. Many times it is plain that the effort is a stretch. This is done to downplay the conflicting perspectives. And so usually when those perspectives are brought to light, the one doing it is a person without faith or who is seen by others to be without faith. But I am here to tell you that I believe in the virgin birth. I think it is impossible for Christ not to have been born of a virgin; that the virgin birth is the very center of Jesus's ability to be the very Creator. Hopefully I will get a chance to explain this matter. It is indeed very exciting and is supported by the latest important scientific discoveries. I believe in the power of prayer and in miracles. I believe in being born again. I believe in the resurrection. I believe Christ is the only way to find salvation. His love and compassion are the only way for mankind to be saved that ever has existed, in old times or new.

So I am coming to you with this information today with that kind of purpose and that kind of faith in my background. I want to remind you of a couple of things from the last session to get us underway again today. The Levitical law in the Bible came directly from Babylonian law. I read to you from one of the Bible dictionaries that called into question whether Moses received the Levitical law by divine revelation. In fact, what is written in the Old Testament law didn't come from Moses but came from the law of Hammurabi. And we heard that they had formulated the law after the pattern of the law of blood sacrifice, which was commonly practiced by many heathen nations surrounding Israel. And all of this was institutionalized in the absence of the writings of Moses. We know this because the Bible is very plain that the very book of the Law of Moses was not found until Josiah's reign, 863 years later.

So they actually took what they said were the revelations of God to Moses and transformed them into expressions compatible with the surrounding heathen religions. The shepherd's hut that was for those who wanted to go and seek the Lord privately outside the camp became a lavish, wealthy temple complex that was the center of political and religious power. All the nations around them had such temples and seats of power centered on blood sacrifice. And it all started out as a chapel 15' x 30' and where the people sat in what was called the holy place.

Also I want to remind you that almost all the prophets were against blood sacrifice and the temple. And I read to you many examples of that. And they didn't just offer their opinion, you will remember, but they spoke in the name of the Lord. Remember this when you go to study those references. Isaiah said, *"To what purpose is the multitude of your sacrifices unto me? **saith the LORD**: I am full of the burnt offerings of rams, and the fat of fed beasts; and I delight not in the blood of bullocks, or of lambs."* He is speaking for God when he says that. And again Isaiah says, *"he that sacrificeth a lamb, as if he cut off a dog's neck."* What he is saying is God feels the same about the sacrifice of a lamb as he does sacrificing a dog; the only thing worse than a dog is a pig in terms of sacrifice.

I want to read to you the one in Jeremiah because it is so important. This scripture is crucial to what Stephen was speaking about. This is Jeremiah 7:21-23. And you have heard this before. He is speaking for God. ***"Thus saith the Lord** of hosts, the God of Israel."* He wants to make sure that he is speaking specifically for the God of Israel, not just any god. *"Cast aside your burnt offerings and your sacrifices, and eat flesh. For I spake not unto your fathers, nor commanded them in the day that I brought them out of the land of Egypt, concerning burnt offerings or sacrifices: But this thing commanded I them, saying, Obey my voice, and I will be your God and ye shall be my people: and walk ye in all the ways that I have commanded you, that it may be well unto you."*

So the prophets spoke for God. And this reading specifically points right at the very time when the Bible says the Levitical law was to have been established. This kind of Scripture begins to show us that we have an elephant in the room. The elephant is "the other guy" in the Bible that nobody wants to talk about. There is this huge issue that has been trailing along behind us through all of the Western Christian history. In the first session, I laid out four scriptures to introduce that issue without addressing it. I did that on purpose because as the series has progressed the issue of "the other guy" has gotten bigger and bigger. I read to you the 31st chapter of Numbers and declared that the god depicted there was not Jesus' Father. I wanted to read chapter 15 of I Samuel but it was too gross to read in church in front of all the tender hearts here.

Did you realize that there are many parts of the Bible that really should not be read in church in light of how vile the god is that they are depicting? Then I said to you that there were people who weren't familiar with the ministry of Christ who wrote later on in the New Testament, out of which I cited for you two scriptures: one that we are saved from the wrath of Jesus' Father and the other that it is a fearful thing to fall into the hands of the living God, who of course is again Jesus' Father. I cited those two New Testament references to illustrate that even in the New Testament there are depictions of "the other guy."

And I purposely said throughout this series that if it is not about Jesus' Father, it is about "the other guy." The reason I call him "the other guy" is because it could be the adversary, it could be someone who crafted their own image of God into the scriptures, or it could be someone who in the church hierarchy in times past edited it in. I don't really care how those references to "the other guy" got there. I have no interest in speculating about those kinds of things. What I care about is for you to recognize Jesus's Father in your Bible. And when you do, the inconsistencies in your Bible will not make any difference anymore, because the part that is about His Father is so extremely valuable and so central to your salvation as Jesus defined it that you will be comforted and your faith and understanding will grow.

Just think of how many hundreds of millions of the world's peoples have rejected the Bible because Christians have typically presented the Bible as one harmonious whole with only one perspective calling it the Word of God when a person who seriously studies can see clearly the contradictions. Do you suppose Christianity would have been ahead to call Christ **the Word of God** instead of the Bible? Read the first four verses of the gospel of John.

Now the opposition that the prophets represented against a blood sacrifice and the temple were the reason why they were persecuted and killed. It wasn't because they gave personal reproval to the leadership of Israel, like saying things about their behavior related to being unvirtuous or something common to all of us. It was because they spoke out against blood sacrifice which was central to their political and ecclesiastical power. They were against the temple and the temple religion because it is a religion of blood sacrifice. The temple is specifically designed to slaughter and burn animals and blood was smeared on everything. I often think of how the place must have smelled like death and of the sounds of the terrified cries of the animals. It has everything there to kill with. It has the water to wash with, and they sprinkle blood on the altar. You have a big place to burn flesh and there is a place for firewood. It was like a slaughterhouse.

Ok, so the primary reason that the prophets were persecuted was because of their threat to the national power structures and their underpinning wealth. Now even Jesus indicated He would not be a blood sacrifice. I want you to remember this as we study today: I am not coming from off the wall somewhere, I am reading to you from your Bible. Jesus said, *"I will have mercy, and not sacrifice."* He said that in Matthew 9:13 and in Matthew 12:7. He was quoting Hosea 6:6, which is one of the references I read to you when I was speaking about prophets who were against blood sacrifice. The word "mercy" in Hebrew means *compassion*. The word "have" in Aramaic means *use*. In Greek the word "have" means *to agree to or possess*. So that statement could say: *"I will have compassion and I will not agree to sacrifice."* The word "grace" means something altogether different. It means *to be cheerful and calmly happy*. That is what grace means.

All right, so here I am and I am preaching to people who love the Lord. The Lord was told me all my days since I was young that I was not to minister to people who didn't love Him. That was to be someone else's job. My job is to preach and to teach people of faith who love the Lord.

So here you come and this elephant is in the room. Your loyalty to Christ, to the Christians who are listening to this, is an integral part of your faith and it has been seen to be one and the same as your loyalty to the Bible - a Bible that has no contradictions. And here you come and you are on the wrong side. Not in your heart. Not in your love for the Lord but in your theology. You are on the wrong side, because the prophets were against blood sacrifice and most of you, most of the Christians in this world, believe they are saved by His blood. And even Jesus said Himself that He would not use sacrifice to save you but He would use compassion. He would love you even when you failed, or fell short, or sinned, or were a thief dying beside Him, or a woman brought before Him to be stoned, or were the occupier and enemy to His nation whose servant was dying.

Now I was thinking about this because we are in the tribulation times and tribulations are advancing rapidly in our world. And the horrible conditions of the last days are spreading. They are getting more severe on a daily basis. And they are coming. They are already here in many nations. And tribulation conditions are coming to our nation soon. And here you are, here are the people who love the Lord, here are His very own people who He treasures, and they believe the very things that the people believed that killed the prophets. They believe in blood sacrifice, because they hold that their Bible says so in certain places. I am going to read to you today every reference to blood sacrifice in the New Testament.

So I was thinking about this when I was driving my buggy home and came around the corner by those big pine trees. I was feeling sorrowful that so many people, millions, love Him and have been taught to ignore Christ's perspective in their Bible. He is the One they love. Is there no room for His point of view? They are taught to ignore what He says when He says I will have mercy and not sacrifice. To ignore it when He says my Father loves His enemies, He is kind to the evil and the wicked. When Jesus defines salvation it has nothing to do with blood. I've read that to you. I am going to read it again. I will read it to you over and over. Christians are taught to ignore Jesus's words and now they are in a predicament. And as I thought on these things the Spirit of the Lord flooded over me and He said, "*I will not condemn them. I will love them. I will comfort them.*" He said to me, "*Please teach them.*" So here I come today to teach.

Now, I want to read something to you here. The Levitical law is directly responsible for the New Testament applying blood sacrifice to Christ. Remember now, the accusation against Stephen concerning God came from what he said in Acts 7:38-39 and 41-42.

The key elements of which are "God turned," and gave up on Israel because of blood sacrifice and that the Angel of the Presence, who is the Son of Man who is standing on the right hand of God, gave Moses the Law - not God. And abhorrently to the Sanhedrin, it was asserted that they had betrayed and murdered that very Angel of the Presence in the being of Jesus of Nazareth.

So here we go with the last blasphemy accusation. And remember the Levitical law is not from God. I'm going to read to you from Hebrews 9:22. This is a pivotal verse in your New Testament. This verse ties blood sacrifice from the Old Testament under Aaron the idol maker, to the New Testament and to Jesus Christ. This verse represents the gateway to grafting Old Testament views of God into the New Testament; it brings "the other guy" forward. It is very simple. Hebrews 9:22, *"And almost all things are by the law purged with blood; and without the shedding of blood is no remission (of sin)."* The word "remission" in my Bible is footnoted to be *forgiveness.* So the author of Hebrews is saying almost all things by the Levitical law are purged with blood. And in the temple in the Old Testament, before the coming of Christ, there was no forgiveness of sin without shedding of blood, which means Christ couldn't do it without blood. So that verse right there ties it all together.

Now we see that this was defined in terms that were not Jesus's own. Other people said this about Him who didn't know Him, who didn't live during His lifetime. And they wrote in the New Testament. I will give you just a little example; some New Testament authors signaled that grace was the foundation and the bottom line of salvation. They would say "we are saved by grace." And yet in your Bible there is not one single reference during Jesus' entire ministry of Him ever uttering the word grace. Christ never said the word grace a single time. Isn't that amazing? If Jesus thought we would be saved by grace, you would think that He would have at least uttered the word.

Mercy is #1656 in Strong's Greek section. It means *compassion.* Grace #5485 comes from #5463 and means *to be cheerful, to be calmly happy.* To be cheerful and calmly happy is a lot different than compassion. Christ certainly has grace, we are not saying here that He doesn't have grace. His Grace has blessed me every day of my life, but it is not the vehicle of salvation. Christ did not define being *cheerful and calmly happy* as the foundation of salvation. He just did not do that - somebody else did.

So there are many references in your Bible from persons who would define salvation as coming from blood sacrifice. And here we come to the all the references concerning blood in the New Testament. I want you to remember this list. I want you to take note also of the many times I mention a reference that only occurs in a book of the New Testament one time. The one time dynamic is evidence of editing. I may deal with that in my next session.

One time in Matthew, *"this is my blood"* at the Lord's Supper
One time and Mark, *"This is my blood"* at the Lord's Supper
One time in Luke, *"testament in my blood"* at the Lord's Supper
One time in John 6:53-56 *"drinketh my blood"*
One time in Acts *"purchased with his own blood"*
Two times in Romans, *"faith in his blood,"* *"justified by his blood."*
Three times in I Corinthian's, *"communion of the blood,"* *"in my blood,* and *"the body of the blood of the Lord."*
Twice in Ephesians, *"redemption through the blood,* and *"brought nigh by the blood."*
Two times in Colossians, *"partakers of flesh and blood,"* and *"peace through the blood."*
Five times in Hebrews, *"partakers of flesh and blood,"* *"by his own blood,"* *"shall the blood of Christ,"* *"without the shedding of blood no remission (of sins,)"*and *"with his own blood."*
Two times in I Peter, *"sprinkling of the blood, "*and *"precious blood of Christ."* That is the greeting of the letter.
One time in First John in the greeting again *"the blood of Jesus."*
Four times in the book of Revelation, *"from our sins in his own blood,"* *"redeemed us by his blood,"* *"made white in his blood,"* and *"the blood of the lamb."*

Those are all the times in your New Testament that blood sacrifice is mentioned or alluded to in relation to Christ using the word "blood." Now how can we understand all this? Especially when the prophets and Christ were against blood sacrifice? And how can we understand what all of this means? How should a person deal with it?

Well here is some information. The missionaries who went to the Gentiles out of Israel had some unique problems that they had to deal with. And all of these references (except the ones where there is just once, including Peter) all came out of that effort to be missionaries to Gentiles. This is the problem they had: in the Hebrew culture, **God is the divine kinsman**. All covenants in Israel, in the Hebrew culture, are covenants of kinship. God is a member of our immediate family. He is my Father, our Father. Christ is also a member of our immediate family. He is my elder brother – kinship; unto us a child is born unto us a son is given - kinship; He is the Son of Man - kinship. My wife is bone of my bones flesh of my flesh, when I get married she becomes my kin. We are related by blood.

The word "covenant" in your Hebrew dictionary is #1285 in the Strong's, it is the word "birith," and it means *to cut the palm of the hand together* - kinship. The kinship group in Hebrew is seen to have the same blood. The word "covenant" is #1285, and it comes from #1262, which means *to eat, to make a compact of kinship*. **You partaking of communion really means you are acknowledging kinship with Jesus and His Father**. God has the same blood as we do. So the word "blood" in Greek, #129 in your Strong's, means **either** *blood* or *kinship*.

If you go to John's writings, including Revelation, and you read what John wrote, you will find an interesting dynamic. I am going to read it to you. This is I John, all the writings of John can be interpreted in a special way. This is really interesting; I may get into this in more depth later. But I am going to read this to you now, I John 1:7, "*if we walk in the light, as he is in the light, we have fellowship one with another, and the **kinship** of Jesus Christ his Son cleanseth us from all sin.*" The word for blood also means kinship. That reference could have just as easily been translated properly that way. They could have written it that way legitimately. But you see, their mind set was on the blood of sacrifices, so they chose to interpret it blood when kinship would have been a correct translation.

So all the references in John are like that, as is the second reference in Peter. The next one of Revelation 7:14, "*And I said unto him, Sir, thou knowest. And he said to me, These are they* which came out of great tribulation, and have washed their robes, and made them white in the **kinship** of the Lamb." You don't make clothes white by washing them in blood. But you can make them white in terms of being pure through your kinship with Jesus. See how that works?

And in Rev. 1:5, *"Unto him that loved us and washed us from our sins by our **kinship** with him."* And in Rev. 5:9, *"Redeemed us to God by our **kinship** with him out of every kindred, and tongue , and people, and nation."* And in Revelation 12:11, *"And they overcame him (the devil) by their **kinship** with the Lamb."*

Ok. So all of the references I cited about blood in your New Testament are not properly about kinship; but most of the ones with more than one reference just plainly meant blood. You just can't say properly that without the shedding of kinship there is no remission of sin. These kinds of references can only mean blood and they came almost entirely in the writings of those involved in the Gentile Mission, or, as I conclude, were edited in, especially in the writings of Peter. After all he was supposed to be the great historical first Bishop of Rome. It was so obvious that the early church, as indicated by Stephen when he termed the death of Jesus to be a murder, that they simply did not view the crucifixion as a sacrifice.

And to add to that, blood in association with Jesus came along so much later they simply had to place token expressions of it in the gospels to make it appear that blood was the intent from the start. And they had to put it into the mouth of Jesus Himself. They even edited the New Testament in such a way as to make it appear that Jesus carefully planned His own death. I personally think this editing took place during the time of Constantine when the persecuted Christians faced the prospect of becoming a state religion and would have done anything to comply with his theology.

Ok, the problem that the missionaries had who'd gone to the Gentiles is that the very last thing Gentiles wanted was to be kindred to their kind of god or a member of his immediate family. They would not on their life want to be kindred to gods like Molec, who burnt their children alive. Their gods argued and fought. Marduc was a god of war; their gods killed each other. Who would want them as a member of their immediate family? Who would want to see themselves as a blood relative to Greek and Roman gods? So the whole kinship message among the Gentiles, the Greek and Romans, just was not going to fly. That idea simply could not be anything like a central missionary message. A person could not go among them and be a missionary and convert them to the idea that God is your Father, which is clearly and explicitly the entire thrust of all of Christ's ministry and teaching. It was even His personal definition of eternal life or salvation.

So how could the later authors in the New Testament convert the Gentiles to the personal message of Jesus, especially when those managing the Gentile Mission did not know Jesus during His life, or hear Him directly for themselves? Can you see why it would seem so natural to graft the Old Testament views into the New Testament? All the Gentiles had similar views of God and blood sacrifice and would much more readily accept that message than one of kinship. So "the One who sent Him" was left out, and **Jesus became the end instead of The Way**. It was just too tempting to offer that which would be accepted, especially for those who sought to be prominent and seen as authoritative in the Gentile Mission.

There is another problem that faced the Gentile missionaries. Gentiles did not associate repentance or forgiveness with any god, which was a message of theology unquestionably central to Christ's ministry. The Living Water would be a completely foreign concept to them. There wasn't any god in the Greek Pantheon or in the Roman mythology that they repented to and asked for forgiveness from. If there was anything similar to repentance and forgiveness, it would have been totally out of fear. Is Molec going to require me to sacrifice my only begotten son for a remission of my sins as it says of him in Micah 6:7? Could it be said it is a fearful thing to fall into the hands of Molec? Yes, I can think of nothing worse. Would people want to be saved from his wrath? You bet.

So grace replaced repentance in the Gentile Mission and the Christian god took on the character of Molec, who required blood. Grace is to *be cheerful and calmly happy* because you don't have to repent, somebody else did it all for you. You are then saved from repentance. The blood applies to you so now you don't have to achieve humility and virtue by your works in your daily walk. You don't have to love or be a relative of your Divine Kinsman and in that love be motivated to continually seek to be a better person for Him. So they had **grace and sacrifice and not mercy.**

Reproval became an insult and sign of condemnation and an offense. But in the Hebrew culture, the Divine Kinsman was someone who loved you and someone to whom you were obligated to through a covenant of love to please and obey as a member of your immediate family. When you caused Him anxiety by your actions or behavior, you confessed and acknowledged it to Him and asked His forgiveness. And you were accustomed to Him readily forgiving and loving you and maintaining your loving relationship.

He provided for His family as a Father. He redeemed His children through the example and ministry of the Man that He became by manifesting His Father. He leads you through every day by His kind and all-knowing Spirit. He blesses and heals and teaches and safeguards His children. He loves His family. He is a tender and understanding and gentle and compassionate parent. That kind of God you love and you want to do what He wants you to do. And you are sorry when you don't because you love each other. One can actually seek reproval and view it in a positive light out of a desire to please the One you love. And because of this love between you the result is forgiveness and purity and holiness. **Molec made not one person holy.** And so this Divine Kinsman idea with repentance and forgiveness just was not going to be an effective missionary message to the Gentiles.

Now I would like to give you a very clear example of this, one of the clearest examples that you can find, and this is in your Bible. I am going to read it to you the difference between Christ's perspective and that of "the other guy." I am going to read to you Matthew 21:33–45. This is really startling. Sit up in your chair and listen to this. You have read this a thousand times and you probably haven't recognized what it is saying. I am going to read through verse 45. *"Hear another parable:"* this is in your red letter edition; Christ is speaking, *"There was a certain householder, which planted a vineyard, and hedged it round about, and digged a winepress in it, and built a tower, and let it out to husbandmen, and went into a far country. "* Basically he did everything he could to make it a perfect vineyard. He had a tower to protect it. He had a winepress in it so it could produce a benefit so you wouldn't have to borrow your neighbors. He made it exactly what he wanted it to be.

"And when the time of the fruit drew near, he sent his servants to the husbandmen, that they might receive the fruits of it. And the husbandmen took his servants, and beat one, and killed another, and stoned another. " And this is talking about the prophets. This is a parable about God making His world and sending His prophets. The husbandmen in this case are His very own people.

Again, he sent other servants more than the first: and they did unto them likewise. But last of all he sent unto them his son, saying, They will reverence my son. But when the husbandmen saw the son, they said among themselves, This is the heir; come, let us kill him, and let us seize on his inheritance. " There is some real heavy stuff right there. However we will get to that in a minute.

And they caught him, and cast him out of the vineyard, and slew him. " And Jesus said to the people who were listening to him, *"When the lord therefore of the vineyard cometh, what will he do unto those husbandmen?* And the people listening to Him answered, *"They say unto him, He will miserably destroy those wicked men, and will let out his vineyard unto other husbandmen, which shall render him the fruits in their seasons. "*

Then this parable goes into a very mysterious direction that is very hard to understand. *"Jesus saith unto them, Did ye never read in the scriptures, The stone which the builders rejected, the same is become the head of the corner: this is the Lord's doing, and it is marvelous in our eyes?*

Therefore say I unto you, The kingdom of God shall be taken from you. " He is talking about the kingdom of God here. *"And given to a nation bringing forth the fruits thereof. And whosoever shall fall on this stone, "* which is the head of the corner, *"shall be broken: but on whomsoever it shall fall, it will grind him to powder. And when the chief priests and Pharisees had heard his parables, they perceived that he spake of them."*

When they answered that God would miserably destroy those wicked men and give it to others, Christ was sustaining their answer by saying therefore I say unto you the Kingdom of God shall be taken from you. Also, the whole Stephen/Christ versus the Sanhedrin conflict is exactly like when they killed the prophets and the son in the parable, then they could be rid of the heir and have their temple religion the way they wanted their inheritance to be. Interesting don't you think? Jesus was prophesying what it would mean for them to not reverence Him and to kill Him. There is a lot there.

There is more than one way scholars view this parable. Some view that it was crafted to be an anti-Semitic statement, but I view it in another way. This is how I view it. I am going to read to you Romans 5:9-10, *"Much more then, being now justified by his blood, we shall be saved from wrath through him. For if, when we were enemies, we were reconciled to God by the death of his Son."*

Whoa. One says God is going to destroy those miserable wretches who killed His Son but the author of Romans is saying God, who was their enemy, is now going to be their friend because they killed His Son. He is going to love them now - just exactly the opposite. Again we have the two opposing perspectives: Jesus and the author of Romans. Did you get it? Did you hear that? Let me read that again. *"Much more then, being now justified by his blood, we shall be saved from wrath through him. For if, when we were enemies, we were reconciled to God by the death of his Son."*

So here is a father who says, I will quit being your enemy and I will love you if you will kill my son, my beloved son, my only begotten son, in whom I am well pleased. Would any of you say that? Would you start loving some enemy only on the condition that they killed your son? Not only killed him but unjustly tortured him to death? Just what kind of a God, who is depicted as being a loving father, would do that? Would any father or parent do that? With this parable, in Jesus' own words, the entire basis of salvation in Western Christianity is out the door. **But what remains is**

Jesus's Father: the God of love who became a Man to walk amongst us.

The Pharisees and the scribes who answered Jesus had it right. They knew what kinship meant for someone to have somebody kill their son, especially their only son. They said He will destroy those miserable wretches. Actually their behavior brought on their own destruction. The other perspective says we were His enemies now we are His friends; even the leaders of the temple religion could know the absurdity of that Romans scripture. It would be completely irrational to a Hebrew, but it may be within an acceptable framework of the Gentile view and also to Solomon who burned his children to Molec. So who are you going to listen to? Jesus is the one who spoke that parable. Remember I asked you, are you going to **listen to Jesus**? Are you going to **follow Jesus**? Are you going to **obey Jesus**? Are you going to **believe Him**?

I would like to ask you some questions. Let's use our brains here a little bit. The phrase that says "the truth shall make you free" is talking about your mind - your thinking. Your freedom comes from your mind. So that is what this phrase is talking about. So please allow me to ask you some questions. Please don't be offended by these questions. If we are saved by His blood, then it was His death that enabled Him to forgive sin, or to bring salvation, right? He couldn't do it without death because God said, I am angry, I won't be appeased without blood, innocent blood, there will be no remission of sins without the shedding of blood. So unless we killed Jesus, God could not forgive us, or would not forgive us. Was Jesus' execution just? Dying on a cross is literally being tortured to death. Did He deserve to die because of His behavior? Or was it just a crime of murder as Stephen said; a **betrayal and a murder**? Do you murder a sacrifice?

Remember that now when you read Stephen, he says it was a murder. And he was clearly representing the views of the early church as it was expressed before the Gentile Mission. If you took a sheep to the temple to offer it, would you hate the priest for killing your sheep? Does anybody say when they are at the temple and they have a sheep there to kill that I am going to murder this sheep? So are you willing to say that the Creator of this earth had to depend on man to commit the crime of murder before He would forgive your sin? Do evil trees bring forth good fruit? Did an abominable crime, very cruel in its function, enable Christ to save the world? Does your salvation depend upon a crime? Or, dear ones, does it depend upon the vastness of the love that created you? Does death bring life or does life bring life?

The philosophy of the Gentile Mission is irrational. It goes like this: We sin. God is angry because we sin. He requires us to commit murder before He will forgive our sin. Was it the unforgivable sin He required as referenced in I John 5:16 and Mark 3:28?

On the other hand, the philosophy of the Nazarenes is rational. It goes like this: God created us with agency, which is a capacity to choose and be holy or bring sin. And God so loved the world that He prepared to love us in spite of our sin from before the beginning, by having The Way of our forgiveness create the world. He did this so we all could be forgiven should we choose repentance. And He brought the Man that He became into our world to teach us how He loved us in spite of our sin. And He demonstrated to us, by His submission to our agency (the cross), that His love in spite of sin is infinite. He said of those who murdered Him: forgive them for they know not what they do. He was not angry because we did something He created us to have the capacity to do, He only and always loved us in spite of our sin and built our forgiveness into the universe – the living water of reproval, repentance, and forgiveness.

Many times they tried to stone Christ. What if they would have succeeded and stoned Him? Would the blood from the stoning have been what saved you? What if Jesus died of old age and there wasn't any blood? Would mankind have lost their salvation from the first man clear to you? If He died of old age, would He have been resurrected? If he died of old age? You bet He would. He said, *"for as the father hath life in himself: so hath he given to the son to have life in himself."*

There are no circumstances that Christ could have encountered in His life on this earth that could have added to or detracted from His ability to forgive and bring salvation with His love, except if He Himself had sinned. And there is no sequence of events He could have experienced that would have prevented His resurrection. He was resurrected by exactly the same forces that were called into play which brought forth Lazarus, only in Jesus' case no one had to call them forth. His resurrection was not dependent upon how He died. And in another place He said, "*I have power to lay down my life and take it up again.*"

So again, what if the Sanhedrin would have repented? What if they would have said, oh, we have been all wrong, here is our much anticipated Messiah? What if they would have been born again? What if they repented of their sins and turned the temple into a teaching facility to teach what the prophets taught about the One True God, and quit blood sacrifice and took on seriously the teachings of Jesus about the First and Second Commandments and the character of His Father? What if they all, each one, turned their lives around and said to the Lord Jesus, come and be our high priest after the order of Melchizedek? Would their repentance and their love for Jesus have prevented your salvation, because they didn't kill Him? Do good trees bring forth evil fruit? Would all mankind be lost because of virtue and love? What about these questions? What does your intelligence tell you?

Why did Jesus say, "*I have finished the work which thou gavest me to do,*" in His prayer in John chapter 17, before He was crucified? Why did He say that, if being crucified was the source of salvation? It was because His death was His last effort to manifest the character of His Father in His submission to man. He said in the garden, "*I have manifested thy character unto those which thou gavest me.*" It was His last effort to demonstrate His love for His Father and the example set by John the Baptist to be fully obedient in His mission as our Savior. He said, I could have called ten thousand angels, and it is certain they would have rescued Him. Put your sword away. I am not resisting evil; I am submitting myself to show the love of my Father. I am making obvious to you the character of my Father. I am going to be kind to those who are unthankful and those who are evil. He didn't say, it is important that my blood be shed, the whole world's salvation depends on it.

Ok I want to read to you now Matthew 9:2-7, "*They brought to him (Christ) a man sick of the palsy, lying on a bed: and Jesus seeing their faith said unto the sick of the palsy; Son, be of*

181

good cheer; thy sins be forgiven thee. And, behold, certain of the scribes said within themselves, This man blasphemeth. And Jesus knowing their thoughts said, Wherefore think ye evil in your hearts? For whether is easier, to say, Thy sins be forgiven thee; or to say, Arise, and walk? But that ye may know that the Son of man hath power on earth to forgive sins, (then saith he to the sick of the palsy,) Arise, take up thy bed, and go unto thine house. And he arose, and departed to his house."

What blood did He use? There was no sacrifice there. So **Christ could forgive sins before the cross.** Clear back in Jacob's time you will remember he said that he was redeemed *"from all evil"* by the Angel of the Presence. **Christ has always been able to forgive.** I want to read it. It is in Genesis 48:15-16, *"And [Jacob] blessed Joseph, and said, God, before whom my fathers Abraham and Isaac did walk, the God which fed me all my life long unto this day, The Angel which redeemed me from all evil, bless the lads; and let my name be named on them."*

It was the Angel of the Presence that redeemed him; Jesus's ability to forgive has everything to do with life and nothing to do with death. He did not need death to reconcile us to God. Reconciling someone to God meant demonstrating the true character of His Father to them so they could really know Him in view of the prevailing image of "the other guy." He used His life and love to do it; His life in you and His Love for you and around you. Jacob didn't do any blood sacrifice any time in his life, only moral sacrifices of covenants of kinship. So what blood did He use to redeem Jacob? He is the God of the living, remember?

Ok now, I want to read you another one. This is in Isaiah 63: 8-9 and boy this is a sweetheart scripture. Oh how I love Isaiah. *"For he said,"* this is God speaking, *"Surely they are my people, children that will not lie:"* He is speaking of His family, His children, *"so he was their Saviour. In all their affliction he was afflicted, and **the angel of his presence saved them in his love and in his pity he redeemed them**; and he bare them, and carried them all the days of old."* There is Christ, by the way, fully functional as the Savior in the days of Moses. He saved them in His love and redeemed them with His compassion: **no crime, no death, no blood – just love.**

That reading right there says he was afflicted with our afflictions. This is the key to understanding Isaiah chapter 53, which is a prophecy about Christ which everybody puts right on the crucifixion. *"With his stripes we are healed"* and so forth and someday I hope to explain, if you want, chapter 53. What chapter 53 is talking about applies to every person in every age, not just the crucifixion. The 63:8-9 reading is plainly saying He was afflicted with the Israelites afflictions while they were in Egypt. With His stripes I am healed when I have stripes. When I am afflicted, He is afflicted. When I grieve over my sin, He is rejoicing over my repentance. When I am forgiven and am restored back to the Spirit, He is comforted with me. He feels your feelings with you, every feeling. Always. Love!

Ok now there is another point that I wanted to read to you just moments ago, both in the first chapter of Isaiah and his last chapter. In both places He says, *"I delight not in the blood of lambs."* That's in Isaiah 1: 11. In 66:3 He says, *"he that sacrificeth a lamb, as if he cuts off a dogs neck."* These readings are a direct contradiction to Christ being a Lamb of God meaning blood sacrifice. He was the Lamb of God because His character was like a lamb, gentle, mild, harmless and innocent. Jesus said, I send you as lambs among the wolves to be harmless as doves. And everyone assumes because of the blood sacrifice mindset that the lamb reference is a reference to blood sacrifice. He is even called by some scholars the Pascal lamb of Passover.

The writings of John and Peter are the only mentions in the Bible where Jesus is called the Lamb of God. There is also a quotation in Acts from the Isaiah reading that alludes to it. The Lamb of God that John the Baptist declared was in the minds of most Bible translators a sacrificial lamb. But Jesus was very active during the Old Testament, completely without sacrifice, fully functional and able to bring salvation. He was called the Angel of God or the Angel of the Presence many times throughout the Old Testament. Scholars have a term for Jesus in these Old Testament contexts, they call it the Christophany. I am just going to read or cite a few for you. I just read Isaiah 63. In Genesis 21:17-18 He told

183

Hagar, "*I will make of him (her son) a great nation.*" That was not God but an "angel of God." It had to be Christ. I read to you Genesis 48:16 "*he redeemed me from all evil.*" Genesis 28:10-22 is where Jesus is speaking to Jacob when He wrestled with him during his ladder experience. Christ is so prevalent in the Old Testament that scholars are perplexed with the Christophany.

Where does an active uninhibited Christ in the Old Testament blend with the New Testament view of the Gentile missionaries about Christ and how does this square with the Levitical law? They struggle with this. Genesis 16:9-13, the Angel said, "*I will multiply thy seed exceedingly.*" Exodus 3:2, the Angel in the bush is Christ as you saw in Stephen's narrative. Exodus 14:19, the Angel Moses used to bring them through the Red Sea was Christ. And that is verified in Isaiah 63. Exodus 23:20 and I Corinthians 10:1, I already read those. Judges 2:1-4, Jesus is active. Judges 6:12-23, Christ salutes Gideon and says to him "*Peace be unto thee,*" very similar to how He is quoted in the New Testament after His resurrection. Zechariah 3:4, "*I have caused thine iniquity to pass from thee,*" Christ told Zechariah. So these are just a few of the many references; there are many more. Christ was very active in the Old Testament forgiving, healing and bringing salvation. If you can know that in 1500 BC He was afflicted with somebody else's afflictions, then you know He has always been that way.

There is also clear and concise information in the New Testament about Christ being the center of the salvation process in the Old Testament. Let me read it to you. This is I Corinthians 10:1-4, "*Moreover, brethren, I would not that ye should be ignorant, how that all our fathers were under the cloud, and all passed through the sea; And were all baptized unto Moses in the cloud and in the sea; And did all eat the same spiritual meat; And did all drink the same spiritual drink:*" This is a reference to a meal in relation to a covenant on the same level as the Lord 's Supper. "*For they drank of that spiritual Rock that followed them: and that Rock was Christ.*"

In Malachi 3:6 it says, "*For I am the Lord, I change not.*" So we know Christ forgave his sins and brought salvation then as He always has. He forgave because He loved. Remember, I will have compassion not sacrifice. **So all mankind from the first man**

184

has been saved by Christ's life not His death. The Lord says we are to love our neighbor as ourselves. And we are to forgive them 70 x 7. If you want to be the true children of your Father; and if you think your father requires blood sacrifice, then you won't forgive them until someone has paid the price; but if you forgive them because you love them, like He does, then you can forgive them in almost unlimited terms just because you love them. Why would God ask you to forgive somebody in a way that He won't? Why would He require blood but expect you not to? Why would He say, I require blood before I will forgive them but I want you to forgive just because you love them? God is love. Do you suppose that the Creator of this earth needs somebody to give Him the ability to forgive sins?

So I am going to read to you John 5:24 again. I want this to be fresh in your minds as I end, because there is something to say here before I close. *"Verily, verily, I say unto you, He that heareth my word, and believeth on him that sent me, hath everlasting life, and shall not come into condemnation; but is passed from death unto life."* To hear and believe is mental. The truth shall make you free.

John 17:3 is another good old verse. *"And this is life eternal, that they might **know** thee the only true God, and he, whom thou hast sent."* Notice the word "**know**." And then go to I John 5:20, *"And we know that the Son of God is come, and hath given us an **understanding**, that we may **know** him that is true, and we are in him that is true, even by his Son Jesus Christ. This is the true God, and eternal life."*

So here are these words; to know, to learn, to understand, to hear, to listen, to believe; all those words are expressing your need to use your mind and intelligence to be free. **There is not any person in this world who has ever lived that needed anything more than the love of Jesus Christ.** They never needed any blood; they didn't need rich temples; they haven't needed powerful religious institutions with clergy to mediate between themselves and God; liturgies can't replace Jesus; books can't replace Him nor can any man. Jesus is the only one who can take you where you are going in your path to salvation and His Father is where you are going. The love of God empowers Him to do all things. And His

185

love is always present for you, but you have to seek Him and keep His sayings and the First Commandment to love Him with all you are or ever hope to be. If we think we are saved by His blood why don't we shower gifts on the Jews every Good Friday and thank them profusely for killing Him because without them killing Him we would not have salvation? The Holocaust was a complete failure of human reason.

Now I want to share one more thing, to introduce the next session with these words: the key to the virgin birth of Christ is if He had been born of a woman and a man, He would have had to create Himself. He would have had a beginning. He has no beginning and no end. He is eternal. He brought Himself into the temporal world. He brought Himself here. He didn't create Himself. And recorded in the 8th Chapter of John, after the chapter 6 discussion Christ had about being the Creator, there was a man who shouted out to Him in the temple *"who created thee, thy self?"* I will read that to you in the next session. Thank you.

Session 9
Revealing the Creatorship of Jesus and His Father
February 15, 2015

Good morning. We come now to our ninth session in this series. This is a pivotal session and it is about the Creatorship of Jesus. Today our topic will take us into areas almost completely unknown to the modern Christian world. I approach this session with some trepidation.

First, I am well aware of my inadequacy in presenting so deep and profound a topic. Second, I am very sensitive to what this information may mean to you and the challenge it will give you, in light of the traditions that have come down to you. I do not come here today to belittle anyone's positions or beliefs. I have no inclination whatsoever to present to you the idea that I have a correct doctrine and yours is inferior. This topic is just too far reaching in its scope and importance for us to approach it in those small ways. Grasping the meaning of the Creatorship of Jesus will change your life.

My experience is that this understanding is essential for anyone to really begin to comprehend the nature of Jesus' Father. This information can awaken in you a much deeper relationship with the universe He created and the magnificent variety and diversity of mankind that He loves. If I can impart to you today what is in my soul you will never be the same. You will love the Lord more and experience Him and His Father's love more deeply. That is what makes today's risk worthwhile to me. The risk in my heart is that I may trouble or offend someone; but how can I hold back when the Spirit of the Lord has instructed me in these things and asked me to teach those who love Him. So with that said here we go.

Christians simply have not developed the Creatorship of Jesus and there are profound reasons why. Yet how does one address such a huge empty place in Christian theology without being forthright and speaking openly about the dynamics that have given rise to this enormously important aspect of Jesus that has been so ignored? We have talked a lot about blood sacrifice during this series. Now here comes the apex of that discussion. Either you are saved by the blood of Jesus or He is the Creator. Those two ideas are mutually exclusive. The Biblical record and intelligent reasoning tell us it can't be both. Almost universally, Christians believe they are saved by His blood when He died as a human sacrifice to appease an angry god. They typically have a Roman gallows on top of their churches. Does He save you by His love and compassion or with His blood? Remember Isaiah 63:9, *"The angel of his presence saved them in his love and in his compassion he redeemed them."*

At first it may seem entirely strange that blood sacrifice has any connection to the Creatorship of Jesus, but you will find today that one effectively eliminates the other. I simply cannot deal with the issue of Jesus being the Creator without exposing the truth of the historical narrative about blood in your Bible.

If I could describe the relationship between the two concepts, blood vs. Creatorship, in as few words as possible, it would go like this. John says at the beginning of his gospel that Jesus is the Word and **the Word was God**. And in the context of that statement, he says Jesus is the Creator two times. **Jesus is the Man that God became** so He could walk among men and redeem them with His love and compassion. That is the Creator side. On the blood side, there is no forgiveness of sin without the shedding of blood. God is angry because we sin; someone, in this case His Son, has to die to pacify Him. On the Creator side, the early church rightly held the saying *"Hear, O Israel: the Lord our God is one Lord."* God is One. On the blood side, Jesus, the **Word**, **is not God**. God and Christ must be two different persons.

It is one thing to say we are enemies to God but we can be friends with Him if we kill **His Only Begotten Son** and quite another thing to say we can become friends with God if we kill **Him** in the form of the Man that He became. **Killing the Creator of this world as a human blood sacrifice to pacify who?** He started out to be deified; in fact, He was the fulfillment of the prophesy in Isaiah 9:6, *"For unto us a child is born, unto us a son is given: and the government shall be upon his shoulder: and his name shall be called Wonderful Counsellor, **The mighty God**, **The everlasting Father**, **The Prince of Peace**."* So they expected for 740 years

188

before Christ's birth that their Messiah would be the everlasting Father, the mighty God, and that God would become a Man and walk among us as the Prince – Jesus, the Son of Man.

This is what happened. Scholars and religious leadership have constructed a historical narrative that projects the idea that, as time went on after Christ's resurrection, His person and His function became exaggerated. In short, it evolved and He became deified. They say He didn't start out to be the Word that was God in the form of a Man, the living bread that came down from heaven to give life to the universe (John 6:33) but He became that in the minds of the church as they developed their theology. Many even say that the exaggeration included His virgin birth – and they call into question His Son-ship, the resurrection and, of course, His Creatorship. But the historical Biblical reality indicates something else entirely. Those who ascribe to this exaggeration process must hold that God and Jesus are two different persons. They would have to be for Jesus to be a human blood sacrifice.

So to make it clear, they say Jesus started out one way and ideas about Him grew and changed until the Word was God. John says the Word was with God because God's experience as a Man was always with Him, as He is eternal and all things are present before Him. So the experience He had, as the Man that He became, was an identifiable aspect of His person and was always with Him.

The Bible record shows quite the opposite historical pattern from those who espouse the blood sacrifice position. In the Bible, Jesus started out to be the Man that God became. In John 14:8-9 it reads, *"Philip saith unto him, Lord show us the Father and it sufficeth us. Jesus saith unto him, Have I been so long time with you, and yet hast thou not known me, Philip? he that hath seen me hath seen the Father; and how sayest thou then, Show us the Father?"*

And Jesus also said, *"I and the Father are One."* And those who heard this knew exactly what He was saying and they answered and said that they wanted to stone Him for making Himself God. He **was** born of a virgin. Isaiah was right. He **was** resurrected. Remember He said He came to give life to the universe? There are numerous passages like this that I could cite, all showing He started out being the Man that God became.

So let's look some more at the Biblical record. Those who assert that Jesus became God, or was deified over time, hold that the accounts of Him were written after His Ascension and had time to build and expand what was thought about Him. They say those concepts, brought into existence by those involved in the Gentile Mission and all such references, were edited in and those concepts began to prevail. Blood was central from the start, for which they had to be two different people. But aside from John 6:51-58, Jesus did not teach at any time anything about His blood. I have singled out those verses in John very purposefully and we will investigate them thoroughly. It will be enlightening.

Remember, the word "blood" appears only one time in each of Matthew, Mark and Luke's records. Blood and sacrifice were no part of His spoken ministry. Remember He said twice, "*I will have compassion and not sacrifice.*" And the Greek word here for "have" means *to agree to*.

In fact, after those verses in John 6, the word "blood" in connection to salvation is not heard from again for a very long time. Not during the 40 days He spent after His resurrection before His Ascension. Not during the whole period in Acts with Peter's ministry to the Gentiles. Not during the great Pentecost experience. Not during the entire time the church was spreading to the Samaritans and into Caesarea. Not during Paul's conversion experience on the way to Damascus. Not through his early ministries outlined in Acts. Not during the ministry of Peter at Samaria and Antioch. Not during any of the church's early work among the Jews. Not during Paul's first missionary journey or his second one at Philippi, or Thessalonica, Berea, Athens, Corinth, or at his return to Antioch; all of which is recorded in Acts.

Blood sacrifice associated with Jesus first appears again in Acts 20:28. This is some 27 years later after the events of John 6. If blood sacrifice was the central foundation of salvation, why did it not constitute the major thrust of Jesus' ministry in the gospels and define the whole early development of Christianity? The answer is because the Biblical record shows the reverse pattern of development. Jesus started out deified and evolved into a human blood sacrifice. All this had, and still has, the overriding effect to eliminate the Creatorship of Jesus. Remember, you kill the Man that God became in order to pacify who?

So rather than the first ten verses of the Gospel of John being edited in, it is now obvious that it was John 6:51-58 that was edited in. The one time occurrence of the word "blood" in Matthew, Mark and Luke shows editing because it is an afterthought posing as the original central thesis of the plan of salvation. And it kind of helped to write it in the greetings of Peter and I John, especially Peter who they defined as the first Bishop of Rome and the founder of their views. I already told you about the proper kinship translation in John's writings. Jesus had ample opportunities to say something about His blood and there were many people who asked Him, specifically, what they must do to find salvation. Again, no death, no blood, rather you should sell all you have and give to the poor, just love! And note that James, the Lord's brother, who was the successor to Jesus in the high priesthood, never used the word "blood" in your Bible in relation to salvation. But he did say just the opposite; or rather he decreed the opposite. He decreed that the Gentile church would be accepted without circumcision if, and only if, they abstained from blood in four specific ways all having to do with blood sacrifice. Already James was worried about the direction the Gentile Mission was going.

So the reality of the Biblical record demonstrates clearly that the blood sacrifice idea directed toward Jesus was, in fact, the exaggeration that developed long after His ministry. The issue of God being one or two persons is the driving force behind this development toward human blood sacrifice and this to support what Christianity had become in the Gentile Mission. Jesus had little, if anything, to do with what the concepts of salvation became in the Gentile Mission. One just could not find any credibility among the Jews by proposing that in order to find salvation man must kill and ritually cannibalize the very Creator of heaven and earth as is indicated in John 6:51-58.

So before I go any further, let me give you a brief introduction to the theology of Jesus' Creatorship. You may not

191

realize just how hard that is to do, but I have asked the Lord to help me and I shall trust Him and make the attempt.

Why didn't God create the world Himself, even though the entire creation story in the Bible as you read it the words are *"I God said"* let there be light and so forth? And *"I God saw all things were good."* The Biblical account squarely puts it in terms of God. So doesn't it seem all the more remarkable that the New Testament authors so readily accepted the idea of the Creatorship of Jesus? They simply had to understand Genesis 2:3-5 and the recitation of the first day of creation as it appears in the original Torah, which I will read to you later. So let's see, what does it really mean for Christ to be the Creator? Will the answer to that question really shed any light on the matter for you? Hopefully it will.

First of all, in John 4:24, Christ says *"God is a Spirit."* That is the only such description of God in the Bible. God created all the spirits of life. Now think about that for a moment. A Spirit created all the spirits of life: the spirits of all people, the spirits of all animals, the spirits of all the insects, the spirits of all the trees, the spirits of the hills and the wind, the mountains and the rocks – even all things. When we get to that part, you will be reminded that Jesus even said that the rocks would cry out if the people quit praising Him. He ought to know! And He, God, by His presence brought into effect all the elements of the universe that were the material that Jesus used to give element form for those spirits of life to live in. Giving element form is what is meant by the Creatorship of Jesus. "Element" is the actual substance of our tangible world.

There is a really good reference Paul uses in I Corinthians 8:6, *"But to us there is but one God, the Father, **of whom are all things**, and we **in Him**; and one Lord Jesus Christ, **by whom are all things**, and we **by Him**."* Why is that scripture so good? Let me explain it to you. The elements of creation cannot be created or made. Any good scientist will tell you that. No element is brought into being or disappears, they only change form in their associations together. So when we speak of Jesus being the Creator, we are referring to Him giving element form; trees, our bodies, rivers – all things. That specific expression of God, as a human person who experienced being in the flesh in the temporal world, is designated to be the One to give element form for a very profound reason. Are

192

you starting to understand it? He influenced the natural substance of the universe to find form.

So it can be understood this way. You have God's presence giving the elements mass, as scientists would say. That means there is **a presence** in the universe that causes atoms to adhere together and to be an identifiable substance; (**of** whom in the above reading,) God, the Spirit, creates the spirits and influences existence to be the building blocks that Jesus, the Man, (**by** whom in the above reading) gives form, so those spirits will have a home to live in; a body, as we would say. That is His very role as Creator. They then could have the gift of life. *"I came to give life to the universe."* The spirits of life God made could not experience the gift of life without a place, a form to live in. While God's presence can bring the building blocks to bear, it does not cause them to interact. Only the love of the Man, Jesus, does that.

For those of you who are up on the latest scientific developments, **the presence** of the Father that gives the elements mass is called after the two scientists that predicted it – the Higgs Boson. And **the function** of giving those elements form, through their interaction, is accomplished by another force that is called by them <u>W</u>eakly <u>I</u>nteractive <u>M</u>agnetic <u>P</u>articles. Ironically, the Creatorship of Jesus has the initials of WIMP in the scientific world.

The oxygen and hydrogen atoms are influenced by His love to love one another and they join out of their love, to form water. All the atoms in existence are joining together in all their forms because they are influenced by the love of the Man, Jesus. This gets more profound folks as we go along. The spirits God made could not experience life without a place and time; and after Eden, it had to be a place with time. God is eternal and He is in every place and all things are present before Him. And He cannot create the illusion of time.

So, Jesus had to give the elements form in this way so when there was sin, creation could transform from the natural, spiritual world of Eden into the temporal world that we know. The spirits of life could have form, in spite of sin; a form that expressed the essence of their spirits so they could truly know their gift of life.

193

They needed a temporal world to live in. They needed a loving society of diverse spirits living in various forms in harmony with natural fellowship and support and companionship to become an expression of the loving kindness of Jesus' Father **in spite of sin.** Just like Christ in His life and ministry did everything in relationship to His Father, His Creatorship was completely for His Father. And someday you may come to fully understand what that means. Perhaps I can say it in this series.

And with all this, the question still remains: why didn't the Father of Jesus create the world Himself? When you read things like Jesus saying, *"you have never heard my Father's voice nor seen His shape at any time;"* or read in Psalms 68:2, *"As smoke is driven away, so drive them away: as wax melteth before the fire, so let the wicked perish at the presence of God,"* or again as you read in Psalms 97:5 even the temporal world cannot be in His face-to-face presence, *"The hills melted like wax at the presence of the LORD, at the presence of the Lord of the whole earth."* This is talking about our temporal earth.

So you see that nothing sinful or wicked can be in the presence of God. Or when you consider the saying, *"no man has seen God and lived,"* you can know full well that no evil or guilty or unclean thing can come into the presence of Jesus' Father – our God - hence, the need for God to come in the form of a **Man** and be called the Son because of the flesh. Jesus can cleanse, forgive and make you pure with His marvelous love and forgiveness called salvation. And again, His definition of salvation is to know His Father. His entire mission as our Savior and Redeemer is to bring us back into the presence of His Father. What would that mean to us if we never knew His Father?

As I continue to approach answering why God didn't create the world Himself, let me give you some Biblical background in support of that which I have said at this point. What I have just outlined for you about God being a Spirit and creating all the spirits of life, is shown in your Bible. I will go over that next session. It is spoken of very clearly, but you may not have openly considered it.

God created all things spiritually before they were temporally upon the earth. You will need to take seriously Genesis

194

2:3-5. *"God"* here means God the Father. *"And God blessed the seventh day, and sanctified it: because that in it he had rested from all his work which God created and made."* God's part of creation was all done. *"These are the generations of the heavens and of the earth when they were created, in the day that the Lord God made the earth and the heavens. And every plant of the field **before** it was in the earth and every herb of the field **before** it grew; for the Lord God had not caused it to rain upon the earth, and there was **not a man** to till the ground."*

After God created all the spirits of life, the earth was still without form and void. There was not a man to till the ground. Element had not found form yet. All the spirits of life that are ever to be on the earth were in the beginning with God. He created all things only spiritually first. We do that. We get a blue print before we construct something. In these three verses comes the format for Jesus to give element form. A mist rose up to cover the ground – remember the oxygen and hydrogen molecules loving each other being influenced by the love of Jesus; water – the Living Water. He brought the Living Water. Does this sound familiar?

Let's go back to the idea of God having someone guilty or sinful or unclean come into His presence. If anyone could do that He would not have needed a Son. We would not need Jesus to make us pure and holy by our repentance and His boundless love and forgiveness if we could come and go into the presence of the Father at will. But nothing sinful can come into His presence.

So He had to have a Son for two very special reasons. First, to create and give element a form that could be transformed so that sinful man could have a place to live. Second, He had to have a Son to give us the opportunity to choose salvation and be made pure in His love and compassion in that temporal world. Remember reproval, repentance, and forgiveness. We cannot enter into the presence of God without Jesus. He is the only way. God prepared **a Way** for His children to have eternal life with Him by the Man Jesus that He became.

Again, let's say God did create or give the world's elements form. Our first parents lived in Eden. They sinned. If God created the world where would they go? When they couldn't be in the

195

presence of the Father any more where would they go? There would be no place to go because the world the Father created could not transform into the temporal earth. But then enter Jesus. The Man that God became created the world and gave it form. The Man who had legs to run, eyes to cry, a mouth to laugh or say profound truths; He created the world. A Man. A Man who was exposed to all the lives of those who had sin and error; who are unclean, who like sheep had gone astray and needed a good Shepherd, and a host of other things. When it was this Man who created the world, the world could then transform in the face of sin from the spiritual world of Eden into the temporal world we know.

Now our first parents had a place to go and an opportunity to work out their salvation. Remember Jesus was always able to forgive. By Him we are first given a temporal world in which to choose whom we will serve. Then we can be brought back into the presence of God in Eden because He came **to live** with us in Jesus. A God who is a Spirit cannot produce anything temporal. A God who is eternal, without time, cannot produce a world with time. Jesus was in time in a temporal world. And He loved. And He loved and He loved. *"Whoever has no sin let him cast the first stone."* And Jesus wept and He said, *"Lazarus come forth"*. God expressed Himself in our temporal world as one of us because He so loved the world not because of His anger that needed appeased. He followed His loved ones into the temporal world as one of us, because of His vast love for us in spite of our sin. It may be better to say Eden left our first parents and was transformed by sin into our temporal world, rather than to think they were kicked out. With a temporal world to live in we could be loved in spite of our sins and waywardness. We could be rescued from the effects in our lives of choices that make us unlike Jesus' Father.

Now there would be death and resurrection, thorns and roses, and cold winter winds and soft summer breezes, and pain mixed with the joys of life and the seasons. They went from being spiritual people in the presence of God in Eden to being temporal people in a temporal world because Jesus, the Man, gave a natural world form allowing it to become temporal. The Man. The Creator. And He was in the beginning with God and He was God. And thus God was called the Son because of the flesh, being the Father and the Son. It is all about love.

So now with that introduction to the theology of Creatorship let us proceed to uncover how the Creatorship of Jesus came to be so underdeveloped in Christianity. This may be anticlimactic, after such deep thoughts, but it is essential for us to understand how something as profoundly basic as Jesus being the Creator came to be marginalized almost out of existence. The Biblical record can tell us.

First, let me give you a perspective from the Bible about the issue of Jesus' Creatorship in the early church. I want to draw your attention to a dispute the church had with those involved in the Gentile Mission, which is found in Acts 15. This is the dispute over circumcision. Circumcision was a long established tradition with a scriptural foundation yet it was a huge issue for the church. I will read it to you. I am reading selected verses from Acts 15, starting at the beginning. *"And certain which came down from Judea taught the brethren and said, Except ye be circumcised after the manner of Moses, ye cannot be saved."* By the way, just as a note, Christ said in John 7:22 that circumcision was not from Moses. It says it was from the fathers. I think he was referring to Abraham. *"When therefore Paul and Barnabas had **no small dissension and disputation** with them,"* this is going to be a big deal. *"They determined that Paul and Barnabas and certain other of them should go up to Jerusalem unto the apostles and elders about this question. And being brought on their way by the church,"* which means the church officially sent for them and they were summoned by the top church leadership. They had to appear. It probably took several months for the summons to be declared, and for it to be communicated and for them to arrange and travel to Jerusalem.

"They passed through Phoenicia and Samaria, declaring the conversion of the gentiles: and they caused great joy unto all the brethren. And when they were come to Jerusalem, they were received of the church, and of the apostles and elders, and they declared all things God had done with them. But there arose up certain of the sect of the Pharisees which believed (which means some of the Pharisees were converted, a fact left out of the Gospels) *saying, That it was needful to circumcise them and to command them to keep the Law of Moses. And the apostles and elders came together for to consider this matter. And when there had been **much disputing.**"*

197

Ok, this is a really hot topic, *"Peter rose up, and said unto them, Men and brethren, ye know how that a good while ago God made choice among us, that the Gentiles by my mouth should hear the word of the gospel, and believe. And God, which knoweth the hearts, bare them witness, giving them the Holy Ghost, even as he did unto us. And put no difference between us and them, purifying their hearts by faith. Now therefore why tempt ye God, to put a yoke upon the neck of the disciples, which neither our fathers nor we were able to bear? Then all the multitude kept silence."* After Peter spoke everybody sat quiet because he evidently had a lot of influence. They *"Kept silence and gave audience to Barnabas and Paul, declaring what miracles and wonders God had brought among the Gentiles by them. And after they had held their peace."*

Everybody sat silent because Paul is trying to persuade them, God has done miracles so I have to be right. And the Pharisees said no we are right, and Peter jumped in and had his say. And after that they had all held their peace and were quiet *"James,"* the Lord's brother, *"answered, saying, Men and brethren harken unto me."* Now he was the high priest of the church. Peter, James and John were three top leaders of the church. *"Simeon hath declared how God at the first did visit the Gentiles, to take out of them a people for his name. And to this agree the words of the prophets; as it is written."* And now he is going to quote a prophecy in Amos 9:11-12 where it talks about the Gentiles coming to God and into the possession of the shepherd's hut. *"After this I will return, and build again the shepherd's hut of David, which is fallen down; and I will build again the ruins thereof, and I will set it up: That the residue of **men might seek after the Lord**, and **all the Gentiles,** upon whom my name is called, saith the Lord, who doeth all these things."*

Now remember, the shepherd's hut was a place where people could seek the Lord as James is saying here. It is amazing to scholars that the prophet Amos is willing to apply the shepherd's hut to the Gentiles. So Amos is clearly tying it in to that righteousness established by Moses. *"Known unto God are all his works from the beginning of the world. Wherefore my sentence is."* In other words, James is issuing a high priest decree. *"Wherefore my sentence is, that we trouble not them, which from among the Gentiles are turned to God."* Now listen to this verse 20. *"But that we write unto them that they abstain from pollutions of idols, from fornication, from things strangled and from blood.*" So he is saying they can go ahead without circumcision but these four things we are going to require of them. All four things have to do with blood sacrifice. **Abstain from pollutions** of idols or sacrifice to idols, **abstain from fornication.** It was typical to have what one could call religious fornication directed toward fertility gods and they were very common among the Canaanites and also common during certain periods with the Romans and Greeks. **Abstaining from things strangled** had a special purpose in blood sacrifice. Strangling was commonly used throughout the centuries. And of course, to **abstain from blood** which has implications with regard to the belief of being saved by blood.

So here is this controversy over something that had a clear precedent. For centuries and centuries, circumcision had been practiced and instituted in Israel, as well as in Egypt and elsewhere. Here James is turning all this toward blood and not circumcision. Isn't that an amazing thing? I rehearsed to you about this controversy so you could better get a Biblical perspective regarding the Creatorship of Jesus Christ. The controversy of circumcision was really a small issue compared to Christ being our Creator. That is why James redirected the issue towards abstaining from blood, to support the Creatorship of Jesus. Circumcision is a small issue with big contention. Even though it has been a practice since ancient times, and notwithstanding Jesus Himself was circumcised, it brought heavy disputes to the early church. But on a huge baseline theological issue of Jesus being the Creator, an all-encompassing issue that should bear on every belief in the early church, they all agreed. And this is an issue with only an obscure scriptural precedent – Genesis 2:3-5; and the issue is that Jesus is the Creator.

As the Bible stands, there is no record of Jesus ever teaching it. Now isn't that amazing? There was no direct traditional precedent and yet Peter, James and John, the leaders of the church, and the authors of Hebrews, and Paul, who wrote the book of Colossians, Ephesians, and I Corinthians in which His Creatorship is cited all agree completely. Even the prophetic record is silent on this issue except for an indirect reference in Isaiah that Christ is the Creator.

I want to read to you just to refresh your memory. You have heard this many times before but this is important for this topic today. I am going to read or cite scriptures stating Jesus is the Creator from all those people I listed. This is the classic scripture, it mentions Jesus is the Creator twice, John 1:1-10 and it is significant that it says *"the Word was God." "In the beginning was the Word, and the Word was with God, and the Word was God."* This is saying that the Man that God became has a special role as a person in the flesh and that expression of God was with God. That expression of God was God.

"The same was in the beginning with God. All things were made by him; and without him was not any thing made that was made. In him was life; and the life was the light of men. And the light shineth in darkness; and the darkness comprehended it not.

*There was a man sent from God, whose name was John. The same came for a witness, to bear witness of the Light, that all men **through** him might believe,"* through Him, again pointing to His Father, *"He was not that Light, but was sent to bear witness of that Light. That was the true Light, which lighteth every man that cometh into the world,"* meaning every religion and every human culture, *"He was in the world, and the world was made by him, and the world knew him not."* The world did not know Jesus' Father nor did it know, really know, Jesus.

Now I want to turn to Colossians, which has a really good scripture for this. It is even more descriptive than the John reading. Colossians 1:15-17, *"[Jesus] is the image of the invisible God, the firstborn of every creature: For by him were all things created, that are in heaven, and that are in earth, visible and invisible, whether they be thrones, or dominions, or principalities, or powers: all things were created by him, and for him. And he is before all things, and by him all things consist."*

That is pretty clear and that's Paul. So Paul and John agree. John actually walked with Christ. Paul never knew Jesus personally during His earthly ministry. And Ephesians 3:9 and Hebrews 1:2 both speak of Jesus as the Creator. With no historical prophetic precedent, it must be a certainty that Jesus, at some point, declared His Creatorship for these divergent individuals to completely agree, again, if they understood Genesis 2:3-5 that might have had an influence. I personally believe that the resurrection cemented the issue but we are coming to that. Also, the original Torah doesn't give any direct indication Christ is the Creator. So with no precedent, they all agree. Doesn't that seem amazing? Have any of you ever thought about that before? Paul on that issue is in total agreement.

Now I am ready to address the 6th Chapter of John. The 6th Chapter of John is absolutely pivotal to Christian salvation. I am going to focus on verses 51-58. These are the eight most appalling verses in your Bible. We have talked a lot about blood sacrifice so far. All the prophets were against it. It led to the apostasy in Israel from a tabernacle/shepherds hut to the temple, and from priesthood coming down through the prophet Moses to Aaron the idol-maker. Stephen squarely addressed that. And I have said that blood sacrifice and the Creatorship of Jesus are mutually exclusive. It has to be one or the other. And remember Jesus said that to know His Father is life eternal or salvation. So when addressing these eight verses, either Jesus' Father is a God who is angry and demands that we kill His Son to be appeased, or He is a God of love. Which Father do you want to know?

So I am going to approach this reading from three different angles. First, I am going to expound to you specifically why John would not have written these verses. Then, I am going to open up the evidence from the Bible that they are an over-write. And lastly, I'll show you that the Biblical historical evidence is clear that these verses were edited in.

So here we go. I will now read these verses to you. "*I am the living bread which came down from heaven: if any man eat of this bread, he shall live for ever: and the bread that I will give is my flesh, which I will give for the life of the world. The Jews therefore strove among themselves, saying, How can this man give us his flesh to eat? Then Jesus said unto them, Verily, verily, I say unto you, Except ye eat the flesh of the Son of man, and drink his blood, ye have no life in you. Whoso eateth my flesh, and drinketh my blood, hath eternal life; and I will raise him up at the last day. For my flesh is meat indeed, and my blood is drink indeed. He that*

201

eateth my flesh, and drinketh my blood, dwelleth in me, and I in him.

As the living Father hath sent me, and I live by the Father: so he that eateth me, even he shall live by me. This is that bread which came down from heaven: not as your fathers did eat manna, and are dead: he that eateth of this bread shall live forever."

In light of this reading there is evidence in your Bible, with additional insight from Jeremiah's Torah that this reading has been edited in. We know the early church was well versed in Jeremiah's Torah - it is called Jubilees. I've told you about it. There were more copies of it found in the Dead Sea Scrolls than any other work found there. An important reason why we know that John would never have written these eight verses comes from the decree of James that I have cited for you. When you recall his decree, you will note that the real issue with the Gentile Mission was abstaining from blood, specifically in four ways that are directly tied to blood sacrifice. By now in our studies you will also certainly be familiar with the Mosaic Covenant – listen to my voice and I will be your God and you will be my people - and Jeremiah's New Covenant - which is basically, every person will know the Lord for themselves.

So now let me put this information all together. There is a third covenant in your Bible. It is the covenant God made with Noah; the Noahic Covenant. It doesn't say, hear my voice and all will know me; it is about something else. And it is foundational to the decree of James and is absolutely the reason behind why he said what he did. This is a covenant that God made with Noah right after the Flood. In it God is addressing the reasons why there was a Flood. And this covenant is about why there won't be another Flood. Here it is: Genesis 9:3-6, *"Every moving thing that liveth shall be meat for you, even as the green herb have I given you all things. But flesh with the life thereof, which is the blood thereof, shall ye not eat. And surely your blood of your lives will I require, at the hand of every beast will I require it and at the hand of man; at the hand of every man's brother will I require the life of man. Whoso sheddeth man's blood by man shall his blood be shed; for in the image of God made he man."*

202

What he is saying is if you will abstain from blood, there won't be another flood. The rainbow is a sign that God is not going to bring a flood again. And if you will see to it that you have the proper relationship with blood in your lives, there will not be another Flood; all the green things are given you for food and the way you use the life of animals is going to be required of you, indicating to me a reference to blood sacrifice and using the life of the animal wrongly. So here in this covenant, God is saying when you see the rainbow, His side of the covenant is there won't be any more flood and our side of it is we will abstain from blood. Isn't that amazing? It is our concept and use of blood in religion. It is our use of blood. Who would have ever thought that the main thing on God's mind after the flood would be blood? So when you see a rainbow, you all think well there is not going to be another flood. That is His part. What about thinking about your part when you see that rainbow? Are you going to abstain from blood or are you going to be saved by blood?

Now in Jeremiah's Torah, that the Jews and the early church possessed, this issue is greatly expanded upon. You are going to be surprised about it and at how much it is spoken of. James had all this memorized. Let me read it to you now, this is in Jubilees, which was perhaps the most common form of the Torah used among the sect of the Nazarenes, or the Essenes, during the time of Christ. I realize that you don't consider this scripture but the early church did, and it is most certainly the reason why the sect of the Nazarenes, among whom Christ was numbered, did not participate in temple sacrifice. (Note: see Acts 24:5 for Paul being called a ringleader of the sect of the Nazarenes, and Matthew 2:23 for Christ to be numbered among them. There are volumes of evidence of this but that's another topic.)

So I will read it to you. This chapter 6 starting with verse 6. This is another account of the same covenant, it contains the same promise and conditions found in your Bible but they are expanded upon. *"And behold I have given you all the beasts and everything which flies and everything which moves upon the earth and in the water and fish and everything for food, like the green herbs. And I have given you everything that you might eat; but flesh which is filled with life, that is, with blood you shall not eat. Because the life of all flesh is in the blood, lest your blood be sought for your lives.*

203

And Noah and his sons swore that they would not eat any blood which was in any flesh. And they made a covenant before the Lord God for ever in all the generations of the earth in that month. This testimony is written concerning you, so you might keep it always lest you ever eat any blood of the beast or birds or cattle throughout all your days on the earth. And the man who eats blood of the beasts of cattle or bird throughout all the days of the earth shall be uprooted, he and his seed from the earth. And you Moses commanded the children of Israel not to eat any blood so that their names and their seed might be before the Lord God always. And there is no limit of days for this law, because it is forever. And he gave a sign to Noah and to his children that there should be not again be a flood upon the earth. And set his bow in the clouds for a sign of the covenant which is forever." And he just said this covenant is forever. "*Therefore it is ordained and written in the heavenly tablets that they should observe the feast of Shabuwa in this month.*"

Remember, Shabuwa in Greek is Pentecost and it was the most important holy day for the early church. (Read Acts 2.) Let me continue reading, "*Once a year in order to renew the covenant,*" to abstain from blood, "*in all respects year by year. And from this day of the death of Noah his sons corrupted it until the days of Abraham. And they ate blood. And Abraham alone kept it. And Isaac and Jacob and his sons kept it. Until your days and in your days the children of Israel forgot it until you* (Moses) *renewed it for them on this mountain.*" That is the real extensive commentary on blood. And it is not just about eating blood as a diet. Eating blood was an integral part of blood sacrifice. And sprinkling blood all around and on people was always a part of blood sacrifice. The Gentile Mission even evolved to the point where they would say they were washed in His blood.

Allow me to add to this a bit of a reading further on in the scroll because it clarifies that this is not just diet. This is in the last blessing of Noah to his children before he died. Here he is describing conditions that brought on the Flood, and in this reading he mentions moral sacrifice. "*And everyone sold himself in order that he might do injustice and pour out much blood and the earth was full of injustice. And afterward they sinned against beasts and birds and everything that moves or walks upon the earth. And they poured out much blood upon the earth."* This is a clear reference to blood sacrifice. *"And all the thoughts and desires of men were always contemplating vanity and evil. And the Lord blotted out everything from the face of the earth on account of the evil of their deeds.* **And on account of the blood which they poured out in the midst of the land he blotted out everything".** Clearly blood sacrifice was the cause of the Flood. *"And we are left, you and I my children and everything which entered with us into the ark. And now I fear for your sakes that after I die you will pour out blood of men upon the earth. And you will be blotted out from the surface of the earth."* Now listen to this. *"For all who shed the blood of man and all who eat the blood of any flesh will be blotted out, all of them, from the earth."* This next part is in direct contradiction to the Levitical law of sprinkling blood on the people. *"**And let no blood from any of the blood which is in anything be seen upon you** on the day when you sacrifice any beast or cattle or that which flies upon the earth."*

Now why would I be dealing so much about blood when our topic is Jesus the Creator? Why was God so intent on this blood issue? When Noah came out of the ark, why would God be so urgent on the use of blood? The reason is because blood sacrifice and the use of blood was that which caused the Flood. The use of blood is what James' decree was about. James is issuing directives on the very same thing in regard to the Gentile Mission, in all four of those points I read to you in his sentence. They used blood to create the Nephilim, which is translated as giants in your Bible. And I am not going to cite all the references. The Gentiles drank human blood to gain power over their enemies and to bring violence. They used blood from animals that were strangled for a specific purpose. It had to do with conquering their enemies. The use of blood was the most prominent use of element in the pre-Flood times among the wicked and it was common among the peoples of the Gentile Mission.

And because of that, God is saying if you stop this practice of the use of blood, blood sacrifice, there won't be another Flood because that is what caused the Flood. That is what spiraled man down into the irretrievable abyss. There was no other recourse than to allow the destruction of those who were doing it. Ok now isn't it amazing that people don't recognize all this and yet James affirmed

205

it in the New Testament. So he said, the Gentiles can come into the faith but this one thing we must insist on. **We have to insist that there is no pre-Flood wickedness in the church.** The Gentiles were well-known to be practicing those things at the time.

So it is plain that for the early church this blood issue was of central concern with the Gentile Mission; and Peter, James, and John were pillars in the church. In light of all this, it is very unreasonable to attribute verses 51-58 to John. If he wrote this, he would have been acting directly against James' decree and against an important, fundamental theology they all adhered to. That is some of the Biblical evidence that these verses were over written.

How did we get those eight verses in John 6? First of all, historically, these verses represent a practice and a doctrine that began and first came into existence more than 300 years after Christ in the days of Constantine. This doctrine was invented in those early days of the period when the Roman church began to be the state religion. And it was for the purpose of promoting the idea that the church had the power to bestow salvation. It wasn't a relationship between you and Jesus' Father. It became a form of domination and control by the church.

Let me explain. This doctrine expressed in these eight verses is the scriptural foundation for what is known as the **doctrine of transubstantiation**. And I am going to read this to you from the Bible dictionary. The Roman church in the days of Constantine became the official church of all of the Roman Empire. The church had to consolidate their power. And one of the ways they did that was they said their priests could say certain words and bread and wine would be transformed into the flesh and blood of Jesus Christ. And it was asserted that no other expression of Christianity had this authority or power; "we are the only true church!" And then: *"Whoso eateth my flesh, and drinketh my blood, hath eternal life."* And of course, all of this fit very well with the religious background of the Romans and Greeks. And it was easily accepted that the Roman clergy had such power that they could say certain liturgical words and change the bread and wine to be the actual body and blood of Christ. Very similar things were done in the wickedness that was before the Flood. And some expressions of it were still to be found among the Gentiles of this time. And James was aware of all of this. And it is called transubstantiation.

Now I want to read to you out of Nelson's Bible dictionary; it is a conservative one. The International Bible dictionary is the liberal one. And the old one from Smith's Bible dictionary has references in it. And it is even in the Jehovah's Witness Bible study book. They all agree on this. This is very interesting to me this transubstantiation view; this view is a doctrine of the Roman Catholic Church. Zwigly, Calvin, Luther and the Westley brothers, Meno Simmons, none of the original reformers who established protestant religions believed these eight verses in their infallible Bible. You can understand why because they all were taking the stand that the Roman Catholic Church did not have exclusive authority to bestow salvation.

So this is a conservative view here that shows the author doesn't believe it either. They just don't believe it. They say this is a Roman Catholic doctrine. Ok, this is what it says: *"This view holds that the bread and wine becomes the actual body and blood of Christ when the words of the institution are spoken by the priest. This doctrine known as transubstantiation holds that while the physical properties of the bread and wine do not change the iconic reality of these elements undergo a spiritual change. While this view may help to foster a serious attitude toward the Eucharist,"* which is the communion, *"it fails to grasp the figurative nature of Jesus's language."* In other words, they are saying Jesus didn't mean literally what those verses are saying.

So in verses 51-58 is the new doctrine of transubstantiation. Where did it come from? Even more importantly, why did it appear in this very important place in the sixth chapter of John? Why did someone choose to insert it in that specific place? First of all, there is no doubt that it doesn't belong here. This idea, this doctrine, this practice didn't come for 300 more years. It simply could not have come from the Jerusalem church. It came from a fully developed expression of Gentile Christianity. There was nobody that believed this in Christ's day or even a close time afterwards. So the Protestant reformers, even though it is written in their Bible, also did not believe it. And they didn't practice it. And they explain it away as symbolic language and that reading in the Nelson's goes on to tell you how they do think about it.

So what happened was the really bad "other guy," in those eight verses in John, brought back into the church the central evil that caused the Flood in spite of James' decree on blood. They brought it back and put in Christ's own mouth and into the writings of the beloved disciple and Apostle John. How utterly appalling. Why did they put it in that particular place? Ok, you are going to find this very interesting and I am going to show you what is missing and was replaced in verses 51 to 58 in John chapter 6 was, in all probability, Christ's declaration of his Creatorship. Somewhere in that part of chapter 6, Christ declared Himself to be the Creator. All of the biblical evidence points towards it.

The Gentile Mission developed their doctrine in such a way that they painted themselves into a theological corner when they pursued transubstantiation. On the one hand they maintain that Mary was the mother of God, but on the other hand transubstantiation requires Jesus and God to be two different persons. It was all but impossible to sell the idea to people that you had to sacrifice and kill the Creator of the earth and drink His blood and eat His flesh in order to receive salvation or for some, a happy afterlife. It was just not going to fly. They could accept blood sacrifice but not in the context of killing the Creator. His Creatorship had to go or be minimized into oblivion. During Paul's day, the sixth chapter of John was still intact without the over writing and, because of the dramatic nature of the resurrection, the Creatorship of Jesus was uncontested in the early church beyond the resurrection.

So you could have John, Ephesians, Colossians, Hebrews , and I Corinthians, all in agreement on the matter. But the blood issue was the biggest scandal in the early church between the apostles and the Gentile Mission, hence James' decree. So as I was saying, it was a hard sell that God could only be appeased from His wrath by killing His Son, who was the **Creator** of all things, and by eating His flesh and drinking His blood. Remember Noah specifically said not to drink man's blood? Also, you will remember in the original Torah reading that people were not to even get blood on themselves. But the common practice required people to be regularly sprinkled with blood or to think of themselves being washed in His blood.

So they achieved two things when they set in place the doctrine of transubstantiation in John 6. They achieved restoring the pre-Flood wickedness into the church to accommodate those they wanted to conver,t and they achieved eliminating Christ as Creator from His own mouth in order to establish supreme church institutional power over salvation. They left in all the verses saying He is the Creator but took out the source of that information from Christ declaring it Himself. I personally think they knew they could leave the Creatorship verses in and His Creatorship would still be minimized into oblivion by other forces.

Now my third point is: I want to show you some of the evidence surrounding the claim that these verses were altered. There is evidence in your Bible that these eight verses were overwritten. I am going to tell you what some of the evidence is. Now I want to read to you about Christ getting threatened with stoning. It is very important that you follow me in this because this evidence is strong.

This is John 5. On a Sabbath Jesus healed a man who'd had withered legs for 38 years. The man found out who had healed him and in 5:14-18 it says, *"Afterward Jesus findeth him in the temple, and said unto him, Behold, thou art made whole: sin no more, lest a worse thing come unto thee. The man departed, and told the Jews that it was Jesus, which had made him whole. And therefore did the Jews persecute Jesus, and sought to slay him, because he had done these things on the sabbath day. But Jesus answered them, My Father worketh hitherto, and I work. Therefore the Jews sought the more to kill him, because he not only had broken the sabbath, but said also that God was his Father, making himself equal with God."*

Then Jesus proceeded to give an important and definitive discourse on His relationship with His Father clear through the rest of Chapter 5 of John. He was not the least bit defensive nor did He feel threatened by the prospect of them wanting to kill Him. He just calmly explained, in detail, His most complete discourse on His relationship with His Father that can be found in the New Testament. And again, His ability to be calm in the face of threats to His life is demonstrated in Luke 4 starting with verse 16. Jesus read from Isaiah a prophecy about Himself and then He said, *"This day is this scripture fulfilled in your ears."*

Then He went on to expound that **His Messiahship would also be applied to the Gentiles** and then comes verses 28-31. *"And all they in the synagogue, when they heard these things, were filled with wrath, And rose up, and thrust him out of the city, and led him unto the brow of the hill whereon their city was built, that they might cast him down headlong. But he passing through the midst of them went his way, And came down to Capernaum, a city of Galilee, and taught them on the sabbath days."* He was very confident and cool in the face of their life threatening intentions. So far all this has happened before John Chapter 6.

Remember, I am pursuing this line of thought as I am opening up to you evidence concerning the Creatorship issue in chapter 6. Jesus' response is different with chapter 6; way different. His responses after chapter 6 were markedly different even though He was not threatened with any violence. After chapter 6, you're going to see an amazing change come over Jesus. The reference that I'm going to read now will be showing just how Jesus was profoundly affected by what He said in place of what is written in John 6:51-58. You will find this very telling.

I'm going to read to you John 6:59-69. This follows immediately after the verses on transubstantiation which ended on verse 58. *"These things said he in the synagogue, as he taught in Capernaum. Many therefore of his disciples, when they had heard this, said, This is an hard saying; who can hear it?"*

Remember, I maintain that what they heard was not the discourse on blood but his declaration of Creatorship. These are His very own disciples, ok? *"When Jesus knew in himself that his disciples murmured at it, he said unto them, Doth this offend you? What and if ye shall see the Son of man ascend up where he was before?"* A thing He never would have said if the issue was blood. This is the evidence that affirms that the resurrection and ascension settled this issue so they could all agree. What He is saying is if you see me ascend to heaven then will you believe the profound things I just said to you?

As you will see as we move on He is talking about being the Creator. Can you imagine having a Man standing before you, no matter how good He is, telling you He is the Creator of all that exists? It is one thing to say He is the Son of God but another to say He is the Creator when there is no traditional scriptural precedent outside of an understanding of Genesis 2:3-5 and a reading in Jeremiah's Torah. Hence, does this offend you? That is what He is saying when He asked will you believe me?

Now I am going to keep going, verses 64-66, "*But there are some of you that believe not. For Jesus knew from the beginning who they were that believed not, and who should betray him. And he said, Therefore said I unto you, that **no man can come unto me**, except it were given unto him of my Father. From that time many of his disciples went back, and walked no more with him.*" He used this phrase "*come unto me*" because He knew many would leave Him and perhaps only those who knew His Father would accept what He said in Chapter 6. This again connects knowing His Father with accepting His Creatorship. It was definitely a bigger issue than a meal of a moral sacrifice. This was a very big point of contention. They all knew what eating bread and drinking wine meant when affirming a covenant. It was an integral part of their religious culture and the doctrine of transubstantiation was still three centuries away. That issue, no matter how it was stated, could not have caused such an extreme response.

Remember, He had just the day before fed 5000 people with a child's lunch. Now continuing on, "*Then said Jesus unto his twelve, Will ye also go away? Then Simon Peter answered him and said Lord, to whom shall we go? thou hast the words of eternal life.*" He even expected His apostles to abandon Him. And He wouldn't have anticipated that if He was establishing a sacred meal with a moral sacrifice, that was very common and they had done that with Him many times. They knew what that was. The issue here was not about the Noahic Covenant. That issue would not have

211

caused them to leave Him. But the Creator issue was very startling and required an entire reassessment of their expectations of Him.

Let's keep going and you will see that there is clear evidence that He declared His Creatorship in place of the blood dialogue - we are coming to it. It wouldn't have offended them at all if He was serving the bread and wine and had said do this in remembrance of me - a covenant to remember the Man that God became. The word "covenant" in Hebrew comes from the root word that means *to eat.* At the Last Supper He was establishing a **kinship relationship**. Jesus says after the Last Supper in John 15:14-15, *"Ye are my friends, if ye do whatsoever I command you. Henceforth I call you not servants; for the servant knoweth not what his lord doeth: but I have called you friends; for all things that I have heard of my Father I have made known unto you."* He was the Son of Man. Just this rationale alone tells us that those eight verses have something amiss. But there is more, of course.

This turns out to be the most dramatic event for Jesus in all of His ministry; for Him and all of His followers. In that chapter 6 reading, what He did say there instead of what those eight verses say turns out to be the most traumatizing event we know of for Christ in the Gospels, of course along with His death, and the most controversial. But the events surrounding His resurrection and ascension ended the controversy and His Creatorship was openly accepted by all in the years to follow.

All the more amazing is the fact that Paul, John, and the author of Hebrews, agree that Jesus is the Creator. It stands to reason that because of the diversity of this group and in light of their agreement on this Creatorship issue, Jesus at some point during His ministry declared His Creatorship. But where? This group of authors are very diverse in the time of their writing, and in their worldviews, and in their actual personal experience with Jesus. Nothing short of a declaration of Creatorship could have been behind their consensus. The scholars who do not simply ignore the Creatorship issue most commonly dismiss it by reporting that the idea came along much later in the context of deifying Christ and someone went back and altered John's record, it being the earliest account of His Creatorship. There was just too much to alter. But when you closely examine chapter 6, there is evidence it was chapter 6 that was altered, not chapter 1 of John.

And now allow me to show you more. I'm going to read verses 32-40 of chapter 6. This is extremely important evidence to place His declaration in the context of chapter 6. It shows He was leading up to it here before those eight verses of 51-58. Here are verses 32-33. *"Then Jesus said unto them, Verily, verily, I say unto you, Moses gave you not that bread from heaven; but my Father giveth you the true bread from heaven. For the bread of God is he which cometh down from heaven, and giveth life unto the world."* The Greek word here translated as world is "Cosmos," better translated "the universe including man." Christ in these verses (32-33) is leading up to telling that He is the Creator. He said that He came to give life to the universe including man. He came to give life to everything in creation. He came to give it life. Well, only the Creator can give life to all creation. So He is leading up to such a declaration with verses 32-33.

Ok remember that this discourse in chapter 6 was all about power in the minds of those assembled. He had just fed the 5000 the day before; He walked on the water, His disciples went across the sea, He got into the boat with them out in the water after they departed, and when He arrived others followed. Some didn't follow Him because they loved Him, they followed because they were fed miraculously; and not just because they were hungry or they were fed but because they viewed that feeding the 5000 as a very important prophetic sign, because there was a prophecy among them that said when someone would arise again like Moses, to feed food like manna, that would be the Messiah. And they likened it to the manna from heaven. This is why Jesus said what He did in verses 32-33.

And to add to that, they knew He did not depart with His disciples and yet He arrived with them. This added to their expectations. And they considered Him to be the Messiah upon whose shoulders would rest the government. And in Chapter 6:15 it says, *"When Jesus therefore perceived that they would come and take him by force, to make him a king, he departed again into a mountain himself alone."* And they would have done it. This was before He left to go over the sea with His disciples. Jesus must have known in His heart when He arrived at the point of making His declaration in the synagogue that the issue of Him disclosing His Creatorship would separate fact from fable. The Creator of this earth simply could not be the king of the government as they interpreted Isaiah, as badly as they may have wanted it, in light of the Roman occupation. It must have taken a lot of courage for Him to approach His declaration of Creatorship.

So this whole chapter 6 dialogue is all about His confronting their response to this expectation in prophecy that arose from feeding the 5000. They had taken Isaiah's statement that the government would be upon His shoulders all wrong. His role was not to be head of state but Lord of a kingdom not of this world like He told Pilate. The Jews to this day still hold to that erroneous view of the meaning of Isaiah's statement. Here in this context, His declaration of His Creatorship would clarify the issue between His being a head of state or Lord over a spiritual kingdom. All this is the backdrop for verse 33 and verse 48 of chapter 6. John 6:33 says, *"For the bread of God is he which cometh down from heaven, and giveth life unto the world."* And verse 48 says simply, *"I am that bread of life."* The stage is set for His declaration of Creatorship. So I am maintaining that His declaration was struck out and replaced with what is found in 6:51-58.

Here is more evidence to support that position; again, this will show just how dramatically this event had affected Jesus. I'm going to read to you from the seventh chapter of John and into chapter 8. I have marked only selected parts to read to shorten it for us. This reading is, of course, describing the aftermath of what occurred in chapter 6. You will find that Christ's response was markedly different than anything recorded of Him previously in the gospels. I am saying that this marked difference is attributable to more than a dialogue about the Lord's Supper and the meaning of the bread and wine as indicated in verses 51-58. See what you think.

This is going to be a sad thing for you to hear in some sense because what I want to show you is Christ's response to having declared His Creatorship and having experienced such a dramatic reaction of rejection even from His disciples, and even more so from His three brothers, who were Apostles. It is sad for me because I love Him and what He went through touches my heart. In those moments, He was truly alone anticipating even that His longtime friends and fellows the apostles could leave Him. I wish Peter would have said, "Lord we believe all you have said about being the very Creator and we will stand by you no matter what comes," instead of, "*Lord where would we go?*" But the apostles were so stunned by His declaration that they had to have time to soak it all in and they couldn't at that moment answer Him affirming what He said in chapter 6. "*After these things Jesus walked in Galilee for he would not walk in Jewry because the Jews sought to kill him.*" Never before when His life was threatened did He avoid going somewhere because they sought to kill Him. They were going to stone Him in the temple many times yet He did not hesitate to go back there. He didn't care a thing about it. But this time it was different, even though there was no actual personal threat recorded. He decided He wouldn't walk among the Jews.

"*Now the Jews feast of tabernacles was at hand. His brethren therefore said unto him, Depart hence, and go into Judea, that thy disciples also may see the works that thou doest.*" Do you suppose His brethren wanted Him to try to reclaim some of His disciples who left Him? Why all of a sudden did His brothers want His disciples to see His works, they had seen them many times before? In John 7:5 it says, "*Neither did his brethren believe in Him.*" Most scholars say that His own family did not believe in His Messiah-ship. But three of His brothers were among the apostles. Matthew 13:55 tells us who they were. "*Is not this the carpenter's son? is not his mother called Mary? and his brethren, James, and Joses, and Simon, and Judas?*" It was Simon, not Simon Peter; James, not James the brother of John; and Judas, the author of the Book of Jude, not Judas Iscariot. Robert Eisenman, in his book <u>The New Testament Code</u>, has a lot of evidence that this is in fact the case. It's wonderful information. Perhaps they, as His brothers, were also stunned. It is one thing to have your older brother be the Messiah and the Son of God, your mother always taught you that, but another thing for you to have your very own brother stand before you in public and declare that He is your Creator and the Creator that gave life to the universe. Family dynamics probably made that more difficult for them than it would have been for anyone else.

215

They said, *"For there is no man that doeth anything in secret."* They knew that He was very shaken and distraught over what happened in Capernaum. And Jesus was downcast. They knew that the reaction He got from declaring His Creatorship had grieved Him. *"Then Jesus said unto them, My time is not yet come but your time is alway ready. The world cannot hate you; but me it hateth."* This is the only time in your Bible Jesus responded to trauma this way. He said the world hates Him. He felt hated. In John7:7-12 it says, *"Because I testify of it, that the works thereof are evil. Go ye up unto this feast: I go not up yet unto this feast: for my time is not yet full come. When he had said these words unto them, he abode still in Galilee. But when his brethren were gone up, then went he also up unto the feast, not openly, but as it were in secret. Then the Jews sought him at the feast, and said, Where is he? And there was much murmuring among the people concerning him: for some said, He is a good man: others said, Nay; but he **deceiveth** the people."*

This kind of public sentiment is not described in regard to other occasions in Jesus' life. So it may be assumed that news of the declaration of His Creatorship reached Jerusalem before Him. Before it was the Pharisees and scribes saying He is misleading the people, but the context of these divergent opinions in this passage it seems to be from the common folks. None of this would have been instigated by a discussion of a moral sacrifice.

The next passage in 7:13-17 is also indicating this. *"Howbeit no man spake openly of him for fear of the Jews. Now about the midst of the feast Jesus went up into the temple, and taught. And the Jews marvelled, saying, How knoweth this man letters, having never learned? Jesus answered them, and said, My doctrine is not mine, but his that sent me. If any man will do his will, he shall know of the doctrine, whether it be of God, or whether I speak of myself."* Jesus is in a rare position to defend Himself. It has to be clearly in relation to the chapter 6 discourse. And certainly it has to be about an issue as large as Creatorship.

"He that speaketh of himself seeketh his own glory: but he that seeketh his glory that sent him, the same is true and no unrighteousness is in him." He is feeling like He has to clarify that He is not seeking His own glory. He is saying, I am not trying to be

something I'm not by telling you what I said at Capernaum. *"Did not Moses give you the law and yet none of you keepeth the law? Why go ye about to kill me?"* He is still thinking about the severe rejection He experienced with His disciples leaving Him and the prospects of His apostles doing likewise. There is no other place in the gospels where Jesus asks people about them killing Him except in John after chapter 6. Before that He could be calm. Now He is dwelling on His rejection by His loved ones. Then in verses 25 & 30 it says, *"Then said some of them of Jerusalem, Is not this he, whom they seek to kill? Then they sought to take him: but no man laid hands on him, because his hour was not yet come."* He still has it on His mind.

Ok now I am going to keep reading. John 8:38-40 is more fallout from chapter 6, *"I speak that which I have seen with my Father: and ye do that which ye have seen with your father. They answered and said unto him, Abraham is our father. Jesus saith unto them, If ye were Abraham's children, ye would do the works of Abraham. But now ye seek to kill me."* Here in chapter 8, Jesus is still reeling from His rejection in the chapter 6 reading. He is still preoccupied. This behavior is unknown of Him in any of the rest of the Gospels. All of this response on Jesus's part was not simply from the issue of the bread and wine of the Lord's Supper. With verse 33 & 48 in John 6, it is clear now that the issue was His declaration of Creatorship. There is another real strong verse that gives us more evidence. This is a key verse. This is John 8:53. A man in the crowd spoke out and said, *"whom makest thou thyself?"* A question that would not have followed a discussion on bread and wine but certainly is a very good question addressed to a Man standing before you had declared that He is the Creator.

I believe when Jesus stayed home and did not go with His brothers; He began to work through the trauma and rejection from the Chapter 6 reading. He was alone with His Father. So this defensive and preoccupied frame of mind gave way to calmness as expressed late into John 8 and through Chapter 10.

So let me read to you of this return to calmness and wisdom in the face of threats to His life. I will read from John 8:58-59. Christ was once again very calm and collected with His self-control and His ability to remain calm and wise in these kinds of circumstances. This is John 8:58-59 and 9:1. *"Jesus said unto them, Verily, verily I say unto you, Before Abraham was, I Am."* You will remember what led up to that. *"Then took they up stones to cast at him: but Jesus hid himself, and went out of the temple, going through the midst of them and so passed by. And as Jesus passed by he saw a man which was blind from his birth."* And He healed this man who was blind from his birth as He was running away from a threat to His life. It took all of His love, all of His emotions, all of His attention to heal this blind man. So the threat to His life was handled with such poise that He could offer Himself in this great healing that shocked the Jewish establishment. He was so in control of His behavior that, while He is running from the threat of being killed, He is able to not think of Himself. He was not looking back over His shoulder. He is able to look at someone in these circumstances and have deep compassion emotionally and He threw His life into that man's life and healed him. He is the one who they had to call his parents to be sure it was really the blind man. It was really a big deal. This is an example of His being calm under stress.

And again John 10:27-33 and 37-40 to demonstrate this He says, *"My sheep hear my voice, and I know them, and they follow me: And I give unto them eternal life."* Here is a Man standing in front of them saying that He has eternal life to give. Also, I think Jesus was bold enough in this instance to say that He had eternal life to give because He had already proclaimed His Creatorship and processed through the repercussions. *"And they shall never perish, neither shall any man pluck them out of my hand. My Father, which has given them to me, is greater than all; and no man is able to pluck them out of my Father's hand. I and my Father are one. And then the Jews took up stones again to stone him."* He was often facing stoning; stones must have been readily available. *"And Jesus answered them,"* He is really cool-headed. *"Many good works have I showed you from my Father, for which of these works do you stone me? And the Jews answered him, saying, For a good work we stone thee not; but for blasphemy; and because thou, being a man, makest thyself God."* If you wonder if the people knew who He was talking about when He referred to His Father, this tells us they did. It wasn't just because He said my Father and I are one but He said He had eternal life to give people and they knew only God could do that.

Then you read on to verse 37-40, "*If I do not the works of my Father, believe me not. But if I do, though ye believe not me, believe the works: that ye may know, and believe, that the Father is in me, and I in him. Therefore they sought again to take him: but he escaped out of their hand, And went away again beyond Jordan into the place where John at first baptized; and there he abode.*" So He was very calm and very much in charge of His behavior. This interim of disquiet by the Lord, in the aftermath of the events in John 6:51-58, taken together with the extreme reaction of His disciples and apostles clearly demonstrates something was communicated as monumental as Creatorship was originally in place of those verses.

So it now becomes apparent that the place of those eight verses was not simply about the Lord's Supper. Jesus said something there to the effect that He is our Creator. We will never know exactly what He said but you can bet it is something appropriately following verse 33 that says He came down from heaven to give life to the universe. Paul, who is often at odds with the apostles in the Gospels and with Jesus' teachings, is in this case eloquent in his description of Jesus' Creatorship, even excelling John, in the Colossians 1:16-17 reading. With the events I just read you with the kind of reaction the people were heard to say "*Thou hast a devil;*" they said this more than once to Him after the chapter 6 dialogue; they said it in 7:20, 8:48, 8:52, and 10:20. This had never been said of Him before in His ministry. Also, He was not accused of deceiving the people anywhere in the Gospels till after chapter 6 of John. And Jesus said in verse 49, "*I have not a devil.*" The reaction His disciples and apostles had just does not follow what is presently written in 6:51-57. So it is almost certain that Jesus declared His Creatorship in chapter 6. No Jew would have said He had a devil for affirming a moral sacrifice.

Ok, I believe that because those moments in Capernaum where Christ finally said that He was the Creator, because of the intensity of that, is why they all agreed that He is in fact the Creator and the issue was settled at the resurrection as Jesus said it would for any among the church who had doubts about it. In our next session, I am going to start to help you know how a Christian can start to develop a daily life expression of the Creatorship of Jesus. I would be surprised if many of you did not already have an intuitive

219

sense for it, however, where it takes us in the next session will be entirely unexpected and excitingly new. Thank you.

Session 10
Uncovering the Mystery of the Righteousness of Jesus
March 8, 2015

Here we come now into delving into why Christianity has been so compromised that the Lord's expectations for them remain unexpressed when He said that greater things would we do than He has done. The reasons we have been compromised are two fold and they can be summed up by addressing something brought into the early church by the Gentile Mission and by something entirely eliminated by them: both that which they brought **in** and that which they have taken **out** completely transformed the religion of Jesus and the early church. It is the religion which you have inherited. They took out righteousness and they brought in death, and Jesus' view of His Father was minimized out of any definition of salvation except to say in the end we get to live with God because of Jesus. Knowing Jesus' Father in this life takes second place to knowing **about** Jesus.

Before I get into explaining these two things, I want first to give you a perspective for that which is really happening in these last two sessions of this series; and that could be said for the session on Jesus' Creatorship as well. In these next two sessions I am attempting to bring information that has the potential to empower Christians in a depth and on a level that can result in their achieving those expectations. I come here today authorized by the Spirit of God and the Council of the Community to disclose information not in the public mind since the days of the early church. I feel compelled by the Spirit to disclose to you at this time specific understanding of how great healings and miracles were done by those of the sect of the Nazarenes. And of course they were also called Essenes. They were known as healers. Jesus was the premier healer among them. I am certain the Lord fully intends His people, here in our day, to follow His example and those of the early church, to love and understand spiritual realities on a level that enables them to bring sight to the blind, hearing to the deaf, and to raise the dead. Never has there been a greater need. Never in history has mankind faced such over powering forces that result in the need for physical and spiritual healing.

Let me say right here that what you will be hearing will not by mystical. It won't be New Age and it will not feel like far eastern religions. It will be very practical and Bible based. It will be expressing an entirely unknown depth for the Christian world in terms of a relationship with Christ and His creation. I will be getting right down to the bare bones of being kindred to Jesus and His Father.

Perhaps after hearing all of this there will be few who will be determined enough to put the kind of effort into it to actually accomplish it; but the prospect that there may be some makes my effort today worthwhile. I will be making public today, for the first time, the Essene view in these matters. And I will be illustrating the Nazarene perspective of the world. I hope the Lord has led me to know just how to do it so that people, with study and the witness of His Spirit, can come to understand those matters in a way that builds faith and empowerment.

Christians need to develop a culture, an expression of true religion, and a way of life that reflects the Creatorship of Jesus; and this in the framework of His definition of salvation - namely knowing His Father, and I might say, confronting the reality of His Father. What would a Christian expression of Jesus' Creatorship be like in practice and in everyday living? The early church, under the ministry of Jesus, building upon the prophets who worshiped the One True God, developed a unique expression of religion, a culture, a language, and a way of life that is founded on the Creatorship of Jesus with always having His Father in sight. So how, now in our day, do Christians express the power of Christianity? Changing peoples' lives and bringing rebirth is vital. Does God expect His people to triumph over the evils of this world to the extent that they can give His world back to Him? Are Christians called upon to do more in concert with the angels of heaven? Does our dear Lord need help with healing His people who are now in the most desperate circumstances? What does the Lord expect of His people? Savior is a secondary role for Jesus; first He had to create you. Salvation must be built on His Creatorship.

So now we come to the two things that have compromised Christian spiritual power. The first one entails that which the Gentile Mission brought **into** the church. They established death to be the central pathway to salvation and eternal life. Does saying that seem startling to any of you? The plan of salvation for the Gentile Mission is centered on death. I know that death is a dreary topic but I must speak of it just a bit more to finally lay it to rest. Recently, archaeologists uncovered a Minoan site in the Mediterranean where a priest sacrificed a person and a bowl of blood was being taken to be placed at the feet of an idol in an attempt to stop an earthquake, but the building fell down on them preserving the whole scene. That is a culture whose remnants and influence remain right in the midst of the lands of the Gentile Mission.

Let me emphatically assure you that the church in Christ's day did not believe that death was the central force which brought eternal life. By bringing it into the church, the Gentiles stripped the church of its power and its legitimacy before God. That is why I have hammered on the topic of blood all through this series. In doing so, I have just added my voice to the voices of the prophets and Jesus and to the voices of the early church. Now you do not have to consciously think of death to be disempowered. The whole environment of death-thinking is sufficient to do it. A person who worships death simply cannot raise the dead back to life. Death thinking inhibits a person from experiencing the deeper and more profound aspects of being born again. You will see that righteousness is the pathway to those depths of holiness and empowerment.

So Christians should be very careful how they associate death with Jesus. Jesus said I am the **living** bread. He says I can give the **living** water. He says I am the truth the way and the **life**. I come that you might have **life** and have it more abundantly. I am talking about **life** here. I have come down from heaven to give **life** to the universe. He says if you believe not ye shall not see **life**. He says if you know my Father you have passed from death to **life** already. John says of Him, in Him is **life** and the **life** is the light of men. Christ spoke a lot about **life**. Jesus said let the **dead** bury the **dead**. He said in Proverbs 8:35-36, this reference is attributing this saying to Christ, "*He who finds me finds life. He who hates me loves death.*" That is what it says in Proverbs. Have you been taught to love His death?

Jesus did not use the words "die" or "death" in relation to Himself even one time in the Bible. If He would have considered that His death would be dying for our sins, wouldn't one think He would have used those words? Caretakers of the Biblical record among those of the Gentile Mission tried to promote the concept of His death as being that which would bring salvation. They could have chosen to do the same with His life. An example of this is found in John 12:32-33, *"And I, if I be **lifted** up from the earth, will draw all men unto me.* (This next verse is not Jesus' words.) *This he said, signifying what death he should die."* They are saying this to indicate that it was His death that would draw all men unto Him. But the Greek word "hoop-sos" is the word here translated as "lifted up." It means *to be exalted.* It is Greek # 5312 and it comes from #5311, "hoop-so-o," which means *to dignify someone.* No one is exalted or dignified by experiencing capital punishment. The ascension of Jesus is what is being spoken of here. That is really what will draw all men to Him. Jesus spoke of His ascension in John 6:62 clearly indicating His anticipation of it. There is no greater expression of His **life** than His ascension.

And so the reason I bring this up is because a part of why Christianity has neglected the Creatorship of Christ, or not been able to develop it, is because of their view of death and how they prioritize it in their thinking of Him. Christ's ministry was centered on life but the majority of Christians center on His death. Hundreds of millions worship His death. Some of us here were recently invited to attend a worldwide celebration of the death of Jesus on what is called Good Friday. They call it Good Friday. I call it Bad Friday because they killed my Lovely One on that day. Resurrection day should be called Good Monday because on it He lived - had life again. The power of Christianity comes from centering on His **life** here and now. Churches should have round stones like the door of His tomb that was rolled away on top of them instead of a Roman gallows. He lives. He gives life. He is life itself for the universe. He restores my soul back to life when a part of me is dead. He lives. Christ overcame death long before the resurrection. Otherwise how could He meet Moses and Elijah on the mount of transfiguration? How would they have gotten there unless they were first resurrected by Him? How can He say God is the God of the living and not the dead, in relation to Abraham, Isaac and Jacob? He overcame death before the world was created, otherwise how was Enoch translated into heaven without death? See Hebrews 11:5.

So there are reasons why Christianity hasn't developed the Creatorship of Jesus. And the place of death in their view of Him is one of them. It is not because Christians are inept. It is not because they just don't get it. It is because there has been a very sophisticated and a very highly developed force against the truth, against Jesus, against righteousness, against the people of the Lord experiencing the abundant gift of life which He has made available. All this has come by the cunning powers of darkness and death.

The adversary has been enabled to rob the Lord's people of their endowment in the power of Godliness. Death does not beget life. Death begets death. Life begets life. People must be conditioned to be dead inside in order for them to kill their fellow men in war. The dead kill and bring death. The living love and bring life. So be careful how you associate death with Christ. The meaning of the death of Jesus is vastly overshadowed by the meaning of His life. His death did not enable Him to be the Creator. It was His life that generated the universe. It is too easy to focus on His death and lose sight of the vastness of the meaning of His life and the consequence of your very existence that sprang out of His life.

Now I want to talk about the second thing that has contributed to Christianity losing its power by not developing the Creatorship of Christ. First of all, and I am going to give you some different things here, almost everyone associates the "atonement" with death. And it is surprising that the word "atonement" doesn't appear in the New Testament. Isn't that amazing? Some Bible versions have it once in Romans 5:11 and that reference is Strong's #2644 in the Greek, it means *to reconcile*. It doesn't have anything to do with the real meaning of the word "atonement." In this Romans verse it was mistranslated, it should have been *to reconcile*. The word "atonement" by its very definition in the Hebrew language, or Aramaic which Jesus spoke, has nothing to do with death. It has everything to do with life. When you look up the word "atonement" it is number #3722 in your Strong's, under the Hebrew dictionary, the word "kaf-ar" means literally *to cover with bitumen*. Isn't that shocking, *to cover with bitumen*? Bitumen is a waterproofing used on cisterns and water channels. It is a pitch-like substance. The reason I am telling you this again isbecause as we go through this and talk about why Christianity hasn't developed the Creatorship of Christ, this word "atonement" and the typical Christian idea of atonement is central.

In the holy land, they had cisterns because water was hard to go get and carry. And cisterns made water available at your home. And they, most of the time, carved them out of the rock that often had fissures and cracks. And they plastered the inside of them to prevent leaks. And sometimes it was sandstone or porous material so they had to cover the interior of their water cisterns with bitumen. And they had to have an atoner, one who did it as a trade, to come periodically. And he had to cause their cisterns to hold water. So the atonement actually means to waterproof something.

So where did this concept of atonement being associated with death come from? It comes directly from the Old Testament, Leviticus 17:11. This scripture catapulted the atonement being blood into the New Testament with those of the Gentile Mission, with no validity whatsoever. And it has no valid association with Jesus's death. I am going to read it. This is part of the Babylonian law that proceeded from Aaron the idol maker's time. *"For the life of the flesh is in the blood and I have given it to you upon the altar to make an atonement for your souls. For it is the blood that maketh an atonement for the soul."* That verse put the idea of the atonement into the category of death and blood. It is purely a Babylonian concept to cover your spirit with blood. Could blood really waterproof your soul? If it was supposed to apply to Christ, why does the word not appear in the New Testament? And why did Jesus not ever even allude to it being blood if it was central to His mission?

Actually He did clearly speak of it with its real definition of being to cause one to hold the living water. Remember He said in John 4:14, *"But whosoever drinketh of the water that I shall give him shall never thirst but the water that I shall give him shall be in him a well of water springing up into the everlasting life."* When this Old Testament concept was brought into the New Testament theology, something or somebody had to die and spill blood for atonement for their souls. But the real meaning actually is to prepare your life and soul to hold the living water. And the Son of God has as His central mission of salvation **to reprove you** and **forgive you** and bring into you His Spirit for you to feel forgiven when you **repent**, which is the condition that will allow you to hold the living water, or *to spiritually cover you with bitumen*. And this new life is being born again, you are a changed person and you will never thirst again and be desperate to feel His love and forgiveness. I personally don't long for what the living water feels because by Him it is always with me.

And so remember this when we continue here today, that the atonement is talking about Jesus's ability to spiritually condition your life through reproval, repentance and forgiveness, so that you can hold in your soul the refreshing, restoring, reviving wonder of utterly pure, cool Living Water. Concepts of death and blood are the first things that began to dilute the Christian spiritual power that comes from living the Creatorship of Christ. This idea has intruded upon the Lord's people springing forth out of the Gentile Mission's attempt to make the gospel compatible with those who had a long history of worshipping pagan gods that required death.

The second concept that rendered Christianity powerless to minister, like Jesus did in His healing ministry and of raising the dead, probably began during the time of the Maccabees and was carried over into Christianity. The temple religion changed the definition of righteousness. **Righteousness** is going to be my topic for today. Never have you heard something so central to your empowerment. Never will you consider anything so capable of endowing you as what I am going to teach and describe to you today. Those in the temple religion changed the definition of righteousness to be keeping the Levitical law. When you look it up in the dictionary this definition still stands, any I have found anyway. The one that I looked up says the definition of righteousness is *"to act in accordance with divine or moral law."* But when you look up righteousness in the Hebrew part of Strong's which represents biblical Hebrew, #6663 the word "zedek" means *to be right.* That's it, *to be right,* nothing to do with keeping the law.

So there are these parallel perspectives in your Bible that keep showing up that we have discovered, all the way through this series. Righteousness is either 1) to act in concert with divine or

227

moral law or 2) righteousness is a feeling expressing a right relationship with the life that Creator Jesus put into all things. When you look up #6663, you will also find that "zedek" also means *to cleanse or clear yourself, to turn to righteousness*, and *to do that which is altogether just.* **The idea or concept of righteousness originated long before the concept of law arose in Babylon.** The Lord told Noah that he was righteous in Genesis 7:1 long before any concept of law. In Matthew 23:35, the Lord Himself called Abel, Adam and Eve's son, righteous. What Pharisee would claim any of their law originated with our first parents? With righteousness diminished and done away with, Jesus' Creatorship is lost to Christianity. Without righteousness being *to be right* in all your relationships, a major awareness of religious expression was denied to the Lord's people.

Let me say a few words to help you understand how such a powerful concept as righteousness could be lost to Christianity. The Hebrews didn't, and in fact couldn't, write about it in any other way than they did in your Bible because righteousness was embedded in their language and old culture to the extent that to them it was obvious that literally everything in their language and culture was expressing it in spite of foreign influences. They could not conceive that there was anything else. Righteousness was so obvious to them and such an overarching part of their lives that they could not grasp that any person would not be fully aware of it.

Ok let's now talk about how to retrieve it. How do you gain an understanding of righteousness? What is the Biblical evidence to show us what it really is? What was Jesus's definition of it, and that of the early church and the old Hebrew culture? What did they have for a definition? First of all, Jesus's central quality of His personality throughout the Scriptures, in prophecy, everywhere was His righteousness. Surely if righteousness was keeping the law and Christ fulfilled the prophecies proclaiming Him righteous, He and the Pharisees would have had the same definition in common. They would have embraced Him not killed Him. The Pharisees main goal in life was to attain perfect righteousness in keeping the Levitical law. Christ's main goal in life was to help us attain perfect righteousness in our **right relationships** of love for His creation and for all people, and especially with His Father. That is the correct definition. That phrase is used over and over in the New

International Bible Dictionary under the word "righteousness." They both were very intent to obtain two different definitions of righteousness. This is the war of the Torahs again. Remember Stephen in Acts 7, "*with the coming of the just one.*" Here look up the word "just" in your Greek; it will be #1342, it means *righteousness.* And in the Hebrew #6662, it means the same thing – *to be righteous.* So Stephen was really saying to the Sanhedrin "*with the coming of the righteous one.*" I think the Sanhedrin was very aware of the two different definitions and were further enraged by this comment because their very issue with Jesus was that He was not keeping the law, especially the law of the imposed Torah.

Here is some evidence supporting the real definition. In Isaiah 53:11, Jesus is called "*the righteous servant.*" I'm telling you these things to establish for you the idea that Jesus' central virtue is righteousness. In Hebrews 7, Jesus is a high priest after the order of Melchizedek. In the word Mel-chiz-zedek, "zedek" is *righteousness.* Melchizedek means *that which rules over me is righteousness* or *my king is righteousness.* So Jesus's priesthood is defined by righteousness. The ultimate holy expression of priesthood is defined by righteousness. In Isaiah 61:3, the people of Messiah are called trees of righteousness. Ok, how do you get trees to keep the law? In Isaiah 11:5, Jesus is clothed in righteousness. Are you clothed by keeping the Levitical law? In I John 3:10, "*whosoever **doth** not righteousness is not of God.*" This statement demonstrates that righteousness was central to the early church's concept of salvation. Why would Jesus exhort people to be righteous if He knew He would be righteous for them, as it is indicated in Romans 4:5-6 and Philippians 3:9?

In the Gospel of John 16:8-10, Christ says He will "*reprove the world of righteousness, because they see me no more.*" None of those things have to do with keeping the Levitical law. This is a vital verse to understanding His definition of righteousness. He is saying He will reprove them for the kind of relationship they have with Him when He is gone. It is one thing for you to have a *right relationship* with Him when He is present, but another when He cannot be seen and one has to rely completely on His Spirit for that relationship with Him.

229

"Blessed are they who hunger and thirst after righteousness for they shall be filled." How do you hunger and thirst after keeping the law? And what would you be filled with? I hunger and thirst after a *right relationship* with the Spirit of life that the Lord put into all things and I am filled with His Spirit. Hungering and thirsting is not just a craving. It is what you have to do to live. And so do you have to keep the Levitical law to live? I am not saying we do not have to keep any law. Here in community, keeping the law of virtue is vital for us to maintain harmony together. Our principle law is found in the Bible and in the Community Rule written by the early church. But I am saying that it is not righteousness. Does your gift of life depend on keeping a law or does it depend on your close walk with The Man, Jesus, the Creator, the Lovely One of God? To have life more abundantly depends on you having the **right relationship** with your Creator and **being right** with the spirits of life that Jesus put into all things as He said, I came down from heaven to give life to the universe. Don't we all hunger and thirst after that? How does one get clothed with keeping the Levitical law?

On the other hand, when you are wrapped up in, and surrounded with the right relationships with the Lord and His people and His creation, you could easily say you are clothed with righteousness spiritually and physically. I will speak of this more in a moment. Here is something that would be good for you to understand. According to the way righteousness is expressed in Scripture, both in the Old Testament and the New, it becomes clear that the Lord's view of righteousness is to have a right relationship: first, with His Father and with Him, and second, with your neighbor and all creation.

Enter "the other guy." As the leadership of the Gentile Mission became more mature in their ability to appeal to the Gentiles, they did not of course embrace Jesus' definition of righteousness being *to be right* in all of your relationships, and they also abandoned its meaning to be keeping the law of virtue because, as you all well know, they openly required people to do away with the law. So there was no righteousness under either definition in the Gentile Mission.

This matter of the law became very complicated by the time it was dealt with by the Gentile Mission. Jesus did not teach the early church to do away with the law of virtue and love, but the law for those in the Gentile Mission was not the Law of Moses, it was the law of Aaron that sprang out of Babylon. So the law of Aaron should have been done away with long before Jesus' ministry or the Gentile Mission. Jesus spoke dismissively of the law of Aaron. Christians can rightly sense that they shouldn't be trying to keep the Levitical law from their Bible's Old Testament. And while the Law of Moses can largely be found interspersed in the Old Testament and also in the New, it is difficult to separate the two. On top of this, Gentiles felt that they had no business keeping any "Jewish law." Separating the Law of Moses (law of virtue) from the law of Aaron in your Bible is a difficult undertaking. Jesus knew this, so He remedied it for us. He quoted the *shema*, or that is the First and Second Commandments found in Deuteronomy 6:4-9 and He said that, "*on this hang all the law and the prophets.*" So by keeping the First and Second Commandments of love and virtue, you are founded on the very basics of the law of love and you are firmly worshiping the One True God of the prophets. With this we find it easier to separate out the two laws.

And as if all this were not enough, they declared and promoted openly that no one needed to be righteous. Jesus would be righteous for you. And how one could lay claim to the righteousness He had in your behalf was to believe in His blood which was called an atonement. So the whole idea of righteousness became so convoluted that the entire central characteristic of the personality and ministry of the Lord was lost to Christianity. And in this way, "the other guy" stripped the church of its power. Just what you would expect him to do and he has done it right under their noses, because the Scriptures are utterly full of information otherwise about righteousness. It is out of a deep sense of love for the people of the Lord that I have embarked on telling you these things.

Then to recap a bit and to continue on: let me ask once again, how does a tree keep the law if the righteous are called trees of righteousness? What does not seeing Jesus have to do with not keeping the law? And how will the skies pour down keeping the law as it say in Isaiah 45:8? So throughout your scriptures the real definition runs counter to what the Pharisees did with their compromising the concept of righteousness.

Now having said all this, the definition of having the right relationship with the life that Jesus put into all things emerges. And this is completely obscure to Christianity. When I begin to uncover this to you, you are going to be surprised, because now I am going to show you some nuts and bolts of the evidence for it in your Bible. So your Bible is yet your greatest treasure because in it is the truth about righteousness from cover to cover. In fact the Bible is so filled with the correct definition of righteousness that the powers that sought to destroy it could not remove it. They would have had to do away with the entire Bible in order to remove it, which, of course, for many that has been accomplished.

So this concerted effort has been very effective because there are many miracles and great healings and such expressions of spiritual power that are gone in Christianity because the power that produces them through Christ in righteousness is gone in the Christian experience. They don't raise the dead anymore; they don't heal the blind and the deaf. With the loss of righteousness, Christianity has been effectively neutralized - sidelined. Think of what an unstoppable surge would occur in the religion of Jesus, in view of the severe world need, if such powers of love, forgiveness and healing were to be expressed today in the way He expected us to do it. And don't be influenced that it is foolhardy to think such power could be in place today.

Now one of the things that added to this loss is sometimes some authors in the New Testament, who were unfamiliar with Jesus' example and teachings, started ideas that fought against righteousness. In Romans in the first three chapters, there is lengthy discussion about righteousness. And one of the things it says is "*sin cometh by the law for where there is no law there is no sin.*" If there isn't someone to say it is wrong, it's not wrong. So the law to author of Romans is the source of evil and sin. There are other places that talk about the same thing. There is one place that says "*that by one comes the free gift to all.*" That is of course what I alluded to earlier about how Christ's righteousness is passed on to all believers of His blood so no one any longer needs to be righteous. What they are saying is only Jesus has to be righteous.

So just what do you find in the Bible when you look, and you really study, and you find out about the righteousness of Jesus and how it was expressed by Him? I am going to talk to you about this and this is very exciting to me. This is one of the biggest blessings that I can ever share with you. So to help you understand where we are going to go here, I want to help you with some knowledge of the Hebrew language. The Hebrew language is a righteous language. What I mean by that is the Hebrew language defines the feelings that are the essence of the spirit of life that Jesus put into things when He gave them life as their Creator. The language in many cases actually defines the feeling of that life, making it possible for you to consciously have the right relationship with it.

In ancient times, maybe not as ancient as some would like to think, the Hebrew language, which I think reflects the original human language, had a way of expressing things that would be very shocking to you. Their word for *strong* is "ayil." It also means *oak tree*. In the ancient times they would look to describe someone and say, "my, he is certainly oak. He has the right relationship with an oak tree." They could have said that because that was a word for strong.

So the Hebrew language, when you look far back, has righteousness deeply embedded in it and, because of that, it is also in the Hebrew culture. And I think that Jesus was born a Hebrew for that reason, He is the prince of righteousness. I don't think He was born a Hebrew because God had racial preference for them. I think He had chosen them because they had a connection and a culture and a language that expressed a *right relationship* with Him, and a connection that was righteousness in its purest expression. Remember righteousness is *to be right in all your relationships*.

So now this is a really fun exercise for me. It may be a little bit of a surprise for many of you. I am going to open up to you the righteousness of Jesus as specifically expressed in your Bible; just a little glimpse of what He did and what His life was like. I am limited by time here but you can study this out for yourselves and add to this. I could spend a lot of time giving you examples if I had it but I will do what I can. So here we go. Jesus said I am the living bread come down from heaven. I am the bread of life. Where would one expect the living bread to be born? In Bethlehem. What does Bethlehem mean? It is Hebrew # 1035 and it means *the house of bread.* He had a right relationship with the place He was born. The word bread is "lechem." It is #3899, *bread,* which comes from #3898, and it means to *overcome and to prevail* and to *consume.* It even has meaning *to fight.* All these meanings are precisely what this little baby Bread of Life, was born to do: to consume human sin and to overcome it and prevail with salvation. His mission in life was expressed by the feelings of the town He was born in. It was the *right relationship.* Isn't that amazing? There is more.

There was a good Christian gentleman named Farrar who was a scholar of the Bible and who wrote in the 1800s. In the late 1870s and in the early 1880s, he went to the holy land. And at the time he went there, there were no cars or roads, only foot paths in Israel. And he spent three and a half years retracing and duplicating what he saw to be Christ's travels in His ministry as found in the Bible. He actually traveled in the pattern stated in the Bible as best he could. He found that Nain was 20 miles away from Jerusalem. And Christ got up in the morning and walked from Jerusalem to Nain and arrived just before noon. That shows that Jesus was a great walker - 20 miles before noon. Farrar's information is valuable just for things like that. He wrote a book called The Life of Christ. So this man Farrar did this. I would recommend it for good reading. It is still available. Some of the things he found were typically very informative. He really liked to go to the inns because Christ's parents went to an inn and found no room there. So he spends a lot of time describing inns, and he found that typically most often the manger was an old kneading trough that they had worn out kneading bread. Then they would use it as a feeding trough or manger. It was a hollowed out wooden piece. So was the Bread of Life born in the house of bread and laid in a kneading trough?

Now on with our information. Was the Lamb of God clothed with a wool blanket? There is a word for sheep - #7353, "rachael," which is the name of Jacob's wife, when you go back to the Paleo-Hebrew, it means to have *authority to divide good from evil.* Did the little Lamb of God have authority to divide good from evil? Wouldn't it have been fitting for the Lamb of God to wear wool? Or did they swaddle the One who had the living water to give in linen? The word for linen is "miqveh," - #4723, and it means *a pool of cleansing water.* Was this all an accident or was He clothed in righteousness? Clothed in righteousness can be wearing garments that you select for their definition of some specific spirit of life that Jesus the Creator put into that which you want to cloth you. Essenes, or those called the Nazarenes, wore linen for this reason.

Jesus fed the 5000 multiplying loafs and fishes in a place called Genesereth. It was called Galilee by the Greeks, which for them simply means *a circular road* - no meaning in Greek with righteousness. But in Hebrew it is called Genesereth, which means *the garden of plenty* according to Farrar in his book on the life of Christ written in 1879. Did Jesus have the *right relationship* with where He fed the 5000? What a place to multiply the loaves and fishes! Now multiplying loaves and fishes was also part of the element of righteousness because fishes, #1709, means *to be prolific* and *to multiply greatly* and He multiplied them greatly indeed. And He used loaves and fishes three times. He used them to feed the 4000 and the 5000, and He used it again after His resurrection on the sea shore. And again, the bread is *to overcome and prevail.* So when He multiplied loaves and fishes, to be right with that element was to help these people to multiply and be prolific in their ability to know God and to overcome and prevail in their struggles to stand clean before the Lord – bread and fish.

Ok, now He went to Nain. This story is in Luke 7:11. In the account that Farrar relates in his book, as you approach the city you have to climb up a hill on a rocky path. The city is on top, so one emerges rather suddenly from the path coming up into the town at the gate. Jesus got up on top just as a procession of a funeral was going by. And Jesus walked out and stood in front of them and He held out His hand and He touched the bier, which is very bold because anybody who touches the dead is unclean, especially for Essenes. It is also unthinkable to interfere in this way with a funeral. Jesus had compassion on the mother and He raised the young man from the dead. And his widowed mother was following along behind sobbing because it was her only son and support. And the Lord raised him from the dead and sent him safely home to dwell with his mother. The word "Nain," #4999 in your Strong's, means *to dwell happily at home.* Did Jesus fulfill the meaning of every town He had association with? How would one, who does not know about *being right,* deal with these extraordinary convergences

235

between meaning and behavior? Are you starting to get it? This is not mysticism. Was Jesus right in His relationship with the city of Nain or was it just by chance that He arrived at that perfect moment and enacted meaning of the spiritual life that gave the city its' name?

One thing is certain; Jesus' rightness with the spirit of life in His environment was critical to His spiritual power and was central to the lad being raised from the dead. Do you think I am crazy? Is your first impression that you could never *be right* in the same sense in your lives? Let's keep going. There was not any detail too small for Christ to be right with the spirit of life in something in creation. Matthew 9:20 says that a woman touched the hem of His garment to be healed. What did He say? He said who touched me? His disciples thought that was a strange thing to say when He was in the press of the crowd. And He said, "*I perceive virtue has gone forth out of me.*" Look up the word "hem" - #7757 - and you get *skirt*. Look up skirt in the English and you find #3671. You follow that word to the root word #3670 "carath," which mean *to go forth out of, to withdraw.* He was in harmony; He was right with even the hem of His garment. Nothing was too small. He is the Prince of righteousness. He is my Hero.

He raised Lazarus from the dead. The word "Lazarus," #499 in Hebrew, means *God is my helper.* Jesus said to his friend Lazarus, I will help you; "*come forth.*" In Mark 2:1-4, they let a man down on ropes from the roof into the midst of the house to be healed. I always thought when I was a little lad that they had to make a hole in the roof. It was so crowded they couldn't get in, so they had to break up the roof, and I was thinking how did they do that without dropping stuff on those below? Their roofs were covered with dirt. Jesus is in there trying to talk. They are letting this guy down from the roof. The word "roof" is #1342, "gah-ah." What did He say to the guy? "*Raise up, take up thy bed and walk.*" Gah-ah means *to be raised up.* He was aware of the spirit of life even with the roof that brought Him a man desperate to be healed by those who loved him so much that they broke up the roof of one of their neighbors. I'm sure they had to go back and repair it later. The people that participated and saw these things all knew that the old definition of righteousness was being presented to them anew. The people of the early church, the Essenes, were completely aware of the spiritual power that comes from righteousness and they lived it every day in both their religion and their Hebrew culture. They had the same struggles as you. They had to find a way to create and maintain a way of life separate from the evils of their world.

Now can you see why those of the early church were so alarmed and dismayed when the Pharisees changed the definition and more especially when those of the Gentile Mission completely took it **out** of church belief? They saw it as disastrous and a frightful affront to Jesus' entire mission. And many of them lamented these diversions from the truth. Here again comes into play problems those engaged in the Gentile Mission were confronted with. The Gentiles had no concept of their God placing a living Spirit of love in their natural environment, one that was identifiable and could be interacted with. Their ideas of creation simply did not include such imagery. They only interacted religiously with those spirits of death in the occult. And I think those of the early church who were scattered, when they heard reports of the Christians being eaten by lions in Rome, would have attributed it to the loss of spiritual power that resulted from doing away completely with righteousness. And the persecuted Christians thought why can't God protect us?

Do not be fooled; a major rift between Jesus and the Pharisees was the difference in their definition of righteousness. They wanted to kill Christ for healing on the Sabbath. That can only mean that for them keeping the Levitical law is more important than being right with the spirit of life that is put into creation to heal and bring life and happiness, which is a very sad narrative. One thing that tells you that the definition of righteousness is not keeping the Levitical law is what Christ said, "*If your righteousness does not exceed the righteousness of the Pharisees ye shall **in no case** enter into the kingdom of heaven.*" The Pharisees were absolutely fanatic about keeping the Levitical law. They were fearfully urgent to uphold and sustain their view of righteousness in light of the public's acceptance of the dynamic nature of Christ's ministry. It was increasingly hard for them to counter it in public with living examples extolling the ancient righteousness. And the threat was magnified by support written in the prophets, especially in David's writings.

Now I want to tell you a fantastic story. It illustrates that not only Jesus knew what He was doing by being right with the life in all things, but also that the multitudes of people were keenly aware of what was going on with righteous Jesus. It was, after all, the Hebrew culture, even if much of it had been lost to Hellenization. I am going to read you six verses from Matthew 21:6-11. This is the account of His entry into Jerusalem. This is a real good illustration of the righteous use of element. When I speak about use of element, I am talking about *being right* by using the material substance in creation that relates to the spirit of life that was given it in creation by Jesus to perform a specific task of blessing and love. Adding that spirit of life, and using it in acts of worship, and blending that spirit of life in what you are doing in love and compassion, say in the context of healing a blind man, joins your love and compassion to the love and compassion that gave that particular element life; and the power of Jesus is expressed through you, because you are in a right love relationship. In this reading you will see an example of the righteous use of element. So we are going to analyze the use of element during Jesus's entry into Jerusalem.

*"And the disciples went and did as Jesus commanded them. And brought the ass **and** the colt and put on them their clothes and they set him thereon. And a very great multitude spread their **garments** in the way; others cut down **branches** from the trees and **strewed them** in the way."* You find out in John that they were branches of palm trees. *"And the multitude that went before and that followed,"* before Him and after Him, *"cried saying Hosanna to the Son of David; blessed is He that cometh in the name of the Lord, Hosanna in the highest. And when He was come into Jerusalem all the city was moved saying who is this? And the multitude said this is Jesus the prophet of Nazareth of Galilee."*

None of the element used in this reading is accidental. The multitude was celebrating the return of the old form of righteousness and the raising of Lazarus. And as I said, this is a moment seen as very threatening by the establishment and their dependence on the Levitical law. So let us analyze this a little bit. They put clothes on the colt and strewed them in the way on the ground for Him and those with Him to walk on. It was their "garments," which is the Hebrew word "ad-deh-reth" #155, which

238

is related to #117 which means something is *lordly, worthy, glorious, gracious,* and *powerful.* No wonder all the city was moved and said, who is this? They wondered who is being represented as Lordly, worthy, glorious and powerful. Usually only foreign heads of state are treated in this manner. Jesus both sat on clothes and His donkey walked on them. In this case garments were being used as the element of righteousness expressly for the spirit of life that the Lord put in them.

And they cut down palm branches. John 12:13 tells you they were palm branches. Palm trees in the Paleo-Hebrew *means to rise up and look we have found and identified the living water.* Palm trees exude the feelings of praise. Did the spirit of life Jesus gave the palm trees join with the spirits and voices and feelings of the rejoicing multitude crying hosanna in the highest? Did that joining magnify the power of that moment when man and creation acted in concert? Certainly it did. That is how all His miracles worked. Blessed is he who comes in the name of the Lord, we have found and identified the Living Water. The palm trees and the people were speaking and acting in unison.

Donkey or ass is #2543, "kam-ore;" go to the root word, #2560, *to cover with bitumen.* Here comes the One who is Lordly, worthy, glorious and powerful Who can give you the living water. He can cover you with bitumen. The reason is because donkeys were humble and seen to be associated with those who are repentant – thus the supporters of the living water. The mother, again, was brought along specifically for its definition in righteousness.

Now the colt. Jesus could have ridden the mother. And the mother didn't have to go with them as the colt was big enough to ride on. So He brought them both on purpose. Colt, #5895, goes to #5782, which means *to openly present yourself.* Jesus was openly presenting Himself to the public. The ancient righteousness was restored to the Hebrew public by John the Baptist. We will maybe speak of John later. Remember John was first to come and restore all things? And the One who has the living water is openly presenting Himself. This is what riding on the colt with garments under Him meant. All this can't be just a coincidence. Jesus' whole life was like this. He is the Prince of righteousness. The multitude all knew what they were doing and what it all meant. And the

239

element enjoined here brought the power of God to bear in Jerusalem. They knew that palm trees felt praise. They were acting in concert with the spirit of life that made those palm trees come to life and grow and emit praise each and every day.

The multitudes were right with all those elements as was Jesus. They knew what it meant, as did the temple leaders, for Him to be sitting on garments and for His donkey to be walking on their garments with palm leaves strewn in the way. Everybody could see this gracious person coming. You wouldn't just put your clothes on the ground for some donkey to walk on for nothing. They know what that was all about. They knew why He also brought the mother donkey along because part of what He intended to say with element at His entry was that He that had the living water to give, is openly presenting Himself. I believe here that Jesus had made a conscious decision to confront this matter of righteousness and the central values of His mission in His task of revealing His Father.

So to consolidate all this use of the element of righteousness with His entry into Jerusalem into a statement it would go like this: Jesus had just raised Lazarus from the dead. Lazarus was well known and the phrase many used was *"Lord by this time he stinketh."* Now this time there was no question that he was dead. Before it could be thought perhaps those Jesus had raised from the dead were just asleep, like Jairus' daughter in Luke 8:52. So this entry into Jerusalem was very deliberate. The crowds were awaiting Him. He asked for a colt. The people sang His praises specifically citing Him as a Son of David, who was universally defined as a righteous king in sharp contrast with many kings which followed, especially Solomon. The expressions of the multitude and of the element of righteousness were joined together – acting in concert. What a thrilling expression of the Hebrew culture it must have been for a public dominated by pagan Rome and subjugated by Hellenization. Those moments exuded freedom.

Jesus fed His apostles on the seashore after His resurrection with bread and fish. And as I told you before bread is *to overcome or to prevail*. And fish is *to multiply greatly*. He said, *"feed my sheep."* Help them overcome; help them to multiply greatly. He cooked them on a fire, see John 21:9. "Fire" comes from Hebrew #216 is "owr", which means *to illuminate* and *to bring happiness* – feed my sheep, teach them, love them, bring them the happiness of salvation.

Jesus lived in Capernaum. What do you suppose Capernaum means? It is a double word, "capern annaham," #3723, # 3722 and #5151 – *to repent and be covered with bitumen*. To cover with bitumen again. The life of Jesus was interlaced with His ability to give the living water.

He turned the water into wine. "Wine," is "chamar" #2560, is *to cover with bitumen*. Are you starting to get it? The one who has living water to give turned the water into something that feels holding the living water in their soul.

And the last thing to touch His lips was vinegar, which is wine that has *run its course*. And the ability of Jesus to minister to people in the flesh had *run its course*. So even with the vinegar, He was right with the spirit of life that is in the vinegar. He was right with the spirit of life that is in the hyssop that carried the vinegar to His mouth. Hyssop, #231 when you go to the Paleo-Hebrew it feels *to be strong in providing for your kindred*. He was laying His life down to provide an example of the love of His Father in submitting to the will of man and He would raise it up again to show evidence of the same thing. Jesus put clay on the blind man's eyes and **released** him from his blindness. "Clay," meh-let in Hebrew, #4422, is *to **release** or to rescue*. Farrar says that human saliva from one who was holy or fasting was seen in the old Hebrew culture to be a primary healing agent.

Righteousness literally penetrates the life and ministry of Jesus. He went to Jericho. A man named Zacchaeus lived there. He **anticipated** the arrival of Jesus and wanted to see Him but he was short and couldn't. The word "Jericho" is #3405, from #7306 which is Hebrew "ruw-ach", which means *to joyously **anticipate** something*. He climbed a sycamore tree so he could see Jesus. The Lord said, "*Come down this day I will abide in thy house.*" While Jesus was there, people were murmuring because Zacchaeus was chief among the publicans (tax collectors) and they said, why does He stay with sinners? While Jesus was in his home, Zacchaeus confessed his sins and rehearsed his repentance to the Lord and the Lord said, "*This day hath salvation come to this house.*" The name

Zacchaeus means *to be made clean and pure*, from #2195 in Greek which is from #2141 "zakak"in the Hebrew. This story is from Luke 19:2-8. By the way, the word "sycamore," when traced back to the Paleo-Hebrew, means *to look to behold the shining light of the living water*. The living water again! I could cite example after example but I have to shorten it for today.

Do you remember Nicodemus? He was the one among the Sanhedrin who found Jesus and was born again. He was the one who they kicked out of the Sanhedrin. He brought things to help with the Lord's burial. "Nicodemus" is #3530 in the Greek and it means *to be victorious among his brethren*. Was he? He's the only one we know of amongst the Sanhedrin who was converted to the Lord. He was indeed victorious among his brethren.

It wasn't just Jesus that was righteous, John the Baptist was righteous. He was clothed with camel's hair. "Camel," from #1580, means *to ripen or bring forward*. In this case, to ripen applies to the ripening of the age. Soon Israel would be plucked up by the Romans. "Hair" is from #1802, "dalath," which means *to let down a bucket to drink water*. John the Baptist brought forward the one who could give you the living water. There it is again.

Now can you see being clothed in righteousness with this and Jesus wearing wool or linen? Now you can perhaps understand a little more hungering and thirsting after righteousness. Christians certainly should want to have a right relationship with the spirit of life their Lovely One put into that which He created. Now do you get it that your righteousness must exceed that of the Pharisees or you can in no case enter into the kingdom of heaven? He said in Matthew 9:13, *"I am not come to call the righteous but sinners to repentance."* He said in Matthew 6:33, *"Seek ye first the kingdom of God, and his righteousness; and all these things shall be added unto you."* In Matthew 21:32 Jesus says, *"John came unto you in the way of righteousness, and ye believed him not."* I John 2:29, *"Every one that doeth righteousness is born of Him."* There it is folks. This reading affirms that the greatest depth of being born again comes in the context of righteous relationships with the spirits of life. And in I John 3:10 *"Whosoever doeth not righteousness is not of God."* If Jesus is righteous for all Christians why would John say **we** must **do** righteousness?

242

Dear folks, here John is actually saying that, unless you are joined and interact with the spirits of life which He put in the elements of the world that He created, you are not of God. I cited you these references to help you see how critical the definition of righteousness is to those who walked with Jesus and from Jesus own mouth. It is something central to His behavior and ministry and foundational to the early church's spiritual power; and it was done away with by those overseeing the Gentile Mission – a sobering narrative for Christians and one that has left you stranded in the tribulation times. So, all the people surrounding Jesus in His life and in His ministry loved righteousness. This is just the surface of the biblical righteousness in the life of Christ. I just gave you enough to give you an idea.

Your Bible is filled with righteousness. It is **a right relationship** with the life Jesus put into creation which includes your fellow man. Your disadvantage with your language and culture does not lend itself to knowing how to be righteous. That is because your language, culture and religion sprang out of the Gentile Mission, not Jesus' personal example in ministry. But God knows this and He will have abundant mercy for you and tenderly love you with all His soul, and take this into account – all of His soul!

Now please know, dear folks, that I am not leading you to a dead end. You only have to be human with sensitive feelings to be righteous. **You can love the Lord and do whatever it takes to know Him, You can feel by His Spirit**. **You have intelligence and intuition** and you can **know the effects of elements**; those four essential things can enable you to be righteous.

Let me explain a little. You can feel. Have you ever been grieving or troubled and gone outside and stood with a gentle wind blowing on your tear stained face and felt comforted? You can feel that. That is righteousness. You don't have to know the Hebrew word for wind, "nesha-mah," means *the breath of God;* you can feel it yourself. Your soul knows. The breath of God is comforting you.   Have you ever felt the joy that a flower has to be picked by some little feminine hand? That moment of fulfillment for the flower is more important to it than remaining on the stem. Your soul knows.

243

The effect something has is also a way of knowing in a general sense and by intuition. Long needle pines, when made into a tea to soak your feet in, can heal your feet from smelling. That can alert you that pine has something to do with *walking in holiness*. Often the effect healing herbs have indicates the nature of the spirit of life that the Lord put in them and calls you to repentance to align yourself with those feelings to be helped by them. Underlying all this is an all-encompassing love for Jesus in your soul.

For those of you that look at life through eyes of humility and love, righteousness is natural for you to feel and participate in. So it is incumbent on you to do what you can. Study the Hebrew language and its righteous definitions. You are just as able to be righteous in your natural environment as Jesus was in His. Some of you who do not have palm trees have some other tree that feels **praise**: cottonwood or aspen or trees that have leaves that wave and flutter in the wind like a rejoicing person with upraised hands.

Now let's move on. Out your window is a tree. I hope anyone listening can look out their window and see a tree. The tree loves you. A Man made that tree; a Man with a mother who knows what it is like to love and be human. A Man made the wind that blows on that tree. A tree in Hebrew is #353 from #352, "eylown" and sometimes "ayil," it means *to be strong*. To be strong is an expression of how much you are loved. The tree always feels that you are loved by God and it is calling you to be strong in your holiness; it is a voice of repentance that lifts and encourages. A Man made the tree and the wind and the wood that is in this building, the hill you are setting on, the ears you're hearing with, the body you live in. A Man made it. Jesus said God is a Spirit. God who is a Spirit didn't make the tree. He made the spirit that lives in the tree and Jesus made the tree for that spirit to live in. He sent His Son to be the Creator - to give element form. So a Man who loves you created it. One who understands all you go through when you are worn down and discouraged and feels with you all that you feel, a Man who had brothers and sisters like you do; He had to be strong to go where He needed to go. Because a Man who loves you built His love into that tree, the tree loves you - identifiably, purposefully, loves you – *so be strong*. Do your repentance. It gives you oxygen to breath, shade, fruit, wood, sap for syrup; and things expressing love too numerous to cite. Trees love you in so many ways.

Here is another instance, the word for "almond" means *to be ever wakeful* or *to see.* According to the idea that Hebrew indicates a spiritual definition, the feeling of seeing and the dynamic of seeing is the very spirit of life Jesus put in the almond tree. It is the cause of the miracle of an almond nut germinating and becoming a tree. I will tell you of a healing later. It could be said therefore that the almond tree is filled with the spirit of life from Christ that is the spirit of seeing with your eyes. So the spirit of life that gives you almonds to eat and makes little nuts grow into trees and produce fruit is a feeling born in Jesus' heart that has to do with seeing.

Everything in creation is like that. And the Hebrew language will give you many, many such definitions of the spirits of life. It actually is a very fun undertaking to investigate it and search out these things. Get yourself a Strong's Concordance of the Bible and if you can also a book by Jeff Benner titled <u>Ancient Hebrew Language and Alphabet</u>. Each and every form that element has taken was made to express some specific aspect of Jesus' love for you, and to give you life. This knowledge has been hidden from Christianity. And righteousness is the way for you to express your salvation here in this life. So many Christians think that they can't know if they have salvation or not until after they die. There is another group that thinks that they have salvation in this life but salvation for the majority only applies to them after they die. They believe they will go to heaven. Salvation, for them, is going to heaven. Many hold that this life is a prison to escape from.

Christ said I come that you may have life and have it more abundantly – here. Righteousness is how one experiences salvation in this life. It is impossible for any Christian community to establish the new covenant without righteousness. This is the new covenant, Jeremiah 31:31-34 *"Behold, the days come, saith the LORD, that I will make a new covenant with the house of Israel, and with the house of Judah: Not according to the covenant that I made with their fathers in the day that I took them by the hand to bring them out of the land of Egypt; which my covenant they brake, although I was an husband unto them, saith the LORD:*

*But this shall be the covenant that I will make with the house of Israel; After those days, saith the LORD, **I will put my law in their inward parts, and write it in their hearts; and will be their God, and they shall be my people.** And they shall teach no more every man his neighbour, and every man his brother, saying, Know the LORD: for they shall all know me, from the least of them unto the greatest of them, saith the LORD: for I will forgive their iniquity, and I will remember their sin no more."*

For every person to know the Lord for themselves and not have to depend on someone else to know Him for them is the new covenant. You have to be right with the spirits of life that He put into your world in order to experience the immensity of His love for you and be joined in your life with His life and know Him for yourself. You don't have to know them all at once. That doesn't mean you can only have the right relationship with things that are holy, you can have a right relationship with something that is not holy by having nothing to do with it. You can have a right relationship with pornography by not having anything to do with it, even to not think about it. That is the right relationship. Those right relationships cause one to be filled with the spirit and presence of Jesus' Father. It is the spirit of life Jesus put into creation that joins you to His Father, hence His definition of salvation. It is repentance that joins you to Jesus. It is the essence of both where you are going and Who is going with you. And so, when Christ said that God is a Spirit in John 4:24, He was demonstrating the importance of Who sent Him. Remember how many times He said "He sent me?" He said this to demonstrate for us who His Father was and is. And the Spirit of His Father is one of the spirits He put into all things that transformed into our temporal world.

Jesus says, I am the door. "Door," is Strong's # 1817 from #1802, "galaw," *to let down a bucket to draw out water* - the Living Water again, to cover with bitumen. He is the Good Shepherd. The word "good" is #2896, and the word "shepherd" is #7462, which together means *to associate with as a friend in loving kindness.* Boy I hope you are listening folks. **Here is your Man.** He is the one who will help you climb out of the abyss of the tribulation times. The Christian holocaust is now underway. You need to allow Him to associate with you as your friend in loving kindness. You're to let your Good Shepherd guide you and lead

246

you. And He is in all of the holy elements of creation for you to interact with. And I will explain more about any exceptions in our next session. He is there to love you. He is there to empower you and give you strength. Above all things, He is there to guide you in your daily walk with His Holy Spirit, so that you can experience His love for you in element - in the wind, the clouds, a mountain, or a sweet river of water or in the smile of the person beside you. And people do this in a very limited way when they don't know what righteousness is and how to be righteous.

I want to tell you a story about a tree that loved me. I have lots of stories like it but this one I want to tell you about happened when I was a sophomore in high school and it is a good illustration of the living spirit of life in a tree. I had to take a short cut through the woods to get to school rather than going a long way around; this was on the Oregon coast in a town called Cloverdale. And there was a jersey bull in that pasture and I had to watch because if he came I had to run. And I could out run him when I was that age. And sometimes I'd have to jump the fence because the bull was right behind me and I would tear my clothes and get into trouble when I came home. But normally I just had to walk. And this time when I was walking there were 6 or 8 inches of new snow on the ground. And as I walked in a straight line, off to one side was a big alder tree. It was probably two feet or more on the stump. They get really big out there. And as I went by this tree, as I approached to go by it, it was afraid. I felt it clearly. And I stopped when I got right by it and I thought, "What is the matter with that tree?" It was afraid; it felt "don't get near me." I could feel that feeling, not hear words, I just felt it so strong it may as well been words.

So I turned from my straight trail and walked slowly toward the tree. My tracks were like a T. And I turned at a right angle and I walked toward this tree. And as I got closer and closer to this tree, the more and more alarmed the tree became. And with more urgency the tree was afraid. And I felt to not get close to this tree. So I walked up as close as 10 or 15 feet away and the feeling became so strong of alarm that I walked backwards keeping my eyes on the tree as I went, looking at the tree all the way back to my trail. And I thought, "wow, there is something so strange with that tree."

247

So I went on to school. And then coming home from school that tree was laying over my footsteps in the snow, covering them completely up clear to the trail; it buried my steps, the whole line of them. Somebody had cut the tree off completely at ground level without a back cut and it was completely balanced just standing there waiting for the wind to blow it over. And the snow was hiding the cut and the sawdust, so there was no trace of it being cut. They had wedged the saw through it. The tree loved me. I could feel its love for me. It didn't want to hurt me. It knew it was going to fall right where I was. The umbrella of an alder tree is very wide and my chances of being able to outrun it in the snow were slim.

What was it about the tree that it could love me? A Man who loves me made the tree. A Man. My lovely Redeemer and Savior made the tree and the tree had feelings and could express them. What else would you expect but love when He was the One who made it and put in it a spirit of life? He came to give life to all things, remember? I could not have outrun it. His love for me in the tree saved my life. A Man who created me and my world wanted me to have the gift of life had made the tree.

When I was young my dad was a mountain hunting guide. He was for much of his life, in the Wallowa Mountains in Oregon. He had 20 square miles allotted to him by the government for exclusive hunting rights on federal land. And we had many horse trails going everywhere there. It was more than 3000 feet from the canyon rim where his cabin and corral stood down to the bottom where the hunting camp was. And this was in what is called Joseph Creek Canyon. This is going to now be a story about a large rock that loved me. In this canyon there were trails that the hunters followed in every direction, because dad had his camp in the center of the 20 square miles. And some of these trails had big cliffs beside them going straight down hundreds of feet. There where switch backs; it was mountainous country. There was one place where there was a shale slide several hundred yards long coming down on one side of the trail and immediately on the other side was a 500 foot cliff going down right beside the trail that cut back under the trail. So you could drop a rock off and not hear it hit until it came to the river. I used to go on this trail with my dad; he had 15 or 16 horses usually. And there was this great big rock, and I mean a big rock. It was probably the size of McGregor's barn, a big rock round and smooth like a big boulder, probably 60 feet wide and 80 feet tall. And it was standing at the top edge of this shale slide. It was shaped like an egg.

And every time I would ride by there with this big old 500' cliff right beside me, I would look up at this great big rock, and that rock was afraid it could fall on us. And I would say, "Dad that rock is afraid it is going to fall on us." And he would say every time, "Awe, that rock has been there a million years. It's not going anywhere." Every year that I would ride by there, I would feel that rock not wanting to fall on us. And my dad would always have the same reply. That rock has been there a million years it's not going anywhere.

So one time we had a church older youth camp down there without my dad. And when we all rode by that place, I thought "Ahah! Dad's not here, now is my chance to find out about that rock". A whole string of riders went by, and me and another guy took up the rear. And when they all had gone by, I told them to keep going to the next nearest point and wait for us. The other guy with me wanted to check out the rock too. It took them about an hour to get there. And they could see real good the whole area of the slide. While they were doing that, Dick and I started up the slide. We didn't go up directly under the rock. I just had to know why this rock was afraid it would fall on us when it had been there a million years.

So we started up; it took us more than an hour to climb up there. Shale slides are very hard to climb because they slide under your feet. It was probably half a mile. And it was hot and we were on the sunny slope. It was in July. And I arrived a few feet ahead of Dick. And when I got up there I was out of breath and hot. So I went behind the rock in the shade and leaned one hand on the rock to catch my breath. And this guy Dick was right behind me about 10 feet from the rock. And I looked up; the rock took up the whole sky and it kind of went behind me as well. And when I just touched it to lean on it, it started to move. At first I wondered if I was just dizzy from the heat and the climb but it was moving in a very slow motion. And I looked at the clouds to determine if I was just seeing things. But it was indeed moving. And Dick said, "It's moving. What did you do? Why didn't you wait for me?" And I said, "I just leaned on it a little". And this huge rock started over. And it tumbled down that shale slide end over end and over the cliff like a ski jump. And when it tumbled it shook the earth. And after it went over the cliff, all was silent for a moment and then it sounded like thunder and a cloud of dust came up above the cliff. It shattered and dammed up the river. And dead fish were everywhere. And boy was I glad we had tied our horses out of the way.

A Man made that rock, a Man who loved us. And the rock had been there a million years and my dad was right. But the rock knew it was about to fall. A strong breeze could have pushed it over on us. Horses and riders panicking on the brink of such a cliff you certainly do not want. If we had walked up underneath it, just sliding the shale away from it may have brought it down on us. We couldn't have run in the shale to get away from it. All the words for "rock" indicate the spirit of life that they have is *to protect you*. See # 4581, #5553, and #6697 in Hebrew in your Strong's Concordance. That rock was utterly filled with the spirit of protection. It just could not stand the thought of hurting us. So not only is He there to love you and protect you, He's there to love you in somebody else's behalf - His Father. He's there to magnify your spiritual power, your power to heal; your power to raise the dead.

Now I have told you two stories: one when a tree loved me and one when a rock loved a group of us. That was done without the Hebrew language or culture. The Hebrew culture can give you definitions of what the spirit of life is in many things, but definitions are not righteousness; they are rather a guide to help you be righteous. **Righteousness is when the spirit of life in you joins and acts in concert with, or shares feelings with the spirit of life Jesus put into something in creation,** which, don't forget, includes your neighbor. I felt what the spirit of life was feeling in the tree and the rock that Jesus put there.

There are four spirits of life in all things good and godly. There is the Spirit of **the Father**, the Spirit of **His Son** our Redeemer, the spirit of **why God created you,** and the **spirit of life of whatever forms** that element has taken, i.e. a rock, a tree, or your fellows, etc. I might say more about this in our last session next week. When you feel the spirit of life in element and you are right with it, you magnify the presence of Jesus in your life and

250

whatever you do you are doing in compassion and understanding as He and the angels of heaven would do.

The same thing happens with wicked people. When they use the spirit of the adversary, they magnify his presence and power in their lives. That is the opposite of righteousness. It is called wickedness. That is the very definition of wickedness and it always has been. Right now there is a wave of wicked empowerment in our world. Oh, for the day when Christ's people are empowered in righteousness. So there is the element of righteousness and the element of wickedness.

Christ is the Prince of righteousness. His spirit of life put into creation only loves, blesses, forgives, heals, and gives the gift of **life**. The spirit of the adversary only hates, curses, accuses, causes dismay, and brings **death**. So our way is clear and the path is straight. The power of Christianity lies in your experiencing and knowing Him in accordance with the spirit of **life** that He put into creation.

I am going to give you another example. I was in Arizona in a ministerial capacity. I was sitting on the porch of the Pinon Trading Post on the Navajo Reservation. And I watched a young woman go in carrying a three or four year old girl, and she had to hold the little girl's head up for her. The girl had Downs Syndrome and could not walk or talk. Somehow this young woman had heard about my ministry there and when she came out of the store she came over to me and asked if I would pray so the Lord could heal her little girl. I told her I would ask the Lord what He wanted me to do. She told me where she lived. It was a little village called Sheep's Head. I told her I knew where it was and that I would come by in a few days to tell her what I found out from the Lord. The Lord told me by His Spirit that He wanted the child's mind to be born and to do the prayers.

So, I stopped by and told them in the village. They asked me what they must do to repent and to get ready. I told them to clean up the hogan where we would be praying and in two days I would come to do the prayers. When I arrived they had cleaned up the whole village. They said they had worked all night. It was spotless. I realized how much effort they had put into it and how

251

much faith they had that the Lord would heal the child. Her name was Eugenia. So I came. I did the ceremony as they would do it in their terms of the element of righteousness. They have the one who's being prayed over sit on a prayer rug. They put cedar on coals to bless with. They held eagle feathers. Eugenia was held on her grandmother's lap the whole time.

I knew what to do. You see, I know Jesus is the Creator and that He put His feelings of immense love into what He created – **just for Eugenia.** So I anointed her with oil and called upon the Lord and expressed how wonderful their faith was. And I called the Spirit of our living Jesus from the cliffs and the sand and the sage and the clouds and the wind to come to restore Eugenia and to give birth to her mind. Up to that time, she could not even hold her head up. I felt the love of our Dear One come to this little girl with great power. Everybody felt it. I asked for the spirit of protection to come from the rock cliffs to protect what the Lord intended for this child when He created her. He did not intend for her to have Downs Syndrome. I asked for the spirit of life in the sand to distance her from evil. I asked for the spirit of life in the sagebrush to bring to her and all her own peace of mind in the Lord. I asked the wind to blow to give her breath to comfort her with a knowledge of her salvation in her later years. And I asked the clouds to look with God upon her to heal her and give birth to her mind. We were very moved and had tears of joy at the presence of the Spirit of the Lord. When I was done, Eugenia was asleep. We had a meal and I left.

A couple of days later, I stopped by and they had me sit down. Eugenia walked across the room and got up into my lap. She looked into my eyes and said, "naw-daw," which is Navajo for corn. It was her first word. She had been walking since she woke up after her ceremony. My, the Lord is so good. She was completely healed of Downs Syndrome and later went to school and was completely normal. I suppose now she is a grandmother.

So because of that healing, there was a village of Navajos that I had never met, that sent a woman to talk to me and she asked me if I would ask the Lord to heal their grandfather. He was in his 80s; he had tuberculosis and the hospital had sent him home to die. The Navajos don't like to go into a room where someone had died so if people died in hospitals, they would not go there. And I didn't know if I could do it, after all he was very old. But I know that repentance can heal, like when you read in the book of James 5:14-16, "*Is any sick among you? let him call for the elders of the church; and let them pray over him, anointing him with oil in the name of the Lord: And the prayer of faith shall save the sick, and the Lord shall raise him up; and if he have committed sins, they shall be forgiven him. Confess your faults one to another, and pray one for another, that ye may be healed. The effectual fervent prayer of a **righteous man** availeth much.*" It says, you will notice, that by the confession of their sins they will be healed.

So I asked the Lord what to do. These people were urgent. This man was alone in his village with only his oldest daughter to care for him. When someone is dying, they all go elsewhere and leave the village empty except for a caregiver. So they sent him home to die. His oldest daughter is the one who came and asked me. The people in the village where I was, unbeknownst to me, were their relatives. And they lived at the opening of Twisted Water Canyon. That is where this very old man was. I don't know the name of his village. So I went out alone to ask the Lord. The Lord said, "The people are too urgent upon me for me to heal him. If his family will rest upon their faith and are willing to give him back to me, I will heal him. If they will do that repentance, I will prolong his days." I didn't know what they would think of this. So I told her that. I said, "The Lord is telling me that if you all will trust Him and have faith in Him and be willing to give your father back to Him, He will prolong his life."

They called a meeting and it lasted several hours. Everyone came from many villages. I didn't realize he was related to so many. And they all decided together that they would do that repentance and be willing to trust the Lord and be willing to give their old father to the Lord if He wanted him now. So I stayed outside and I waited for word of the decision. I was sitting in the sand. They came out and one who could speak English spoke to me. And I didn't know what they were going to say. I didn't know but they might have said, "We don't believe like you do," or something like that. They were all strangers to me except for a few where I was staying. And they said, "We have decided to ask God to forgive us for wanting him to stay." A hard decision. They did their repentance.

So now I had to do my job. So I went over with his daughter and I didn't know what to expect at all. And we went into this little hogan with a dirt floor. And he was laying in the fetal position over against the wall. The room was empty. And he was asleep. I thought he may be dead. I didn't know. And his daughter woke him up. And he gurgled from so much fluid in his lungs. She had to keep wiping off this awful yellow stuff coming out of his mouth. And she said, "The white man is here to pray for you." The word for white man is "belagona." And he said, "How is he going to do it?" And she turned and looked at me; I could understand Navajo and I said, "I am going to do it the right way." And he knew what I meant. And I was just going to anoint him and pray like they do with cedar on the coals where he was laying. And I had a Navajo prayer rug that I brought along that they usually like to use to sit on while they are prayed over. I had used it with Eugenia. And so he started to try to get up. I said, "I can do it right here," in Navajo. And he said, "I thought you said you were going to do it the right way." So he crawled and pulled himself over to the center of the room so he could sit on the rug there facing the door to the east. He took several agonizing minutes to get there. They had a little place to put the coals on. And in my compassion for him, I kept thinking I shouldn't have said I am going to do it the right way. His daughter and I watched in agony at his effort to get himself out there and sitting up on the rug. We watched as he was having such a hard time inching his way over to this prayer rug. Both of us were crying, we felt so much love for him. And finally he got himself over there and he got himself sitting up, and he sat there with his head drooping down, having barely made it. He held his eagle feathers and I put cedar on the coals and fanned the smoke on him with his feathers. I used the element of righteousness in the way they do.

And as I began to pray, I anointed him with oil. I called God the Navajo name for Jesus —which is Degin een Linii, which means *Jesus who is in all things*. He knew exactly what that meant. I began to ask the Spirit of Jesus to come to him from the life that was all around this wonderful old man. The family had previously showed me a row of graves spanning thirteen generations of their family. They were all graves of generations of grandmothers. That is how long his family had lived in that village.

This was about 50 years ago now. He was born there and he herded his sheep there as a little boy and raised his family in that place and everything there felt the spirit of life Jesus had put in all that was there for him. The hills, sand, cliffs, grass, the washes all knew him and the life Jesus had given him. And everything around him knew the desires of Jesus in His heart for this man to have his life prolonged.

So as I prayed, I invited the living Spirit of Jesus to come to bring him life. And I could feel it coming from all the life around me: from the sand, the hills, rocks, clouds – from everything. In addition to what I told you I had asked for with Eugenia, I asked the spirit Jesus put into the hills to give His feet more years to walk on them. I asked the spirit Jesus put into the grass to cleanse him of his sickness. I asked the spirit Jesus put into the streams in the washes to cleanse his spirit of any uncleanness and I asked the clouds to look with God upon him to love him and to acknowledge the repentance of the family he had fathered and taught to love His Lord. And when I was done, he just tipped over and went back to sleep. And I didn't know what had happened. I just knew that the spirit of life Jesus put into all of our natural surroundings came with great power. So did his daughter.

A couple days later, I was playing volleyball with a bunch of youth up in Twisted Water Canyon and somebody hit the ball down into the wash and I went down there to get it. And as I came up out of that wash, my eyes were level with the ground and I could see across the ground a long ways off. I could see a cloud of dust coming our way. So we kept playing and I kept watching it. And pretty soon, I could see it was a horse and a rider. And soon this guy came galloping up on this horse and, before the horse even stopped, he jumped off and they both kind of bounced on the ground together. The horse bounced to a stop because the man was off. And he whipped his lines around a tree and said, "Where is the food?" I said to the guy beside me, "Who is that?" And he said, "That is grandpa, who you prayed for a couple days ago." Everybody knew he was healed except for me. He lived 5 more years. I don't know what he ended up dying from but they said it wasn't tuberculosis. Folks, here is your Man, the Man of love, your Creator – Jesus the Nazarene, the One who can empower you to raise the dead.

Now I have shared these very sacred experiences with you. I don't like to share such things with those whom I am not intimately acquainted with. It feels braggy to me, but the Lord has impressed upon me by His Spirit that you hearing these testimonies is more important to you and to Him than what anyone thinks of me. The Lord did all that I have told you. I am baring my soul to you so that you can choose to find your endowment with Christ-like power. The Lord and His loved ones are the only ones who benefits when He has His people blessed.

So I am going to tell you another story. This story is one where I was only marginally involved and it is a good example because it shows you that you can really be empowered also by the Lord as your Creator. Some time ago, a couple who lived in Michigan came to see me. The wife worked in a day care center. At her work was a little blind black boy, who was three or four years old. He was born blind. This woman loved this little boy. And she asked me if I could give her any advice as to how he might be healed. She said she could not pray for him at work because the building was financed with Federal money and no prayers were allowed in the building. I gave her some almond blossoms. The word for "almond" in Hebrew is #8247, from the root word #8245, "sha-ked," *to be awake, on the lookout, to watch*. The spirit of Jesus that gives almonds their life is that of *seeing*. I told her how to use them and to look for a time when she could pray for this little son.

One day not long after that, the mother had car trouble and asked the woman to take her son to her house and she would pick him up there, as they would close the day care center at a certain time. When she brought the boy home, she had her chance to do her prayers using the element of righteousness. She used it very simply. The little boy just held it in his hand. She did it and the mother came and picked up her son. That was on a Friday. On Monday when the woman went to work, she saw the boy sitting on the floor in a gymnasium. He pointed across the room and said, "I want one of those." She picked him up and carried him across the room and she said, "What is it you want?" He pointed to a blue ball and said, "I want that." She embraced him with many tears. The doctors said for some reason he began to see. He could see colors and movement and shapes. His sight got better and better. This woman related to me that when she prayed she felt the Spirit of the Lord come to this little boy from absolutely everywhere but especially from the spirit of life in the almond blossoms.

Jesus, the Man, is there in creation to help you, to love who you love, and to empower you through your repentance. And it is in the form of righteousness when you are right with His Spirit of life in element. Jesus is the Creator. He is the Prince of righteousness, compassion, healing, forgiveness and life. Without love and repentance, now listen carefully folks, the use of element can drift into New Age or something worse. Repentance is the guiding principal for all the use of element of righteousness for Christians.

Now there are hundreds of definitions of the spirits of life Christ put into the things in creation. Folks, are you listening? Do you realize what I am telling you? I am telling you **how** to heal the sick and the disabled and how to raise the dead. This is not pretend. You must in no uncertain terms come into a close daily walk with the Man, Jesus. You must do your repentance before Him and discern what He wants and what He is feeling and also His view on any given thing. Then you can *be right* with Him and the life He put into the things that bring healing and life. You can't just have it because you want it. You have to walk in what is called **perfection of way**. *"Be ye perfect as my Father in heaven is perfect."* How you do that is you become very familiar and comfortable with repentance. You actually learn to love repentance. Repent for any thought that the Spirit is not with in your mind. Be continually willing to be humble and to repent before the Lord, so as to stay in constant harmony with His Spirit: only love, only bless, and be thankful.

Real repentance is not brow-beating yourself. Repentance is joyous because it links you to the One you love – your Redeemer. **Repentance is changing something in your life from what you have been feeling or doing to what God feels or does instead.** The adversary hates repentance and humility and virtue. He fears righteousness. He wants you to be separate and alien from the Spirit and presence of Jesus in your world. **Repentance is the highest spiritual state one can enter into**. It joins you directly to Jesus. It is the gateway to everything you were created to be. **All this must be undergirded with a real understanding of the**

character of God hence the importance of Jesus' view of His Father. Not the traditional or Levitical view expressed in so many places, but the view and perspective Jesus has of His Father. Just think, if only a handful of you do this, you can change the course of Christianity and bring it back to its rightful place of spiritual power like an unstoppable beacon or wave of love and compassion to bring salvation.

Knowing what righteousness is helps you to know where to look to feel Him, and you can feel it by His Spirit because of His grace and love for you. He knows what you are capable of. We know many definitions of righteousness. And the wind and the clouds and the rain obey us here in community, as they would anyone who is right with what they feel. And the food we eat, many times, is based on the spirit of life Christ put into what specific things we eat. So you can celebrate and be happy and rejoice when you eat any kind of squash, because every kind of squash feels something different about *celebrating and rejoicing* with the life you are given. That is the kind of thing you have that allows the spirit of life to empower you in your health and in your daily walk with Him. Search out the various meaning of the kinds of foods you eat. Plan meals to fill specific spiritual and emotional needs.

When righteousness was done away, because it was perceived and taught that only one person could be righteous, the Christian faith languished. And that also happened when righteousness was keeping the Levitical law instead of the law of love and virtue and being right with the spirits of life in creation; in short, when Jesus is not the Creator, or He is the Creator only as an abstract idea, your power is gone. I am going to read a statement to you found in the International Bible Dictionary on page 109. It reads, "*In Christian theology the atonement is the central doctrine of faith. It can properly include all that Jesus accomplished for us on the cross.*" What happened to being covered with bitumen? There is no other definition for the word "atonement" in the ancient Hebrew.

When you take the living water away from Jesus and replace it with death, you have lost Him as Creator, not theoretically, but literally you cannot be covered with bitumen. You can't connect with the living water because you don't even know that you can; that is you don't know how to connect with the life that He put into all things for you to feel with Him.

Next week in the last session of this series, I am going to do a session on how to divide the spirits of good and evil in our world: how to divide powers. Because not only do Christians need to know how to be righteous, they also need to know how to avoid evil. And in regards to righteousness, oh people, please listen to me and be diligent students of your Bible and appeal to the Comforter to teach you all things. The Lord needs you so badly to be empowered. The evil of this world is closing in on His people worldwide. We are well into the Christian holocaust and your fellow Christians and loved ones around the world are in danger. You need to be empowered with the spirit of life provided so carefully and lovingly for you by your Creator for them and for any who the Lord moves you to minister to. Thank you.

Session 11
Exhorting the Lord's people toward Empowerment
March 22, 2015

Well we have come to the last part of this series. And what is important, and what motivated this series, has been concern for the Lord's people. I recently read in the Wall Street Journal an article that showed a map of the world and it focused on the Middle East. And it had big circles depicting the numbers of how many Christians used to live in each country. Then in that circle was a tiny circle showing how many are left there after all the killing and displacement. One country once had tens of thousands of Christians, but now only 3000 are left in that country. And in some countries they were gone altogether. And some were once in the millions with now just a few hundred left. So they are being decimated all over the world. Even Christians here in the US have dropped in number 15% in just the last seven years. Their world view is being attacked and I am going to say a bit more about it later.

That is partly what has been motivating me in this series because Christians need a framework within which they can be spiritually empowered, not empowered to fight, but to love and effectively minister. I tell you this not to be a doomsayer or frightening but to give you a real sense of urgency to really know your Lord, who He is and what He has done for you in anticipation of the conditions we all now live in. Christ said, *"Greater things will you do than I have done."* That has not happened. Do we love Him enough to put every effort into fulfilling His expectation for us in our service to Him? It is the time for Christians to find a way to be able to be doing things that Christ did.

Now in the last session I talked about righteousness. I want to say a few words about that in relation to what we are going to talk about today. Christ had righteousness in relation to the moment. He had righteousness. As you know, in Hebrew the word "zedek" means *righteousness*. He is the Prince of righteousness. He was right with the context of the moment. What I mean by that is one time He healed a man born blind. The setting for that was He was fleeing for His life from being stoned. He came across this man and put clay mixed with saliva on his eyes and healed him. He had compassion on him. He could have been thinking about Himself and looking behind Him seeing if He was being followed, but He turned His whole self in compassion toward this man. This man had a need. And in having that compassion, He was right in that moment. His feelings were right. He was right in His interaction with the life that was in all things, including His saliva and the clay that caused this man to see. All the stories that were mentioned have this component.

He was also undergirded by being right in a broader sense. He was right *beyond* the moment. He was right in His lifestyle and in His personal thoughts and behavior. He was right in how He viewed the world. He was right in knowing what His Father felt and what He would say or do. He knew the compassion His Father had on the blind man. He was right in His culture as an Essene or, as some would say, a Nazarene. He could always perceive what people were feeling or thinking, because the Father knows all our thoughts. And He could discern the intent of each heart. And when He would say, *thy sins are forgiven,* He could discern even their unspoken sorrow and humility in their repentance. He forgave people when they just had a desire to repent. He was right in His religion because He could always touch and connect with the spirits of life that He had put into all things and draw on them to give life. He was right in what He ate. He was right in what He wore for clothing. He was right in His authority over evil and adverse spirits.

There isn't any reason that you cannot be right in the broader sense too. But you can't do it all at once. First, you must come to understand the powers of the spirits of life in the earth and set out to divide them in your life. This session is intended to bring some of that understanding. Much of this can be found in your Bible. For many, it has been hiding there in plain sight.

With raising Lazarus, Jesus had the foundation of righteousness well established in His life. So when He came to the need of Lazarus, He was prepared in the purity of His soul to be empowered in the moment. He knew that Lazarus had died. When Jesus and the apostles got there, Jesus was able to turn His soul toward a focus on the immediate need of Lazarus and his family. They were His special friends. And after feeling what the women felt, Jesus wept because He felt compassion for the women, for

Lazarus, and for His Father's poor heart in His desires for Lazarus in that moment. And He also felt compassion because of what had been going on with Lazarus and how he was killed. And He was also right, as I have said, in the broader sense or He couldn't have done anything in the moment. But He was intimately connected with all the spirits of life that were there that gave life to Lazarus since his birth. And he could draw on those spirits of life, being joined with them, to bring life back to him. Any raising of the dead is like this. All the creative forces that give and sustain life are the ones that can bring life back or can restore life to its proper order with healing.

So today I want to talk about this broader view of righteousness that goes beyond the present moment. And of course with Christ's culture and in that context He had the advantage of a language that defines the life that is in all things. So most often whatever something was named in Hebrew indicated something about the spirit of life it held. So Jesus had a starting place that we are weak in but we can share with Him His ending place, which is to be joined in our feelings with any given spirit of holiness. God would never expect us to be righteous and then not make it available to us. He would never expect Christians to be empowered joining with the life that He put in all things if we couldn't know and feel what that life was. He wouldn't do that being our kind Father. He is a God of love.

So as I begin to get into this topic of this broader spectrum of righteousness, I am calling it **the dividing of powers**. And if Christians can rightly divide the spiritual powers that their lives are subject to in this world and with what they experience with the Lord, they can be empowered in their lives and in community.

There is kind of a strange thing here today with this that I am giving you because I am going to say some things that most of you have never heard spoken before but some already know. Now isn't that strange that you are going to hear something spoken that you have never before heard, but in your heart, because of the Spirit of God in you, you may already know. The Spirit of God has gone before us. And another strange aspect of today's topic is all that will be spoken today is in your Bible, from cover to cover, but you have never really known it. You have read it but it is hidden from your eyes. Much of it you already may know in your heart by the Spirit. Should be an interesting day, don't you think? So start listening with both ears. With one ear, listen to the words that are spoken and with the other ear, search your soul to hear what the Lord wants to tell you by His Spirit. All this will be in your Bible with some support from the writings of the early church.

So many of you have this innate sense as Christians, a people who love God, to already know much of how to divide the powers of life on earth. This is what I mean. Christians that live in the world already know to be careful what they watch on TV. They already know they have to be careful with their children on the computer and cell phones. They already know they have to have safe things around where there is danger with something unseen like chemicals that would like to take their life. Or they know to guard against things like when a little kid could put a hairpin in a light socket. Or get run over by the car backing out of the driveway. Or burn the house down by not understanding a gas stove. There are all kinds of things that threaten their gift of life. So they already know how to be careful and stay away from bad influences and language and such like smoking and drinking and drugs and raucous music and evil influences and violence and fornication.

But as Christians, all they have is discipline. All they have is boundaries they set - so they program their computer so the child can't call up pornography; or they hope they can't. But boundaries and discipline wear away like the shore line at the beach. And they try to oversee what their kids are watching. They try to control the influences of their lives while in the midst of evil. But that is a very weak and ineffective defense to dividing powers but that is all they can do, that is all they have. And the Lord's people languish in the midst of a wicked world and succumb to evil and lose their children to the world and grope to find their way. And yet some of them eliminate these forces altogether. So they are off the grid. They don't have to worry what their kids watch; they don't have a television. So there is varying degrees of how Christians are able to divide the powers of the earth and refrain and distance themselves from the forces that do not contribute to their gift of life or do not compliment Christ in their lives. Taken as a whole, they are at this moment, by in large, failing. They need to join with the things that enhance His presence in their lives that go beyond traditions and religious habits. They need to separate themselves from the things with do not complement Christ in their lives. They have to try not to drown in the world's wickedness.

It is a fact that the real ability of Christians to divide powers in the earth comes out of the creative role of Jesus and how creation and mankind have responded to Him. The fact that He is the Creator really is what makes it possible for Christians to live a life that is truly righteous and empowered. A life that is effective in its scope to give life, to avoid evil, to enhance the good to the extent that they can save their children from the evil of the world, and to bring healing and abundant life to their families and the Lord's people. I realize all of this is a new thought, as the Creatorship of Jesus is so remote within the context of the Christian tradition. You will be amazed at how plainly stated this is in your Bible.

So I bring this to you out of love and out of concern. I have worried a long time about the Lord's people. We have been motivated to establish a community for the purpose of providing a place of refuge from the evils of this world. This place belongs to Him and hopefully it is one of many such places where the Lord can lead His people to a life that is Spirit filled and overflowing. We know that such places afford a closer walk with the Lord, a place of spiritual empowerment.

So let's begin with information about angels. This might not be where you thought I would begin. Being right with the angels is the foundation for creating a life style centered on the Lord and is one that is successful and effective for Christian empowerment. And now you say, "Huh? What was that again? I have never heard of that before; being right with angels." Let me go on with this because this is very important. When I talk about angels, I am talking about the spirits of life that Christ as Creator put in the elements of creation. It is that life that you can join with and use to interact with in order to bring healing, inspiration and life by the power of His Spirit and presence. I did that, you know, to a small extent with the little girl that had Downs Syndrome and with the man with tuberculosis. I was graced to be right in the moment. I wept at the thought of their need and had compassion. And I used the life that Christ put into many things around me and the Lord brought the healing.

265

So as I begin this information that I'm sharing with you, I will be reading lots of scriptures in your Bible with some passages just being cited to shorten it. I would like to say I use four different Bible dictionaries. The reason I do that is because I get a good overall view of different perspectives. And there are a lot of Bible references. I use the old Smith's version from the 1880's. I use the International version, which is liberal and comes from England. Sometimes I use the Nelson's, which is conservative, and I like the Jehovah's Witnesses because they are good students even though sometimes it is very narrowly focused. The conservative Nelson's is usually very helpful. I use these to study to find points of view and the corresponding references. And of course as I have said I use the Strong's Concordance and on occasion Benner's book on the Paleo-Hebrew to clarify what is found in the Bible.

First of all, these different dictionaries that I just listed for you, all agree that angels are not human. In the International Dictionary it says, *"Angels constitute a company not a race developed by a single pair,"* like people coming from Adam and Eve. All of this information is including scriptures to point this out. In the Nelson's Dictionary it says, *"Angels are members of an order of heavenly beings who are superior to men in power and in intelligence."*

Ok, now I am going to start reading a few things, it says, *"Also angels were created before man."* And this comes from Job 38:4-7. *"Where wast thou when I laid the foundations of the earth? declare, if thou hast understanding. Who hath laid the measures thereof, if thou knowest? or who hath stretched the line upon it? Whereupon are the foundations thereof fastened? or who laid the corner stone thereof; When the morning stars sang together, and all the **sons of God** shouted for joy?"* Sons of God is a reference to angels. That is what they are commonly called. They shouted for joy when they saw the world created. In Genesis 6:2-4, they are called the sons of God. So that is saying that when the earth was created, the angels were there to rejoice. That was a reference to the fact that angels were created before people. You will notice a correlation here that trees, mountains, hills, rivers, animals, and everything in the Genesis story of creation was created before man. Man was the last thing created. In the beginning state, all these angels that were created were holy. But one third of them fell away from God and rebelled against what Jesus the Creator had intended them to be.

I want to read a couple of scriptures about that. This is Jude 6. Jude only has one chapter. *"And the angels which kept not their first estate but left their own habitation he hath reserved in everlasting chains under darkness unto the judgement of the great day."* Some of the angels, some of the spirits of life that Jesus put in everything, didn't like the life He gave them or that they were called upon to love Him and us. They didn't like their first station or what they were created for. They wanted to choose their own view of their purpose of creation - choose the meaning of their own lives, which was not one of love. And in this way, they rejected their Creator and it was as if they cast the Spirit of His presence out from themselves. And with the rejection of their created purpose, went the Creator's purpose in them that was an expression of His love for you. So in effect, they cast out two of the four spirits of life that they had in the beginning.

The four spirits of life that came to dwell in all that Jesus created are: 1) the spirit of His **Father**, which is His spirit of love and compassion for all that exists upon the temporal earth, and 2) the spirit of His purpose and great expectations for **you**, and 3) the spirit of life that gives **life** to whichever form any specific element has taken like a tree or a hill and so forth, and 4), the spirit and presence of **Jesus**. So all that remains in the fallen angels is the Spirit of God and their own spirit. They hate Jesus and you. These are the devil and his angels. Remember God is a Spirit. And He created all the spirits of life. Jesus's role was to give element form. One is a spiritual creation and the other is a natural creation. Without the spirit of God, those fallen angels couldn't exist. And God is gracious enough to allow them to live in spite of their evil. And they became the angels of death that are very often referred to as demons.

Now II Peter 2:4-5 is another example shedding light on the matter. *"For if God spared not the angels that sinned, but cast them down to hell, and delivered them into chains of darkness, to be reserved unto judgment; And spared not the old world, but saved*

Noah the eighth person, a preacher of righteousness, bringing in the flood upon the world of the ungodly." So there also is a reference that these angels fell. And it also is a statement as to why there was a Flood. There are many references to that in your Bible. But all of the Bible dictionaries I cited agree that one third of the hosts of angels fell. And in Revelation 12:4, it says that the adversary drew a third of the hosts of heaven with him when he fell. Now the lead angel, remember these angels are not human, was Satan.

And if you think of Satan as a human being, you may be surprised at what is recorded in your Bible. You will find in Isaiah 14:12-19, it says, *"How art thou fallen from heaven, O Lucifer, son of the morning! how art thou cut down to the ground, which didst weaken the nations! For thou hast said in thine heart, I will ascend into heaven, I will exalt my throne above the stars of God: I will sit also upon the mount of the congregation, in the sides of the north: I will ascend above the heights of the clouds; I will be like the most High. Yet thou shalt be brought down to hell, to the sides of the pit.*

*They that see thee shall narrowly look upon thee, and consider thee, saying, Is this **the man** that made the earth to tremble, that did shake kingdoms; That made the world as a wilderness, and destroyed the cities thereof; that opened not the house of his prisoners? All the kings of the nations, even all of them, lie in glory, every one in his own house. But thou art cast out of thy grave like an abominable branch, and as the raiment of those that are slain, thrust through with a sword, that go down to the stones of the pit; as a carcase trodden under feet."* In this reading the word "man" in verse 16 is Hebrew #376, a proper interpretation in English would be *to be extant* or *the one who exists*, which does not necessarily have to be man. It is literally *one who is extant*.

The name Lucifer is Hebrew # 1966, which means *the morning star*. And taken together with Luke 10:18, Jude 13, and Revelation 9:1, points to the Devil being a meteorite. I know that this is an entirely new idea to you but that is the position taken by the sect of the Nazarenes and the prophets.

268

Luke 10:18, *"And he said unto them, I beheld Satan as lightning fall from heaven."*

Jude 13, *"Raging waves of the sea, foaming out their own shame; **wandering stars**, to whom is reserved the blackness of darkness for ever."*

Revelation 9:1, *"And the fifth angel sounded, and I saw a **star fall from heaven** unto the earth: and to him was given the key of the bottomless pit."*

Also Ezekiel 28:12-15 is about the origin of Satan. The devil has his angels. So the fallen angels have become the fallen spirits called demons by the original Torah; they are spirits of evil. Some of the spirits of life Christ put in things became the spirits of evil. *"Then shall he say also unto them on the left hand, Depart from me, ye cursed, into everlasting fire, prepared for the devil and his angels,"* so said Jesus in Matthew 25:41. Sorry, I forgot to give the reference.

Ok, so one third of the spirits of life that our Creator, Jesus, put into various parts of creation rebelled against Him. And they began to hate Him. They began to want to kill His children. They hate Jesus so much that the more a person is like Him the more the fallen angels want to come against them. They began to be against everything Jesus stood for. They began to be against man's salvation. Remember these are spirits of life that He put into the elements of the earth for the purpose of loving you. They began to be murderous. Jesus commanded evil spirits to depart. But Jesus had a very intimate loving relationship with the holy angels - the ones who didn't fall but who were faithful.

Again, in Matthew 13:41 it talks about Jesus sending forth angels. *"The Son of man shall send forth his angels, and they shall gather out of his kingdom all **things** that offend, and **them** which do iniquity."*

In Matthew 26:53, when they were taking Him into custody He says, *"Thinkest thou that I cannot now pray to my Father, and he shall presently give me more than twelve legions of angels?"*

And Mark 8:38, it talks about Christ's second coming with the angels. *"Whosoever therefore shall be ashamed of me and of my words in this adulterous and sinful generation; of him also shall the Son of man be ashamed, when he cometh in the glory of his Father with the holy angels."*

In Luke 12:8-9 Christ says He will confess us before God and His angels if we confess Him. *"Also I say unto you, Whosoever shall confess me before men, him shall the Son of man also confess before the angels of God. But he that denieth me before men shall be denied before the angels of God."*

Also, angels followed with great interest every moment of Jesus' entire earthly ministry. From all the way from announcing His birth to Mary that she was going to have a child to those who were at the stone that was rolled away; during His 40 days in the wilderness, angels, who are the spirits of life that He put in all things, ministered to Him.

Angels are interested in the salvation of man. Luke 15:10, *"Likewise, I say unto you, there is joy in the presence of the angels of God over one sinner that repenteth."*

Angels are charged with the care of the Lord's people in times of distress. Think about the Christians in Syria and other places right now. Psalms 91:11-12, *"For he shall give his angels charge over thee, to keep thee in all thy ways. They shall bear thee up in their hands, lest thou dash thy foot against a stone."* Hebrews 1:14, *"Are they not all ministering spirits, sent forth to minister for them who shall be heirs of salvation?"*

The affairs of nations are guided by angels. See Daniel 10:12-13 & 20. All these are real sound readings in your Bible. These Bible references are not stretching anything when they say these things. And yet many scholars and Christians don't know who angels are. They have all of this knowledge of angels and they don't know who they are. And the Bible is not obscure; the Bible is filled with what angels are. There are some obscurities there and I will point them out when we get there.

Hebrews 1:6-7 says that the wind and fire are angels. *"And again, when he bringeth in the firstbegotten into the world, he saith, And let all the angels of God worship him. And of the angels he saith, Who maketh his angels spirits, and his ministers a flame of fire."* The best translation of that is in the American Standard Version. The word "in-mah" is the word used there, which is number #4151 in the Greek, and it means *a current of air, a breeze* or *an angel.* But the King James Version translated that word as "spirits." So that verse in Hebrews could be obscure if you have the King James Version. But the real good translation there calls wind and fire angels. And we know this because it is attested to in the original Torah. I will be reading it to you.

Then in Psalms 148 is a very important reading. David lists the leaders of the angels. I am going to read this to you but I want to say some things first. In the writings of the sect of the Nazarenes, which Christ was a part of, there is a full list of the fallen angels. The old term they use is **fallen watchers**, which is the old name for the fallen angels which rebelled against their Creator (see Daniel 4:13, 17, & 23). And here in Psalms 148 is David's list of the angels who remained faithful to God - the spirits of life who didn't fall from their created purpose. So I will read this to you. This list is a little bit different than the list we have but not much.

*"Praise ye the LORD. Praise ye the LORD from the heavens: praise him in the heights. Praise ye him, all his angels: praise ye him, all his hosts. Praise ye him, **sun** and **moon**: praise him, all ye **stars** of light. Praise him, ye **heavens** of heavens, and ye **waters** that be above the heavens. Let them praise the name of the LORD: for he commanded, and they were created. He hath also stablished them for ever and ever: he hath made a decree which shall not pass."*

Now he is going to list some more other angels. *"Praise the LORD from the **earth**, ye [sea creatures], and all **deeps**: **Fire**, and **hail**; **snow**, and **vapours**; stormy **wind** fulfilling his word: **Mountains**, and all **hills**; **fruitful trees**, and all **cedars**: **Beasts**, and all **cattle**; **creeping things**, and **flying fowl**: **Kings** of the earth,"* referencing that which guides man in his life on the earth, *"and all **people**; **princes**, and all **judges** of the earth."* This last phrase is talking about the seasons and time. What David has done there is he

271

says, *"Praise him."* All those angels praise Him; they are alive. They can express their feelings for God. They can speak to say what is on their minds. They are happy. They are excited about God. The mountains are and little hills and the fruitful trees are too. All these things David mentioned are to his mind alive and feeling entities. He is saying to them: express your love for God. He is saying they are alive and calling them angels.

So angels are the elements of creation. They are the spirits of life that Jesus put into all the forms that element took. They are the angels. That is what they are. You may find it interesting to hear how plain this concept of angels being the spirits of the elements is recorded in Jeremiah's Torah. Here you will see the source for the Hebrews 1:6-7 reading that fire and wind are spirits called angels. This is found Charlesworth's edition on Chapter 2:1-3 in Jubilees.

"And the angel of the presence spoke to Moses by the word of the Lord, saying, 'Write the whole account of creation, that in six days the Lord God completed all his work and all that he created. And he observed a Sabbath the seventh day, and he sanctified it for all ages. And he set it (as) a sign for all his works.'

*For on the first day he created the heavens, which are above, and the earth, and the waters and **all of the spirits** which minister before him:*

> *the angels **of the presence**,*
> *and the angels **of sanctification**,*
> *and the angels of the spirit **of fire**,*
> *and the angels of the spirit **of the winds**,*
> *and the angels of the spirit **of the clouds** and **darkness** and **snow** and **hail** and frost,*
> *and the angels **of voices** and **thunder** and **lightning**,*
> *and the angels of the spirits **of cold** and **heat** and **winter** and **springtime** and **harvest** and **summer**,*
> *and all the spirits **of his creatures** which are in **heaven** and on **earth**.*

*And the abysses and darkness – both **evening** and **night** – and light – **both dawn and daylight – which he prepared in the*** *knowledge of his heart.* *Then we saw his works and we blessed him and offered praise before him on account of all his works because he made seven great works on the first day."*

When it says *"which he prepared in the knowledge of his heart,"* it is a clear reference to a spiritual creation - all this on the first day. Your Biblical account is the imposed Torah and it has evolved from this reading. And then another interesting reading indicates the source for all of David's Psalm 148 statements the spirits of life or angels are capable of speaking is also found in Jeremiah's Torah Chapter 3:28-29.

*"On that day the mouth of all the beasts and cattle and birds and whatever walked or moved was stopped from speaking because all of them used to speak with one another with one speech and one language. And **he sent from the garden of Eden** all of the flesh which was in the garden of Eden and all of the flesh was scattered, each one according to its kind and each one according to its family, **into the place which was created for them.**"*

Most importantly, you find here the critical reference to everything in Eden being transformed into the temporal earth *"that was created for them."* For the Essenes, or the early church, this is the precise place in their Torah that pointed toward Jesus being the Creator. They went from Eden to the place that was created for them.

Remember the statement in the Bible dictionary I read to you that said, *"the angels are superior to man in intelligence and spiritual power."* Remember all the things it said of them? I will list some of it again: they are not human; they are superior to man in power and intelligence; they were created before man; Ezekiel said that the angels rejoiced at creation; angels are interested in the salvation of man. The adversary, who is the lead fallen angel, is a meteorite. The angels are charged with the care of the Lord's people in times of distress. The affairs of nations are guided by angels. Jesus will confess His people before the angels; they will accompany Him at His second coming; and they followed Jesus all through His earthly life.

Are mountains, thunder, wind, and trees superior to you in power and intelligence? Can they take care of you in times of distress? Are all those things David listed interested in your salvation? For me, because of the clear witness of the Spirit and that which I have experienced, the answer is yes. The holy forms creation has been given by their Creator are indeed the angels of heaven. Please do not misunderstand; also people who lived holy lives and live in the presence of God are angels. John says in Rev. 5:11, "*and the number of them was ten thousand times ten thousand, and thousands of thousands.*"

So in order to facilitate understanding, we must call the natural forms Jesus gave elements of the earth, like hills and grass, **watchers**. People who have passed who now live with God we must now call **angels**. The people of the early church called the elements of the earth the Watchers of Holiness. They are alive and can speak to you and love you and teach you all things good. And the Bible bears this out. The expression of these things is made clear throughout the Bible. And I am going to read some of that information to you. You will be surprised how much the Bible has to say about this and of how clearly it is stated.

At one point in my studies, I was just going to go through the Bible and write down everything that showed that the elements of the earth are alive and can experience and can speak and feel and express themselves if they want to, but there are too many. That is the conundrum facing scholars. Scholars don't know who angels are even though the Bible says it clearly because of the complete lack of the concept of righteousness. That is where Christians have problems - if they want to deny who angels are.

This hill we are on is more intelligent than we are. Just one shovel full of clay from it knows more about the history of the earth and the course it has traveled than all the scholars of the world combined. I think so. The tree outside has more power to love than we do. Not because it is a tree but because your Jesus, who loves infinitely, made the tree specifically for that reason to love you in a unique way. It was the Man with a mother, who knows how to love. God loved us so much that He became our fellow man. And whatever the Lord made, He gave it life. He said, I am the bread of life which came down to give life to the universe. Whatever He gives life to is alive.

You will recall from my experience when the Lord came to speak with me in the woods, one of the things He said as He stood by me was, as I was touching this tree and as I was marveling over that there was no shadows in the bark, the Lord said to me with His own mouth, "That tree is your brother." I was surprised and I said, "Lord how can that be?" And He said, "Because I have given it life like I have you. And it is going to grow old and die like you will. It has feelings like you have. It loves me like you do." I said, "Oh that is great! I have a brother." One doesn't doubt the Lord when in His presence. That is something I know now, trees are my kindred. This has been on my mind 60 years.

Alright, now I want to say some more here as I go along about angels. The writings of Enoch in the early church and found in the Dead Sea Scrolls influenced almost every author in the Bible, including the New Testament. For a good perspective read Charlesworth's introduction to the Book of Enoch in his collection called Pseudepigrapha. They are quoted from Daniel through Jude and influenced Matthew and many other places. The Book of Enoch from Milik's translation of the Dead Sea Scrolls says that there are 20 leaders of the fallen angels, who are called the Decadarchoi. And there are 24 leaders of the holy angels, who are called the Eerkodeshoi. I will be explaining these names in a moment. I just read 24 of them in Psalms 148.

Those listed by David in Psalm 148 vary somewhat from the reading in the original Torah. Our list of the angels which we use is somewhat different yet in the details. The principle difference in the lists is in how the seasons are viewed and in the lingering gray areas of the distinction between angels and watchers. These 24 leaders of the holy angels are the 24 elders in the Book of Revelation in 4:4, 10; 5:8, 14; 11:16 and 19:4. Here is our list of the leaders of the Holy Angels by order of inscription, the two-thirds who remained faithful:

Element	Name	What they teach:
Fire	Debariel	Prayer
Wind	Rahaviel	Responsibility
Mountains	Malakiel	Faith & Worship
Rocks	Ebedel	Steadfastness
Thunder	Yatsal	Understanding
Trees	Kabodiel	Being trustworthy
Rain	Bawrakel	Patience
Hills	Regel	Diligence
Rivers	Pawnel	Selflessness
Clouds	Abariel	Knowledge
Dew	Anahiel	Tenderness
Grass	Rachatsel	Cleanliness in Jesus
Oceans	Sarahel	Humility
Sun	Oreiel	Preparedness & visions
Fountains	Kayal	Wisdom
Animals	Shemael	Obedience
Fruit of trees	Chafetiel	To be Uncomplaining
Moon	Emethiel	Maturity
Enoch's Calendar	Adahiel	Loyalty & remembrance
Springtime	Chadashel	Confidence
Summer	Osheral	Happiness
Fall	Gavahel	Respect
Winter	Shabethiel	Kindness
Stars	Rachaphiel	Long-suffering

Now a word about how the concept of angels developed.
You will find in Daniel in your Bible that there are three different
times that the word "watcher" is used. And in the Torah of
Jeremiah, the word "watcher" is prevalent in referring to angels.
What developed is the word "watcher" comes from #5894 in
Hebrew, and it is the word "eer" **which means either *watcher* or
angel.** That comes from #5782, to *have open eyes, to be awake* and
to converse, but on the side of the fallen angels it also means *those
who can lift themselves up as masters*. Since early times there has
been a reference to the fallen ones.

In the early days before the flood, the holy people of Enoch
and the holy people on the earth, who loved the Lord Jesus but
called Him by a different name, called all of the elements of

creation watchers because they knew they were awake and alive and could converse. And they were cognizant that the elements held the spirit of life that the Man who God became put into all things. Where the word "angel" began to come in to replace the word "watcher" was when there began to be human beings who died and then appeared to people. Just like when Gabriel came and spoke to Mary.

So the old way was to speak of watchers and the more modern terminology, and by the modern I mean after the Flood, was to call the spirits of life that were resurrected humans angels. And in this way, a distinction began to be made between humans and other forms element had taken that had life. So it became that the word "angel" meant *people* and the word "watcher" meant *other forms of life*. Both words originated in the Hebrew word #5894, "eer." Then, because the influence of the leaders of the Gentile Mission, the concept of there not being life in anything except man prevailed and the term and idea of watcher went by the way. And angels became entirely disconnected from our environment in creation and only meant people who had died.

Now in John 6:33-35, "*Jesus said unto them, verily verily I say unto you, Moses gave you not that bread from heaven but my father giveth you the true bread from heaven for the bread of God is he that cometh down from heaven and giveth life unto the world. I am that bread of life.*" So Christians need to learn to think of Christ as Creator, not just as an idea, but we need to begin to make that the way we live. We can begin to know how to identify adequately what we need to make a Christian culture,: a Christian language, and a Christian way of life based on and in harmony with the elements of the earth that were faithful, which are all around us. Our Savior Himself created them and gave them life specifically for the purpose of loving us and being our companions in Him. They are the angels of heaven and the Watchers of Holiness. So there is a little bit of a leap required to begin to think of angels as the spirits of life that are in all holy things in the creation around you. Your interaction with them is a part of your personal relationship with Christ and, by extension, an integral part of your salvation and your spiritual empowerment.

But first I want to demonstrate for you just how much is in the Bible about this. The Bible is filled with this dynamic of the creation being alive and speaking and acting. They are too numerous for me to cite them all. There are hundreds of such references in your Bible. It is all through your Bible. I will just take them by topic to shorten the list and make it practical for this session. This is just to give you an idea of what is there for you to find in your studies.

First **trees**, ok? In Isaiah 14:8 trees are rejoicing. Isaiah 55:12, trees are clapping their hands with joy. Isaiah 61:3, trees are righteous. Psalms 96:12, trees are rejoicing. Zachariah 11:2, trees are howling in sorrow.

Now **hills**. Psalms 65:12, hills are rejoicing and again in 98:8. Isaiah 55:12, hills break forth into singing. Micah 6:1, hills can hear your voice. Psalms 114:4-6, the little hills skip like lambs.

Ok, now **mountains**. Psalms 114:4-6, the mountains skip like rams. So David and Isaiah had the same expression. Isaiah 44:23, the mountains are singing. Isaiah 99:13, mountains sing and the earth is filled with joy and is joyful. Micah 6:2, the mountains are listening to you. Habakkuk 3:10, the mountains **saw** you and the oceans **spoke** to you.

Jesus said when He was entering Jerusalem that if the people didn't praise Him, the very stones would immediately cry out. Luke 19:40, "*And some of the Pharisees from among the multitude said unto him, Master, rebuke thy disciples. And he answered and said unto them, I tell you that, if these should hold their peace, the stones would immediately cry out.*" I believe all this was due to His raising Lazarus, which was the event exciting interest in the multitude.

When Jesus said the stones would immediately cry out some people might think that all this that I read to you about the elements of the earth being alive and of what Jesus said about the stones was simply poetic and symbolic. But the context of that reading in Luke doesn't smack of being poetic or being symbolic, especially in light of who He was saying it to. When Christ was on the donkey and there were sounds of loud praise heard and His donkey was walking over clothing of the crowd and the palm branches were strewn in the way, He did not have His mind on poetry for Pharisees. And He said, if you stop them from praising me the rocks would cry out. Jesus knew exactly what was on the minds of the Pharisees and the movement in their society toward the Torah of Jeremiah and the ancient definition of the expression of righteousness.

Ok, so the Bible is filled with the idea that the elements of the earth have the real spirits of life. So there are good spirits of life in the things around you, and there are bad spirits of life in the things around you. Dividing the powers of the earth is referring to one's relationship with those powers and how we divide them in the broad sense of our Christian lifestyle. Do you really want a relationship with things around you that hate and your wonderful Jesus, our Creator? That question is essential to address for the Christian community.

So in Revelation 12:4, it talks about the one-third that fell away from God. All right now, the word for angel in Hebrew as I have said, is "eer." And it is from #5782 meaning *angel*. And it also means *a dweller of the city of holiness*. Here is a direct link between angels and the Christian community. Here the indication clearly is that the Lord's people in His holy city will dwell together and interact with the angels of heaven. And the word "kodesh," #6944, means *holy*. So "Eerkodeshoi" (pronounced ear-ko-desh-ee) means the *angels or watchers of holiness*. And the "ee" sound in the end usually in Hebrew designates a specific social group. So the word "Eerkodeshoi" means *the society of the angels of holiness*. That is the name for the 24 elders or leaders of the angels - the 24 elders in Revelation.

The word "Decadarchoi" is another word found in the writings of the sect of the Nazarenes and it is the name for the 20 leaders of the fallen angels and their followers. And it means *the society of the fallen bullies*. And these words are in the writings of the Essenes of which Jesus was a member in the early church.

Now there are 20 leaders of the fallen angels and here is the list of the one-third who rebelled:

Element	Name	Evil teachings:
Meteorite	Semihazah	Pleasure
Copper	Artagoph	Alienation
Coal	Ramtel	Loneliness
Phosphorus	Kokabel	Fear
Marble	Tahamiel	Lying
Petroleum	Ramel	Power of man
Comets	Daniel	Mystery
Generated electricity	Zeqel	Hatred
Oppressive Laws	Baraqel	Bondage
Meteor Iron	Asael	War
Sulfur	Hermoni	False Authority
Mercury	Matariel	Pollution
Uranium	Ananel	Mistrust
Alcohol	Satawel	Illusions
Arsenic	Samsiel	Illness
Lead	Sahriel	Doubt
Steel used for violence	Tummiel	Conformity
Gold used for wealth	Turiel	Self-glory
Aluminum	Yomiel	Laziness
Tomb writing	Yahaddiel	Death

I want you to think about this and see if the Lord hasn't already been telling you in your heart what I am going to tell you now. Remember what I said at the start of today's session? See if He hasn't already been telling you by His Spirit to distance yourselves from these things. Even though you may not ever have heard that the angels are the elements of the earth, and you may have thought they were just humans. See if you haven't had already some of this experience in your heart. It is vitally important to rid your living environment of these elements.

Arsenic is poison – everyone knows that. Lead: if you painted your baby's crib with lead paint and they chewed on it, it would injure their mental abilities or their intelligence. Aluminum is a source of Alzheimer's, it makes little crystals grow in your brain, especially when you drink things in aluminum cans according to Australian researchers. Mercury: you have all heard of mercury poisoning. Copper and all it allows with the use of electricity and the strong electrical fields it produces. Strong drinks, petroleum, and generated electricity. Do you know that because of electricity, you have to beware of what your children are watching and being influenced by? You have to worry about their cellphone; you have to worry about what movies they see. Right now electricity speaks for you. You talk into a little electronic device and it talks to somebody else for you. It heats your house; even if you have gas, it is the pilot light and air blower. It entertains you; it cooks your food; it does everything in your life.

Christians are surrounded with these fallen watchers that hate their Redeemer and are just looking for the chance to destroy their children. Remember, they are living spirits that Christ put into the elements of the earth who fell away from His purpose for them and now they hate you and Him. But the holy angels have concern for your salvation.

Coal causes black lung disease, phosphorous is something that is abundantly used by sorcerers. Comets, sulfur, uranium, meteorites, and marble: all those are identified in the writings of the early church as the 20 leaders of the fallen watchers because and the temple had marble in it they put three dots (…) in place of that name in their writings. And the Hebrews illustrate them in their language many times with derogatory names. I will give you four examples. All the names of those fallen bullies show that the Hebrews were aware of what they felt just as it is in righteousness. Copper is #5178, and it means *filthiness;* lead #5777, means *rubbish;* coal #7815, *to be of a **dark** countenance;* meteorite is defined as *to hunt and hurt and penetrate your world.*

So these things hate the Lord. They want to destroy you and your children more fervently because you belong to Jesus. They want to distract you totally from any connection with the gift of life you have been given and make you complete aliens to the spirits of life Christ put into the things around you. Boy does the Christian tradition leave this out! So what do Christians do? The first thing you do, besides doing your repentance daily, is you try to distance yourselves from those forces that don't love the Lord. You know

281

that petroleum does not love the Lord. You worry about your loved ones when they are driving. And if you go into a car wrecking yard, you see blood all over the cars there. And you feel death and cries of agony. Vehicles don't love the people they carry. They have to be forced by law to do everything possible to save your life from them - seat belts, car seats, air bags, anti-locking brakes, on and on.

Petroleum does not love you. It will burn you to death, suffocate you and injure you in so many ways. Coal doesn't love you. How many families are lonely for their fathers who die in the mines or at an early age from black lung disease? Meteorite iron is the weapon of choice for assassins. Knives made of it are sold all over the world for high prices and are used for killing. The law of oppression, uranium, strong drink - just look at all of these things and how your Christian life is compromised by them to rob you of the empowerment Jesus envisioned for you both as individuals and as a people. And this is to say nothing about what it takes for you to acquire them and maintain them. You have to literally give your life to the world to obtain them when we are supposed to have given our lives to the Lord.

These fallen angels are effectively inhibiting the close walk you need with the Lord. I suppose some would say they are not inhibited. I ask, "Are you raising the dead?" Are you *doing greater things than I have* done, that Jesus forecast about you? Better look prayerfully again. And so the first order of business in dividing the powers of the earth is to diligently seek how to distance yourselves and separate your loved ones from the things that do not love you or the Lord in the spirits of things around you. This is what the Spirit has been telling you, but the thought is easily dismissed because it seems impractical and impossible to do. This is what many of you have already made an effort to do before I said anything. The Christians who love the Lord and want to live the right life all know in their hearts by the Spirit that these things are hurting them and threatening their children.

So why would Christians bring into their personal, intimate, private homes the enemies of the Lord and of their gift of life in Him? If you had a grandmother let's say, or a little daughter or somebody you loved so dearly you can hardly express it, would you invite somebody home to dinner that hated them and would like to kill them? Would you? And yet the people in the Christian world have surrounded themselves with them. So how they travel, what they eat, the clothes they wear, the paint on the walls, what cooks their food and lights the room when they eat, everything is centered and integrated into those spirits that hate the One they love. The fallen watchers hate the source of salvation and the Bible that says they rebelled against Him and are destined to go down to hell. I read it to you in II Peter. They hate what Christians hope for in their children and they deny the second coming.

One of the presidential candidates said, "If we want to be good citizens, we must set aside our religion." The Christian community has been duped and all of this has come on them and they have been caught unawares. Their lamps are out of oil. They have been conditioned to think all this is progress. Some even suggest God ordained all these fallen angels for our use. So they teach you, they entertain you, they influence your mind and they medicate you. And now they are even altering the building blocks of creation to obtain their own purposes for creation in the face of what God wants. In your Bible that is called the giants. In Hebrew "giants" is the word "nephiyl" #5303 which comes from #5307 "naphal" which together means *the fallen bullies*, or the Nephilim. Some of them are genetically modified organisms. Society is now well into thumbing their nose at our lovely Creator.

So is it any wonder that when Christians surround themselves with all these things and partake of them, they base their religion on death? And when death comes near, they are in harmony with it. Take note, the Christian holocaust now is well underway undoubtedly to exceed the Jewish one. Maybe it already has.

One way to *be right* is to separate yourselves from the fallen spirits of life that have rejected you and their Creator. To be right is to join yourselves with all the holy spirits of life that Jesus put into your earthly home to love you and to promote and safeguard your salvation and well-being. So the Lord is worried about what is happening to His people. He is sorrowful. And His people need desperately to find the framework within which they can build a Christian society to be spiritually empowered. That is what we are talking about here. We are talking about Christians being empowered, not with violence and the use of force, but with

283

the power of the Spirit from on high; to know the Lord and relate to Him and His creation in harmony, to achieve His purposes in their lives and His design for the earth and His people. Why did He create man? What does He want for us? Who's going to tend to that? Does everyone who dies at the hands of the wicked need to die or did God intend them to live on like Lazarus or the young man at Nain? Does everyone blind need to stay blind? **Who are you?** Don't you belong to Jesus and His Father? Aren't they members of your family? When one of the Lord's loved ones is in danger of being swept away by evil, we should be able to rescue them.

Isaiah says in 5:29 of us now in our day that, *"Their roaring shall be like a lion, they shall roar like young lions: yea, they shall roar, and lay hold of the prey, and shall carry it away safe, and none shall deliver it."* We are called to rescue the Lord's loved ones and there is nothing evil can do about it – if you know how and you are willing to make the choices to be righteous. Your calling is great and the war against you is coming on strong. The Lord will not abandon you but you must broadly cleanse your lives before Him. When you are righteous the world will not be able to stop you from saving your little ones. Righteousness is way and beyond more powerful than wickedness. And I don't know how it will all work out for us but aren't we all in His hands? When these signs that are now happening in the tribulation times, which are sweeping all different parts of the world, come to us, right now when those forces of evil come to this country, I believe that being in harmony and being joined to the spirits of life will generate life.

So what are Christians going to do now that is different than what they are doing? Millions are being killed and driven from their homes. First of all, the Holy Spirit has to lead you. You have to be in tune with the Spirit – your repentance is a bridge to the Spirit. And you have to see that the Spirit is the center of the wheel. And the spokes reach out to have a relationship with Christ who is in everything holy. But without a center, the wheel is no good for anything. And so the Spirit of God talking to you in your heart can lead you and help you to be aware of the powers that are around you and how to divide them. The Lord can lead you. He would never ask you to do something that He knew you couldn't do, because He loves you.

So you need to come to instinctively know that the clouds, and the wind, the sun and the hills, rivers, seasons, trees, the mountains, rocks, and the grass, and all the Holy Spirits of Life around you, love you. And they can speak to you in your feelings and they can enhance your compassion and your ability to reach people for the Lord and their good. And they will take care of you in adversity like the Bible says, just like they did the Lord. That is why He spoke of it.

So I brought this message all the way from the start so people can focus on life. Life begets life. Death begets death. Leave death alone. Let the dead bury the dead. Christ is your life. Focus on His life, on the Creatorship of Jesus and on the life He put into creation just to love and empower you. He is alive. His Spirit is alive in everything holy. Cling to the holy, reject the evil. And that life can touch you and help you know when you are forgiven and when you are whole and how much you are loved. It can help you know how to pursue His purposes for you and how to find your place of refuge and safety and endowment with the power of His Spirit. He can help you know how to escape the bondage of an evil society so you have the sacred opportunity to construct your own spiritual environment and where to look for such opportunities.

So I am urging you to investigate these things. I know the world can make it seem impossible to escape the life they provide for you but all things can work to the good for those who love the Lord. I hope you will take time and effort to put into practice what you have heard in this series. I am well aware of how diverse all this is from mainstream Christianity. But you know I spoke it from your Bible and from my heart. And I did not engage in any stretch of interpretation but very carefully used the scriptures; every verse. If I made any misprints with numbers I apologize; there were so many numbers in this series. There is no doubt whatever that He knows each circumstance you face. You can depend on your eternal Christ, the Creator of heaven and earth.

And as I close, I want to say that I have opened up my heart to you in this series. I have expressed the theology and world view of the sect of the Nazarenes, which is that of the early church. I have declared the viewpoint of Jesus about His Father. The Spirit comforts me with the knowledge that there will be among you those

285

who will love the Father of Jesus enough to find a way to fulfill the expectations of Jesus for His people in a way that will meet His people's needs in the end of days. Thank you and God bless you fully in every way is my prayer. Amen.